Hardboiled Web Design
by Andy Clarke

Published in 2010 by Five Simple Steps
Studio Two, The Coach House
Stanwell Road
Penarth
CF64 3EU
United Kingdom

On the web: *www.fivesimplesteps.com*
and: *www.hardboiledwebdesign.com*
Please send errors to *errata@fivesimplesteps.com*

Publisher: Five Simple Steps
Development Editor: Chris Mills
Tech Editor: Tim Van Damme
Copy Editor: Owen Gregory
Production Editor: Emma Boulton
Production Manager: Sarah Morris
Design & Art Direction: Nick Boulton, Andy Clarke, Alex Morris, Mark Boulton
Front cover illustration: Kevin Cornell
Part opening illustrations: Elliot Jay Stocks
Printed in the UK by Paramount Print

ISBN: 978-1-907828-00-3

A catalogue record of this book is available from the British Library.

Five Simple Steps

HARDBOILED
WEB DESIGN
BY ANDY CLARKE

"I looked at Berin and laughed. He turned his head and stared right into the muzzle of his own gun. The killer's face was a vile mask of hatred. Berin had his mouth open, screaming with all the furies of the gods dethroned, but my laugh was even louder. He was still screaming when I pulled the trigger."

— *My Gun is Quick*, Mickey Spillane, 1950

Acknowledgements

To Emma, Nick and Mark Boulton and everyone at Mark Boulton Design and Five Simple Steps, for helping to make this book everything I imagined it would be.

To editor Chris Mills and technical editor Tim Van Damme for daring to take a ride inside my head, their editing skills and the years of experience they brought to the process.

To copy editor Owen Gregory, for being Lewis to my Morse.

To Kevin Cornell and Elliot Jay Stocks, for their cover and inside illustrations.

To Geri Coady, for my author photo and illustrations.

To Simon Collison and Jeffrey Zeldman, for their preface and foreword and for being the best friends an old man could have.

To John Allsopp, Maxine Sherrin and everyone involved in the Web Directions series of conferences, and to Eric Meyer, Jeffrey Zeldman (again) and everyone involved in An Event Apart, for the platform to present my ideas at the best web design conferences in the world.

To Faruk Ates and Paul Irish, for developing Modernizr, and to Keith Clark, for the Selectivizr JavaScript library. Both make hardboiled web design possible.

To Authentic Jobs, Scott Boms, Sam Brown, Clearleft, Dan Cederholm, Simon Collison (again), David Desandro, Luke Dorny, Jon Hicks, Jeremy Keith, nclud, Reagan Ray, Dave Rupert, Jeremy Swinnen, Cedric Vandendriessche, Tim Van Damme and Trent Walton, for the work we'll be 'investigating' later in this book.

To the clients of Stuff and Nonsense, for agreeing to delay their projects and being OK with me ignoring their calls and e-mails while I concentrated on writing.

Finally, but most importantly, to my family, because all that really matters is them.

About the Author

Andy Clarke has been called many things since he started designing for the web over ten years ago. His ego likes words like "ambassador for CSS", "industry prophet" and "inspiring", but he's most proud that Jeffrey Zeldman once called him a "bastard".

He runs Stuff and Nonsense [1], a small web design company that specialises in designing highly usable and attractive websites. You'll see examples from some of his designs later in this book. Andy's a renowned public speaker and presents at web design conferences worldwide. He teaches web design techniques and technologies through his own workshop masterclasses, For A Beautiful Web [2] and is the author of *Transcending CSS: The Fine Art of Web Design* [3] (New Riders, 2006).

He writes a popular blog, And All That Malarkey [4], mostly about the web, and tweets as @malarkey.

[1] http://stuffandnonsense.co.uk
[2] http://forabeautifulweb.com
[3] http://transcendingcss.com
[4] http://stuffandnonsense.co.uk/blog

About the Editor

Chris Mills is a mighty metal warrior who works for Opera (the Viking web browser), evangelising open web technologies such as CSS3 and HTML5 and heading up Opera's education activities. Chris publishes design and development articles on Dev Opera[1], and is the creator of the Opera Web Standards Curriculum[2]. Chris is also co-author of *InterACT with Web Standards: A Holistic Approach to Web Design*[3], speaks regularly at web conferences and universities, and is a core member of the Open Web Education Alliance[4], a grassroots organisation that aims to develop a global standard for web design and development education. He tweets as @chrisdavidmills.

About the Technical Editor

Tim Van Damme is a freelance interface designer at Made by Elephant[5]. Not afraid to push limits, friend of all things living, blabbermouth, honest chap, passionate about the web, always in the mood for a chat, blogger at Maxvoltar[6], boyfriend of Gwenny, Belgian and Twitter addict @maxvoltar.

---

[1] http://dev.opera.com
[2] http://opera.com/wsc
[3] http://interactwithwebstandards.com
[4] http://openwebeducation.org
[5] http://madebyelephant.com
[6] http://maxvoltar.com

Foreword

Not every CSS design wizard still lives in his mum's basement and cries himself to sleep each night wearing a soiled Tron T-shirt. For there's also Andy Clarke: dapper, charismatic, and perpetually brimming with ideas, insights and enthusiasm for the design of great experiences and the experience of great design.

The man is a walking epiphany, a King Midas of CSS-powered creativity. And the book you're now browsing may be his greatest gold classic yet. For here you'll learn why, when and how to use HTML5 and CSS3 in your daily work. Daily as in every day. Daily as in right now, today.

Every web designer should possess this book, but be warned, it is not for the timid. If you tremble at the thought of your web layout boasting rounded corners in one browser but not another; if the mere notion of even trying a CSS drop-shadow fills you with a sinner's remorse, *Hardboiled Web Design* is so not for you. Leave now. No judgements. Return to your safe, soft-boiled life. Okay, maybe that was a judgement.

But if you're among the restless, enlightened and daring few who embrace the future of web design, and know that we can't get there by clinging to the past, brother slash sister, has Andy got a book for you.

Jeffrey Zeldman
August 2010

About Jeffrey Zeldman

What can I say about Jeffrey Zeldman that hasn't already been written a thousand times or more? Sure, he was the co-founder and voice of the Web Standards Project during its formative years. Sure, he's one of the most recognisable faces in the web industry with his blog, A List Apart magazine, conference An Event Apart and short books series A Book Apart, "for people who make websites". Sure, he's the author of *Designing with Web Standards*, the book that popularised XHTML and CSS. He's also my inspiration, my mentor, my critic and my friend. What more can I say?

http://webstandards.org
http://alistapart.com
http://aneventapart.com
http://books.alistapart.com
http://zeldman.com/dwws

Preface

Every web designer harbours tales of frustration, limitation and despair. Web design requires skills and knowledge beyond mere manipulation of form, shape, language, colour, message and meaning. What users don't see behind those visuals is just as important as what they do see. We have to think about moving parts and engineering solutions, and consider language, metadata, user experiences, and so much more.

Whether we work alone or in teams, we need to follow rules, constantly extend our skillsets, and sometimes even predict the future, dealing with social networks, web apps, microformats, geolocation, magical new devices and augmented realities. Our work goes beyond borders, accessible at any time from any location, on any number of browsers and devices, at varying speeds, on multiple resolutions. And it is consumed by humans, each with a brain a little different from the next.

The rules will never be set in stone. Technology evolves, and battles over minutiae will rage publicly, whilst also causing us private headaches that keep us awake at night. There will always be misunderstanding, contention, and limits. Our immediate remits will always be open to question, and the pile marked 'things to learn' will grow beyond our ability to cope with it. What programming languages and tools do I use? Am I up-to-date with accessibility and usability best practice? Should I learn that new method everyone is talking about? Will I ever understand JavaScript? We can only do our best.

The web presented a fantastic new opportunity to us, but from the outset we made the mistakes typical of every new industry — we ran before we could walk, and forgot to take notice of the lessons learned by those that came before. We started building things without any thought for the future: no accountability; no standards. Every industry needs to be accountable. Every industry needs standards.

And we stood proud, and caught up. Look at web standards — It's incredible that our core community embraced the right path so early on. We understood the legacy of the content we create, that it should be well-formed and scalable, and that our presentation and behaviour should remain separate and not sully the core content. Our front-end building blocks — HTML, CSS, JavaScript — will be around in various forms for as long as we are.

Many bloody battles continue. Most notably, we've fought with browsers for well over a decade, battling with the very agents that deliver our work to the world. The perplexing and confusing anomalies of browser rendering engines have lost many of us plenty of sleep. Our desire to deliver the exact same details to every user via every browser has shackled us throughout our journey, and it has often robbed us of our opportunity to create truly spectacular experiences on the web.

So, is our industry really all that bad? Well, no; no, it isn't. It's incredible, but we often lose sight of that. We need to accept that what makes the web so unique — so special — is this constant flux. We are working in by far the most pioneering creative medium at this point in time, and it's undeniably exciting. Your toddler, your grandmother, the chap on the TV who says "log on" — they all know that everything happens on the web now, and we're the people making it happen. Sure, this requires us to constantly read, test, learn and evaluate. None of us will ever master all the aspects of web design we'd like, and I can tell you that nobody I know is managing this weight of information any better than you. That said, the smartest ones look at it more positively, learning to embrace this flux, and manipulate it as best they can.

We also learned to apply ideas and principles from print design, which has been worthwhile or vital in many cases. Adopting formulaic layout, grids and typographic rhythm allowed us to begin breaking away from the inflexible 'templated' web that content management systems gave us. We're learning to build more responsive layouts, automatically adapting our page content depending on the device used; we're designing for mobile, and thinking about the order in which we should design for various devices.

As Andy himself said at @media in 2009, "We don't design pages, we design systems." He's right, of course. What we build is rarely finished. We build systems that flex and grow with the client, the business, the organisation, the community and the availability of new devices. Once we understand a system, we can then break its rules and be truly creative. We're beginning to think about the "systems" we use as more holistic, made up of not just their mathematical foundations, but also the flexibility of colour, type families, use of white space, light and shade, form and shape.

By better understanding the possibilities of HTML and CSS, our ability to be creative and bold with systems increases significantly. They give us a platform to express our ideas and communicate with our audience; but being adept with them does not automatically bring about great design. Let's not forget our primary motivation — we design to communicate, whether it is an idea, a message, or a mental model or map to communicate what to do, how to engage with something or make it function. We have to take ideas, concepts, text and images, and present them in a visually engaging form. We impose order and structure to raw content in order to ease its communication to the largest possible audience. We enable others to get things done, and we sometimes create philosophical, emotional and sensory experiences. We need to do these things in the most effective way available to us, but to allow perceived limitations to compromise what we design is not acceptable. We have to be smarter than that.

The most successful web designers combine their tools and principles with a hunger and ambitious desire to break down convention: to challenge, explore, innovate and never compromise. There is tangible craftsmanship at the heart of everything we create, and we seek elegance at every turn. We're aware that every line of code and every decision is open to scrutiny. We prove our mettle as web designers through our ability to adapt to and overcome any challenge, delivering engaging experiences without compromising our own integrity or innovation. Our processes are transparent thanks to 'View Source'. When you elegantly solve a problem, others will go under the hood to see how you did it, or look for errors. If you can make those curious or sceptical interrogators go "Whoa!" you're probably great.

To strive for better, to never deviate from what you believe to be right, to seek to inspire and delight, and to avoid compromise—no matter what the obstacles or limitations—that's all possible. That's happening right now. That's being hardboiled. Let Andy show you how.

Simon Collison
August 2010

About Simon Collison

Simon Collison[1] is one of the world's best freelance web designers, a conference speaker and the author of *Beginning CSS Web Development: From Novice to Professional* (Apress, 2006). He's a deep, deep thinker and makes connections that no one else makes. But there's more to Colly than just the web. For the last six years he's been my sounding board, loyal friend and the closest thing to the third brother I never had. He also once published a photo of me coming out of a sex shop. (I was using the cash machine, honestly, you bastard.) He tweets as @colly.

[1] http://colly.com

About this book

If you've been working on the web for a while, your bookshelves may already be buckling under the weight of books about HTML and CSS. Do you really need another one?

Hardboiled Web Design is different. It's for people who want to understand why, when and how to use the latest HTML5 and CSS3 technologies in their everyday work. Not tomorrow or next week, but today. It won't teach you the basics of writing markup or CSS, but if you're hungry to learn about how the latest technologies and techniques will make your websites and applications more creative, flexible and adaptable, then this is the book for you.

If you care about markup, you're in for a treat because we'll focus on how to use the new semantic elements contained within HTML5 right now. We'll also cover microformats and WAI-ARIA landmark roles, looking at how they'll reduce your reliance on presentational elements and attributes, as well as making your websites and applications more useful without doing anything more than writing HTML.

If you're a designer who wants to learn the creative opportunities offered by CSS3, this book will teach you how to use CSS3 in browsers that support its new properties, and offers a fresh perspective on how to handle older, less capable browsers.

You'll need to be willing to leave your preconceptions at the door, and hungry to learn about how using HTML5 and CSS3 will change the way you design and develop for the web. Is the engine running in your heap? Buckle up, let's go.

First, some assumptions

This book is about using the latest, emerging HTML5 and CSS3 technologies so I'll assume that you're already familiar with writing well-structured, meaningful HTML or XHTML markup and using CSS to implement your designs.

Do you need to know everything there is to know about CSS? No, although understanding selectors and layout techniques will help as you follow along. If you're new to CSS, I hope that you'll be inspired by the examples and will want to learn more about what it means to be hardboiled.

What you'll need

To follow along you'll need a variety of browsers, extensions and developer tools installed on your Mac or PC, so you can see how the 'It's Hardboiled' examples are intentionally different across browsers of varying capabilities, and create your own hardboiled websites. I recommend you have the most current versions of the following installed (the numbers listed below are the most recent at the time of writing):

Apple Safari 5
Make sure that you go to Safari's preferences, click on the 'Advanced' tab and check 'Show Develop menu in menu bar.' This will give you access to Safari's developer tools.

Google Chrome 6
Like Firefox, Chrome has extensions that help us to design websites using a browser and to test them during development. You'll find plenty of Chrome developer extensions online[1], but Chris Pederick's Web Developer Toolbar for Chrome is the official port of his indispensable Firefox extension.

Microsoft Internet Explorer 9
The browser that every web designer loves to hate just got a whole lot better and comes with its own set of developer tools that makes developing on Windows easier.

Mozilla Firefox 3.6
Install the latest version of Firefox and any available beta versions[2]. Firefox is popular for its extensions. Web Developer Toolbar[3] and Firebug[4] are both essential.

---

[1] https://chrome.google.com/extensions
[2] http://mozilla.com/firefox/all-beta.html
[3] https://addons.mozilla.org/en-US/firefox/addon/60
[4] https://addons.mozilla.org/en-US/firefox/addon/1843

Opera 10.6

The most ambitious Opera browser to date with excellent
HTML5 and CSS3 support. Opera also offers its Dragonfly[1]
debugging environment. Part desktop application, part web
application, Dragonfly is stored in local storage and updates
itself when a new version is released.

It also wouldn't hurt to download and install Camino 2[2] for Mac OS X as it uses
an earlier version of the Gecko rendering engine and shows off well why we
shouldn't talk about the age of a browser but instead discuss its capabilities.

You won't need any special code writing software — feel free to use Coda,
Dreamweaver, Espresso (my tool of choice), TextMate or whatever else takes
your fancy.

[1] http://www.opera.com/dragonfly
[2] http://caminobrowser.org

Introducing our case study, 'It's Hardboiled'

Throughout this book we'll be working through a set of examples I designed for the fictitious 'It's Hardboiled' fan site. I didn't intend this to be the most usable or practical website — instead it illustrates the fantastic things we can achieve when we use the most up-to-date technologies and leave behind old-fashioned ideas about browser support, progressive enhancement and how standards are developed.

You can download the 'It's Hardboiled' files and example code from your Five Simple Steps account page.

Piled high with examples, 'It's Hardboiled' will teach and inspire you to start using HTML5 and CSS3 in everything you make for the web today.

You'll also learn by example by investigating how HTML5 and CSS3 technologies are being used today by some of the best designers and developers in the world.

Now pick up your hat, slip on your raincoat and leave what you thought you knew about web design behind, because you, ol' buddy, are about to get hardboiled.

Contents

Part 1 Getting Hardboiled

Part 2 Hardboiled HTML

Part 3 Hardboiled CSS3

Part 4 More Hardboiled CSS3

GETTING HARDBOILED

The Web's changed beyond all recognition from when designers and developers like us liberated it from its dusty academic origins. But the way that we work with design and implementation tools such as HTML and CSS has changed very little.

In **Getting hardboiled**, you'll learn about what it means to be hardboiled. You'll discover why we need to re-evaluate concepts such as progressive enhancement and find out the cold, hard truths about how standards are really developed. You'll find out why websites cannot, need not and should not look the same in every browser and what this means for us and the people we work for. Above all else, you'll learn that change isn't coming, it's already here.

What the hell is hardboiled?

SINCE I WAS IN MY TEENS I've been fascinated by detective fiction. Not the English country house murders or whodunnit mysteries of Agatha Christie — oh no, the Sunday evening television adaptations of those never did it for me — I'm talking about gritty, hard-hitting, anything goes stories from writers like Raymond Chandler, Dashiell Hammett and my own personal favourite, Mickey Spillane.

Turn back a few pages and read the quote at the beginning of this book. That isn't from the notes I made during a client meeting, nor is it from the minutes of a W3C CSS Working Group meeting — although it could quite easily be. No, it's from one of my favourite books, the hardboiled classic *My Gun Is Quick* by Mickey Spillane.

Even if you're not a fan of detective stories, you might know a little about them or have seen a few hardboiled film noir movies. You might be familiar with Humphrey Bogart's portrayal of private detective Sam Spade in Dashiell Hammett's *The Maltese Falcon* from 1941[1].

The Maltese Falcon is the second best detective movie ever made after *Who Framed Roger Rabbit?*[2]

How about Stacey Keach? His 1980s portrayal of Spillane's Mike Hammer on TV was more poached than hardboiled but, still, better a slow detective than no detective is my motto.

Then, of course, there's this guy.

---

[1] http://en.wikipedia.org/wiki/The_Maltese_Falcon_(1941_film)
[2] http://en.wikipedia.org/wiki/Who_Framed_Roger_Rabbit

Want to read some hardboiled for yourself? I hope so, but not until you've finished this book. Start with a classic — the old ones are the best — perhaps Dashiell Hammett's *The Maltese Falcon* or Raymond Chandler's *The Big Sleep*. In the mood for archetypal hardboiled action with a big mug detective, dames and dirty cops? Mickey Spillane's Mike Hammer novels are my favourite. Start with *My Gun Is Quick* and *Vengeance Is Mine!*

In hardboiled detective stories since the 1920s, crime, violence and characters — both good and bad — have been portrayed without a veneer of sentimentality. The term 'hardboiled' means tough, like an overcooked egg. The crimes are tough too, so the heroes have attitude, don't sugar-coat the truth and never play it cute. They — and, by association, we as readers — demand the truth, no matter what it takes and how rotten it might be.

It's always been the heroes — Hammett's Sam Spade, Chandler's Philip Marlowe and especially Spillane's Mike Hammer — who've fascinated me most about hardboiled detective fiction.

What's with him?

Hardboiled heroes are almost always down at heel, usually broke, often drunk and living on a diet of black coffee and smokes — hey, that sounds like most web designers I know. They've a good woman to help them stay on the straight and narrow but don't always treat her as well as they should. When a glamorous redhead walks in the room, a hardboiled hero can't help but turn his head. (OK, this is getting weird. I could be describing myself.)

To a hardboiled hero, jamming a pistol into a guy's temple or ramming a fist into his guts is part of a day's work. When you're 'that guy', the one who can get the job done when no one else can, rules are for sissies — and cops.

Hardboiled detectives sometimes work alongside the police, but they're on the outside because they're also not afraid to break the law when they need to. Being hardboiled means they make their own rules to get a case cracked and see a bad guy behind bars — or dead.

Laws, rules and conventions matter, of course, but sometimes those same rules can get in the way of justice being served. When we can't do what we know is right, we need heroes who aren't afraid to step outside to get the right thing done.

Hardboiled detectives do what cops and the rest of society can't — because a detective's actions aren't limited by the rules or conventions that society has imposed on itself. We cheer them on, no matter how ugly or how brutal they can be — we root for them because we need them. Web designers can learn a lot from hardboiled detectives. This brings us to the title of this book and an approach I've called 'hardboiled web design'.

What's hardboiled web design?

'Hardboiled' web design is about never compromising on creating the best work we can for the web. Hardboiled is about challenging assumptions. Hardboiled is never being afraid to push boundaries, break rules or invent new ones. Hardboiled is stripping our markup to the bone to make it more adaptable to whatever the web might throw at it. Hardboiled is not hesitating to make the most of new technologies.

Being hardboiled won't be easy, but if you're ready to challenge yourself, light a smoke, take a lungful and steel yourself. It's going to be a long night.

Here's to the pencil pushers: may they all get lead poisoning

In life, as well as on the web, we need rules, we need conventions, we need standards — but we should always use them to inform what we do, not define it, and certainly never limit it.

Although the web's roughly two decades old (at the time I'm writing this), we've already developed 'standards' for it — standards bodies like the W3C act as the guardians of so-called 'web standards technologies' like HTML, CSS and JavaScript. We've also built up a series of best practices, such as progressive enhancement and graceful degradation, dictating how to use these technologies to build websites that are usable, cross-browser compatible, accessible, visually appealing, indexable by search engines, and more.

But the world's far from perfect and these standards and best practices are only really 'recommendations'— the W3C even uses this word to describe the specifications they maintain. There's no legal entity and no other body that can force browser vendors and web professionals to adopt these standards and best practices, other than through peer pressure and common sense. If it wasn't for them, this would be a very different kind of book.

We're all fortunate that support for standards in browsers is now more complete and consistent than at any time past — but there's still trouble in paradise. As well as supporting contemporary browsers, we also need to find ways to deal with the older and less capable browsers.

In the past it was standard practice to fight hard to create a website that looked and worked the same across all browsers — no matter what their capabilities. To do this meant making compromises and avoiding using technologies not supported by all browsers.

Is this hardboiled?

Don't kid yourself, sweet cheeks. This isn't the way to evolve our craft or build a better web. This kind of old-fashioned thinking holds us back. It forces us to make excuses for not doing what we know is the right thing. The worst that we, as the current custodians of the web, can do is to allow anything to limit what's possible.

"But we have to do what our bosses and customers want! We have to do what they expect!"

I've been around the block a few times — I know the score. But I also know it's possible to give our clients what they want and at the same time use new technologies such as CSS3 and HTML5 to expand our creative options. This is what hardboiled web design is all about.

Before we look at how to move beyond approaches we take for granted, let's ask ourselves why we've been so reticent about embracing new web technologies.

Nice shirt. Who's your tailor? Quasimodo?

When my last book, *Transcending CSS*, went to print in 2006, there was very little support for CSS3. Only Firefox supported CSS3 multi-column layouts and only Safari supported multiple background images. Even though *Transcending CSS* was described as an 'advanced' book at the time, those two properties were about as advanced as it got.

Four or more years on and the scene has changed beyond all recognition. On the desktop, Internet Explorer's market share dipped to less than sixty per cent for the first time in 2010[1]. Rival browsers have gained market share and mobile internet browsing has grown faster than I bet even the smartphone makers and network providers could ever have imagined.

We've an amazing array of CSS3 properties today that would've set my pulse racing if I'd written about them in 2006. Most have been implemented by contemporary browsers, including Internet Explorer 9.

The Twitter #css3 hash tag[2] buzzes with comments when a new CSS3 demonstration is published — like the Spider-Man cartoon titles recreated using CSS animations by Anthony Calzadilla[3].

---

[1] http://telegraph.co.uk/technology/news/7676289/Microsoft-Internet-Explorer-losing-share-to-Google-Chrome.html
[2] http://twitter.com/#search?q=css3
[3] http://www.optimum7.com/css3-man

If you've time on your hands, why not follow Anthony Calzadilla's lead and recreate a cartoon classic with CSS? I can't do justice to this example, or the many you'll find throughout this book, with four coloured inks. That's why I've included links to online videos[1]

Web magazines and thousands of blogs regularly publish tutorials and demonstrations about what's possible with CSS3. After years of frustration at what we saw as painfully slow CSS3 development progress, we now have amazing CSS tools. You might think we'd be clamouring to do amazing things with them.

You'd be wrong. Think again, chump. Far from focusing on what we can do, most of us focus on what we can't. Far from embracing the possible, most of us complain about limitations. Far from getting excited, most of us whine and moan.

If you'd like to know exactly how Anthony Calzadilla made The Amazing Spiderman animation using only CSS, he wrote an exhaustive (and exhausting) breakdown.[2]

[1] http://hardboiledwebdesign.com/v/listing/
[2] http://optimum7.com/internet-marketing/web-development/pure-css3-spiderman-ipad-cartoon-jquery-html5-no-flash.html

The whole thing stinks like yesterday's diapers!

In June 2009, Smashing Magazine published an excellent CSS3 primer by Inayaili de Leon which referenced a little of my work[1] — that was nice. I can't say the same about Smashing Magazine readers' comments though. In response to Yaili's article we have Exhibit One:

> *"Great article, thanks but I think to wait that the most of [sic] browsers support CSS3 total[l]y to develop websites for my clients."*

And this:

> *"I HOPE css3 will be standard in the near future, right now you can't really use anything of it 'cause not every browser supports it."*

There was more:

> *"I can't wait to start using the new CSS3 standard, but I don't think we can start just yet. Especially when IE isn't supported in some of these."*

Give me strength.

> *"CSS3 looks really good however because of IE it will be long time before I start using it"*

My heart sank. I wondered if the last four years had all been for nothing?

Six months later, Tim Van Damme sent me a preview of the CSS animations he was publishing on 24ways[2]. I was stunned and wrote on Twitter:

> *"Just seen something that, at 12pm tonight, will change the web forever!"*[3]

[1] http://www.smashingmagazine.com/2009/06/15/take-your-design-to-the-next-level-with-css3
[2] http://24ways.org/2009/css-animations
[3] http://twitter.com/Malarkey/status/6666284803

That wasn't intentional hype-mongering. I was speechless, stunned, flabbergasted. OK, maybe I was a little over-enthusiastic, but this wasn't mindless hyperbole. I was excited because here was one of the world's best designers demonstrating amazing new possibilities.

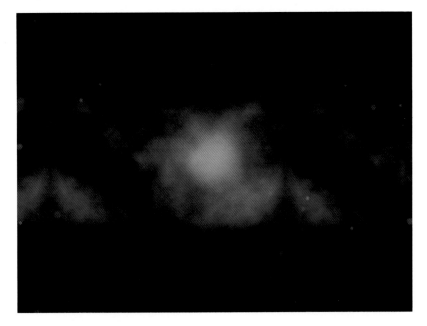

24ways[1], the annual advent calendar for web geeks, is one of the best places to find HTML5 and CSS3 tutorials written by some of the world's best designers and developers.

When the comments began to roll, I got angry. Angry at the lack of enthusiasm and angrier at the lack of ambition. Exhibit Two:

> "Um, what's the point of using some CSS tricks that less than 8% of users can see/use?"

Oh, don't get me started.

> "I really think people are being quite optimistic about this being available in any other browsers any time soon. I think it will be a while before we can use this kind of stuff all the time and have most people see it, it really is a minority at the moment."

[1] http://24ways.org

I could feel my blood starting to boil.

> "[W]e dont yet live in this future, and when my clients' stats tell me that
> 90% of their visitors use IE (and less than 1% use Chrome and Safari
> combined), I sigh and we get on with the job."

I sighed too — at just how mediocre all this sounds.

Who are you callin' a chump, chimp?

Despite designers like Yaili and Tim demonstrating what's possible today with
CSS, what's the most adventurous most of us get? If we're feeling daring we
might, just might get away with adding rounded corners using `border-radius`
instead of garbled markup and images.

Is that the best we can do? Is that the most adventurous we can get? What?
We're working with a client who really lets us push the boat out? We could add
a drop shadow too!

Well, let me sit down while you fetch me a stiff drink*.

Hardboiled? I don't think so.

Frankly, I don't blame people for a lack of ambition. I'm not naive enough to ignore the fact that most of us have bosses or customers who dictate what we can and can't do. I know that we've lived with conventions about what's right and wrong for a long time. But if we're to move the web forward, we should be thinking anew, challenging conventions and at the same time clearing up popular misconceptions. Misconceptions like:

- websites should look the same in every browser
- it's not safe to adopt new technologies until every browser supports them

Breaking it up

I may not be one of the hardboiled heroes I dream about — I never was much good in a brawl — but over the next few chapters I'll challenge many popularly held ideas about how to use new and emerging technologies. Then I'll set out a plan that satisfies our clients' needs while allowing us to push the boundaries.

I'm passionate about how we can make the best designs using the best, most up-to-date tools. So I won't be afraid to tell it like I see it. Don't expect me to be soft-spoken.

---

* Irony

(Give me that) ol' time religion

PROGRESSIVE ENHANCEMENT has been one of the foundations of modern web development and my first exposure to it was an entry posted by Dave Shea on his blog[1], when he introduced what he called 'MOSe' — Mozilla, Opera and Safari enhancement. You should've heard of Dave, because he's the guy who created the CSS Zen Garden[2].

Dave explained his MOSe method as follows:

> "[A]fter creating a basic, functioning page in IE, you add extra functionality [for more capable browsers with advanced selectors]. ...This is the only way we can keep moving forward in the next few years. Let's embrace it."[3]

Dave suggested that we should first create a page that's accessible and usable to low capability browsers, most notably earlier versions of Internet Explorer. Then — by using CSS child, sibling and attribute selectors — apply styles understood only by more capable browsers. You'll notice that Dave discussed how a page should work, not necessarily how a design should look.

Hold that thought.

---

[1] http://mezzoblue.com
[2] http://csszengarden.com
[3] http://mezzoblue.com/archives/2003/06/25/mose

Scotch on the rocks... and I mean ice

Earlier that year, Steve Champeon[1] wrote and spoke about what he termed 'progressive enhancement.' If you haven't heard of Steve, he's the 'other guy' who co-founded the Web Standards Project[2].

> *"Progressive enhancement is an approach to web design that builds documents for the least capable devices first, then moves on to enhance those documents... [to] allow a richer experience for those users with modern graphical browser software."* [3]

This notion of progressive enhancement is what many of us now regard as the ideal way to design and develop websites — starting with a design that can be rendered by less capable browsers, then layering on details that will only be seen by more modern and generally more capable browsers. In practical terms this means starting with widely supported CSS2 selectors and properties, and only using emerging CSS3 properties sparingly. But this widely held interpretation is holding back both our creative potential and the wider use of new technologies.

Even though Steve used the term 'web design', I'm sure that he never intended we should limit our creativity to the capabilities of a lowest common denominator browser. Even if he did, can you guess when his and Dave's articles were written? 2003!*

[1] http://hesketh.com
[2] http://webstandards.org
[3] http://hesketh.com/publications/articles/progressive-enhancement-paving-the-way-for/
* Coincidentally the same year that George W. Bush declared "mission accomplished" in Iraq.

Work's been kinda slow since cartoons went to colour

If you were carrying a bleeding edge MP3 player in 2003, you'd have a massive 30Gb iPod in your pocket or purse. If you were designing, developing or just browsing the web in 2003, here's what software you were using:

- Apple Mac OS X 10.2 (Jaguar)
- Windows XP (SP2)
- Adobe Photoshop CS
- Macromedia Dreamweaver 7
- Microsoft FrontPage 2003
- Internet Explorer 6
- Apple Safari 1
- Mozilla Phoenix/Firebird
- Opera 7

In terms of software, we accept that time marches on and upgrades are both necessary and desirable. But in other ways — particularly the way we think about progressive enhancement — we stick doggedly by received wisdom.

I'm as good as dipped

That isn't to say that there aren't still many aspects of progressive enhancement that remain useful, even seven years since the term was coined:

- basic content and functionality should be accessible to all browsers
- lean, clean, semantic HTML should describe content
- CSS should accomplish all aspects of visual design
- behaviour should be enabled using unobtrusive scripting

When we build by these rules, our content never relies on CSS or JavaScript to be available or accessible. When we use meaningful HTML it will be lighter and more adaptable. CSS makes pages easier to format for every type of browser and device.

Progressive enhancement still has much to offer, but instead of rigidly applying its ideas — especially in regards to visual design — we must continually re-evaluate it as the web, and what we make for it, changes.

I'm not bad, I'm just drawn that way

In Handcrafted CSS' hard man Dan Cederholm re-christened progressive enhancement as 'progressive enrichment':

> *"We should treat these visual details as rewards for the browsers that support the advanced code that creates them. We're visually rewarding users of browsers that are forward thinking. That's the core of the term 'progressive enrichment'."*

Enhancement (or enrichment) commonly starts with layering the 'safest' CSS3 properties like border-radius or box-shadow — perhaps applied using RGBa colour values — over a simple design.

The trouble is, enrichment still treats CSS3 properties as visual rewards for people who use modern browsers.

Enrichment still means starting at the bottom, with a lowest common denominator design for less capable browsers — and that's not good enough anymore. When we use CSS3 simply to "enhance documents [to] allow a richer experience for those users with modern graphical browser software" [1], it's no wonder we normally only manage a few rounded corners. That's because when we start at the bottom and design for the capabilities of the lowest performing browsers first, there's only so far up we can reach.

I had to shake the weasels

The hardboiled approach turns progressive enhancement as applied to visual design on its head. Instead of starting from the lowest performing browsers, hardboiled means working from the top down and designing for the best browsers first. This way we can make the most of everything that more capable browsers and emerging technologies like HTML5 and CSS3 have to offer.

This enables us to reach higher and design better experiences. But how can we design for the best and still take care of people who use older or less capable browsers? The answer is to consider how each progressively less capable browser will render a design. And then, instead of hacking our HTML, CSS or JavaScript to attempt cross-browser pixel perfection, embracing the differences and designing around them.

I can guess what you're thinking. "Isn't this just 'graceful degradation'?"

You've been hanging around rabbits too long

The flip side to progressive enhancement, graceful degradation ensures that when styles and scripts are not available or understood, the content of a document will remain accessible.

Taking a graceful degradation approach means that a website's functionality will always be usable — albeit to a lesser extent and perhaps with a lower fidelity experience — and its content will remain accessible.

---

[1] http://handcraftedcss.com

This is how we handle things down in Toontown

Considering accessibility and how websites function in older or less capable browsers is a fundamentally important part of what we do. But the term graceful degradation, as traditionally applied to visual design, implies that we should compromise.

To hell with being graceful!

The hardboiled approach pushes graceful degradation further and demands that we use our creative talents to design experiences that are responsive and tailored to a browser's capabilities. Hardboiled web design redefines graceful degradation for the challenges we face today.

If we're going to create the inspiring websites that our customers expect, we must look beyond how we've approached progressive enhancement and graceful degradation in the past. Simply 'rewarding' people who use more capable browsers with rounded corners and drop shadows and generally settling for less isn't enough.

Instead we should take full advantage of new technologies, and craft every user's experience so that it's appropriate to the capabilities of the browser they're using. That will likely mean that designs will look different — sometimes very different — across browsers.

For some people this approach might seem radical — hardboiled even — but it makes better use of today's technologies and it's creatively liberating. It allows us to reach higher and design better, more inspiring and imaginative websites and applications.

I'll bake you a carrot cake

When progressive enhancement and graceful degradation were first described, the web was an altogether different place. There were relatively few differences between competing browsers in terms of absolute support for new features.

Today, that's all changed. The gap between the capabilities of older browsers and contemporary ones is wider than ever. In contemporary browsers there's now solid support for CSS3 selectors and properties:

- selectors to bind styles to any element without using id and class attributes
- more ways to work with colour and transparency
- new ways to work with backgrounds and borders
- transforms to translate (move), rotate, scale and skew elements
- transitions to add subtle interactive effects
- animations that were previously only possible using JavaScript or Flash

Support for CSS3 properties in contemporary browsers

	Safari 5	Chrome 6	Firefox 3.6	Opera 10.6	IE9
@font-face	●	●	●	●	●
border-radius	●	●	●	●	●
border-image	●	●	●	●	
box-shadow	●	●	●	●	●
Columns	●	●	●		
Gradients	●	●	●		
Keyframe Animations	●	●			
Multiple backgrounds	●	●	●	●	●
Opacity	●	●	●	●	●
RGBa/HSLa	●	●	●	●	●
text-shadow	●	●	●	●	
transforms	●	●	●	●	
transitions	●	●	●	●	

CSS3 has given us the tools and creative freedom to make amazing things happen. To dismiss the creative possibilities of CSS3 as 'bells and whistles' would be short-sighted and foolish. There are no technical reasons why we can't use every single one of these CSS3 properties today. There really is no need to wait.

So what's stopping us?

Nothing more than a few old-fashioned ideas.

Breaking it up

Neither progressive enhancement nor graceful degradation should be treated as doctrine or applied religiously to everything that we make for the web. Instead, they provided the starting points, and it's now up to us to keep redefining how we adapt and apply their principles to suit the changing landscape of the web.

The way standards develop

PEOPLE OFTEN MISTAKENLY BELIEVE that the W3C innovates new technologies, but its role is primarily as a standards body, not an innovation body. Its job is to standardise patterns of existing technologies. CSS Working Group Invited Expert Elika Etemad sums up the role of that group well.

> *"[T]he Working Group exists for the purpose of standardization. If nobody's interested in implementing something, we're wasting our time writing a spec on it. Also, if only one implementor is interested in implementing something, we can't really make a cross-platform standard out of it."* [1]

For a long time I thought that the W3C's CSS Working Group first innovated, then released working drafts and recommendations. I imagined that when W3C recommendations were complete, browser makers would implement them (or not). In reality, the opposite is true. Implementation comes before a standard is defined, with browser vendors implementing experimental features and then trying to reach agreement. That's why — although most parts of the CSS2.1 specification were implemented in browsers years ago — it only became a W3C Candidate Recommendation in September 2009, when differences had been resolved. This makes CSS2.1 a snapshot of web browser implementations.

> *"The CSS Working Group's work is considered a success if there are multiple independent complete and interoperable implementations of its deliverables that are widely used."* [2]

---

[1] http://fantasai.inkedblade.net/weblog/2009/css-wg-charter
[2] http://fantasai.inkedblade.net/weblog/2007/css-wg-q-and-a

While many of us wait for the W3C's work on CSS3 to be complete and then implemented by browser makers, the reality is that a standard is formed only when there's consensus on what's already been implemented.

If we care about standards and want to ensure that our work conforms to them, what does this mean? How can we use 'web standards' selectors or properties when the standard has not yet been finalised and may not be for a decade?

Should we avoid using emerging technologies until a standard is finalised? If we did we'd miss out on years of creative opportunities. So, we needn't wait for HTML5 or CSS3 modules to become recommendations at the W3C: we can make the most of these emerging standards today.

There's no one CSS3 specification

Unlike CSS1, CSS2 and CSS2.1, CSS3 isn't a single, monolithic specification but is divided into modules. The CSS Working Group develops each module separately and according to the group's priorities:

> "CSS beyond Level 2 is being developed as a set of modules each of which may advance on the W3C Recommendation Track independently. Among them are modules for syntax, cascading and inheritance, and, of course, many aspects of typography, page layout and presentation." [2]

Breaking CSS3 into modules is good news for browser makers because it enables them to gradually implement CSS3 features to fit with their release schedules. It's also great news for us because it allows us to work with CSS3 properties as they're implemented — rather than waiting for a single, large specification to be complete.

---

[1] http://w3.org/Style/2008/css-charter
[2] http://www.w3.org/Style/2008/css-charter#scope

CSS Working Group active priorities

In its 2010 charter, the CSS Working Group set out its priorities along with the 'deliverables' it aims to accomplish.

This isn't a full and exhaustive list. I've chosen the modules that are most relevant to the work we do. (You'll find explanations and examples for modules marked *.)

High Priority Modules

---

*Selectors   Proposed recommendation
                                     (http://w3.org/Style/CSS/Test/CSS3/Selectors/current)

Adds an even greater array of selectors to bind styles to an element. For example, we can select elements based on whether they're immediate siblings of another element or if they're the only child element of their kind. We'll be working with CSS3 selectors throughout the examples in this book.

---

*Backgrounds and Borders   Candidate recommendation
                                     (http://w3.org/TR/css3- background)

Enables us to control the size, repetition and fit of a background image, use images within borders and round the corners of a box. (See chapters 13 and 14.)

---

*Colour   Last call (http://w3.org/TR/css3-color)

Includes transparency and several colour notations including RGB, RGBa, HSL, HSLa. (See chapter 12.)

---

*Fonts   Working draft (http://w3.org/TR/css3-fonts)

Allows us to embed downloadable fonts and adds more advanced text styling and typographic controls. (See chapter 11.)

---

*Multi-column Layout   Candidate recommendation (http://w3.org/TR/css3-multicol)

Generate pseudo-columns without additional markup and control their quantity and width as well as gutters and dividers. (See chapter 19.)

---

*Media Queries   Candidate recommendation
                                     (http://w3.org/TR/css3-mediaqueries)

Extends CSS @media rules to allow us to apply styles based on a device's screen size, colour depth and aspect ratio. Media queries are useful for sending optimised styles to mobile devices. (See chapter 19.)

*Transitions Working draft (http://w3.org/TR/css3-transitions)

Different to animations, CSS transitions enable a property to transition smoothly between two states using CSS instead of scripting, for example the colour of a hyperlink as it changes between normal and :hover states. (See chapter 17.)

*Transformations Working draft (http://w3.org/TR/css3-2d-transforms)

Matching many of the controls available in SVG, this module adds controls in CSS to translate (move), rotate, scale and skew an element. (See chapter 16.)

Medium Priority Modules

*Flexible Box Working draft (http://w3.org/TR/css3-flexbox)

Defines 'box' and 'inline-box' keywords for the 'display' property to allow us to display elements either in rows or columns.

Generated Content for Paged Media Working draft (http://w3.org/TR/css3-gcpm)

Adds advanced properties for printing, including creating footnotes and cross-references.

Generated and Replaced Content Working draft (http://w3.org/TR/css3-content)

Allows us to add generated content before or after an element, or to replace an element altogether. This visual-only generated content can include text or an object such as an image.

Grid Positioning / Template Layout Working drafts (http://w3.org/TR/css3-grid) (http://w3.org/TR/css3-layout)

Previously known as Advanced Layout, these are ambitious new proposals to enable us to position elements on a flexible grid.

Lists Working draft (http://w3.org/TR/css3-lists)

Increases the variety and shape of list markers.

Marquee Candidate recommendation (http://w3.org/TR/css3-marquee)

Primarily designed for mobile devices and required by the CSS Mobile Profile, this module allows you to use CSS marquees to create scrolling content areas and control their speed, style and direction.

Low Priority Modules

---

*Animations   Working draft (http://w3.org/TR/css3-animations)

Specifies how properties change their values during an animation and over how much time.
(See chapter 18.)

CSS3 Text Layout

Adds new properties to control text direction, including vertical text. Although these properties are
predominantly designed for styling non-European languages, they will also be a useful addition to a
designer's CSS toolkit.

CSS3 Text   Working draft (http://w3.org/TR/css3-text)

Aims to expand text styling for non-European languages and scripts. Very little of this module has been
implemented and there's even less impetus to develop it further.

Each CSS3 module is currently at a different stage in the standards
development process based on how much of it has been implemented in
browsers. Plus, new modules are still being added. This is why CSS3 will not
be 'complete' for some considerable years to come. Don't worry, we can start
using a lot of what these modules contain today with a little help from vendor-
specific prefixes.

Vendor-specific prefixes

When I demonstrate CSS3 in later chapters, you'll soon notice a recurring theme — not all browsers support the same properties in the same ways. For example, many browsers, including Internet Explorer 9, support opacity in its native form:

```
a.action { opacity : .5; }
```

But rounded corners need a vendor-specific prefix to work in some browsers. For example, older versions of Safari and Google Chrome require the -webkit- prefix before the border-radius property.

```
a.action { -webkit-border-radius : .8em; }
```

Browser makers use vendor prefixes to test new CSS properties — usually for several iterations — until there's common ground between implementations. Mozilla's Firefox requires the -moz- prefix:

```
a.action { -moz-border-radius : .8em; }
```

Cross-browser border-radius therefore means writing rules several times — vendor prefixed properties followed by the W3C's official syntax (which is supported by Internet Explorer 9, Opera 10.6 and Safari 5.)

```
a.action {
-webkit-border-radius : .8em;
-moz-border-radius : .8em;
border-radius : .8em;
}
```

There are several other vendor prefixes but we generally use those only needed by Firefox, Opera and WebKit. Microsoft even has its own vendor prefix, -ms-, but there's been little reason to use it.

If you find writing multiple vendor prefixed properties tedious, Paul Irish and Jonathan Neal's 'CSS3, Please!' Cross-Browser CSS3 Rule Generator[1] will make your life easier. One word of caution though. 'CSS3, Please!' offers proprietary Microsoft filters too. Don't use them.

---

[1] http://css3please.com

Common browser vendor prefixes

-khtml-	Konqueror
-moz-	Mozilla
-ms-	Microsoft
mso-	Microsoft Office
-o-	Opera
-webkit-	Safari, Google Chrome and other WebKit browsers

While standards emerge, writing long lists of vendor prefixed properties is a hassle, so in March 2010 Peter Paul Koch (PPK) called for browser makers to stop using them altogether.

> *"Vendor prefixes force web developers to make their style sheets much more verbose than is necessary[...] [W]hy do we need to use several declarations for obtaining one single effect?[...] Guys, let's stop the vendor prefix nonsense. Enough's enough."* [1]

I'll respectfully disagree. PPK would find plenty more to complain about if emerging properties were implemented without vendor prefixes and each browser rendered them differently.

Does writing multiple vendor prefixed properties take more time? What, you expected being a web professional would be easy? There's still an upside though — we don't need to write box model hacks anymore.

---

[1] http://quirksmode.org/blog/archives/2010/03/css_vendor_pref.html

Targeting specific browsers

When PPK suggested browser makers drop their vendor-specific prefixes altogether, he missed one critical point. It's not only browser makers who take advantage of prefixes: we can too. This is important because not every browser gets its implementations right first time.

In Firefox 2.0 Mozilla implemented border-radius incorrectly. Until Mozilla fixed the problem in Firefox 3.0, we could choose to target only those browsers whose implementations were up to scratch, denying Firefox 2.0 any rounded corners by omitting the -moz- vendor prefix. In his article, 'Prefix or Posthack' on A List Apart, Eric Meyer makes the point well.

> *"Mozilla and WebKit browsers both support gradients, but they use radically different syntaxes to achieve the same basic result. Now imagine a world where the vendors had implemented gradients without the prefixes. You would have three choices:*
>
> *1. Pick which browser gets a gradient and which one doesn't.*
> *2. Use CSS hacks or browser sniffing to serve up different styles to different browsers.*
> *3. Walk away from using gradients entirely."* [1]

In response to PPK's article, Jonathan Snook got it right.

> *"The vendor prefix does two things:*
>
> *1. It allows browser developers to test new functionality without fear of a changing spec.*
> *2. It warns web developers that things are in flux.*
>
> *[...] As web developers, we make the choice to implement a design with or without vendor prefixes and their existence does not mean that we have to use them."* [2]

Vendor-specific prefixes were originally intended for use only by browser makers and the CSS2 specification warns us (authors) not to use them.

---

[1] http://alistapart.com/articles/prefix-or-posthack
[2] http://snook.ca/archives/html_and_css/not-supported

"Authors should avoid vendor-specific extensions." [1]

Out here in the real world, vendor-specific prefixes are a necessity so that we can use CSS3 properties today. SitePoint also fails to take the rapidly changing landscape of the web into account and suggests we play it safe on vendor-specific prefixes:

> *"[W]e don't recommend that you use these extensions in a real application. It's fine to use them for testing purposes, and for trying out CSS properties that haven't been implemented yet."* [2]

But safe isn't what the web needs now — it needs us to make the most of emerging standards and technologies so that we can create amazing things.

Not all vendor prefixed properties are the same

SitePoint gets it right about one thing — using vendor-specific prefixes shouldn't open the door to using every proprietary prefixed property, no matter how tempting they may be.

Tim Van Damme used WebKit's proprietary custom scrollbar styles in his 2010 redesign[4]. You can read about these properties on Beautiful Pixels' 'A Guide To Using Custom Scrollbars On Your Site'[5] and on the Surfin' Safari blog[6]. You'll find a comprehensive list of WebKit-specific properties on CSS Infos[7].

> *"[Y]ou should use those that are closely related to equivalent CSS properties (be that CSS1, 2, or 3), so that you can switch to the standard property later on, and remove the extension when the browser implements the correct specification."* [3]

This is because as well as using vendor-specific prefixes to perfect their implementations of emerging CSS3 standards, browser makers also use them for non-standard properties inside the workings of their browsers. For example, Apple uses non-standard controls for scrollbars in iOS. While it's fascinating to study non-standard extensions, I recommend you only use properties that are part of the continuing standards development process.

[1] http://w3.org/TR/CSS2/syndata.html#vendor-keywords
[2] http://reference.sitepoint.com/css/vendorspecific
[3] http://reference.sitepoint.com/css/vendorspecific
[4] http://maxvoltar.com
[5] http://beautifulpixels.com/goodies/create-custom-webkit-scrollbar
[6] http://webkit.org/blog/363/styling-scrollbars
[7] http://css-infos.net/properties/webkit.php

Are vendor prefixed properties valid?

In the standards development process, properties prefixed with a - (dash) or an _ (underscore) are reserved for vendor-specific extensions.

> *"An initial dash or underscore is guaranteed never to be used in a property or keyword by any current or future level of CSS."* [1]

Using them will render a style sheet technically invalid, but you should know by now that validation is a tool, not a religion. An invalid style sheet is a small price to pay for all we can achieve using emerging CSS3 standards.

There's no time like the present

In the W3C's standards process it takes years for any specification to reach Candidate Recommendation. Should we wait until every CSS3 module has reached that stage before using its properties? Are we going wait until every new browser has implemented CSS3 properties without a vendor prefix before we take advantage of them? Good luck with that. Meanwhile the web will have moved on and, if we don't make every use of these new technologies starting today, we'll soon find our work has failed to keep up.

Party like it's 1997

Some of us have realised that it's possible to achieve results similar to CSS3 properties in Internet Explorer 6, 7 and 8 — even though those browsers implemented very little of any emerging standards. How are we doing this? By digging out a copy of *Dynamic HTML Web Magic* from 1998. You know the one — it's probably propping up your monitor.

---

[1] http://reference.sitepoint.com/css/vendorspecific

When Microsoft released Internet Explorer 4 in 1997 — at the height of the first browser war with Netscape — a set of proprietary CSS extensions was one of their heavy weapons.

Microsoft hoped these filters and transitions would tempt us to create what the company described as "multimedia-style visual effects" — effects that its rival Netscape couldn't reproduce. Many of these effects are similar to what's now possible in CSS3. For example, the following makes an element appear fifty per cent opaque in Internet Explorer (before version 9):

```
div {
-ms-filter : "progid:DXImageTransform.Microsoft.Alpha(opacity=50)";
}
```

This, on the other hand, adds an effect that's similar to CSS3's box-shadow:

```
div {
-ms-filter : "progid:DXImageTransform.Microsoft ↵
.DropShadow(offx=2, offy=1, color=#333)";
}
```

Microsoft's filters and transitions are still supported by Internet Explorer. This has encouraged some of us to blow off years of dust from *Dynamic HTML Web Magic* and replace that faithful monitor riser with *Flash 4 Magic*. What are we thinking? Possibly we, our bosses and our customers still cling to the idea that websites should look the same in every browser.

In April 2010 Smashing Magazine published Louis Lazaris' 'CSS3 Solutions for Internet Explorer' [1] in which he combined vendor-specific prefixes with Internet Explorer's non-standard filters. This gave readers the false impression that vendor prefixed CSS3 properties and Microsoft's proprietary filters are somehow the same.

They're not.

---

[1] http://smashingmagazine.com/2010/04/28/css3-solutions-for-internet-explorer

Internet Explorer's filters weren't, never have been and never will be part of the W3C's standards process, and advocating their use as acceptable alternatives to CSS3 is dangerous.

Used frequently, Internet Explorer filters can have a serious negative impact on a website's performance. This is particularly apparent on older hardware in less well-optimised versions of Internet Explorer. Even the AlphaImageLoader filter we commonly use to force support for semi-transparent PNG images in Internet Explorer 6, holds up the rendering of a page and freezes the browser while each and every image downloads.

To avoid performance problems associated with the AlphaImageLoader filter, substitute PNG32 images with an alternative format such as GIF or PNG8. If there's no alternative to AlphaImageLoader, quarantine it using conditional comments to target only those versions of Internet Explorer that need it.

Double standard?

Why am I so emphatic that we should embrace vendor prefixed properties but avoid Internet Explorer filters? Don't we need to use any tool necessary to get the job done? I've not forgotten that some bosses and customers still demand that their websites look exactly the same in every browser, but there are other issues to consider. When we hack around differences between browsers by using proprietary filters — even to satisfy a demanding client — we perpetuate that outdated notion that cross-browser pixel perfection is a worthwhile goal, even at the expense of standards.

Breaking it up

When we understand that CSS3 is made up from a series of independent modules, each with its own timetable for development, we can leave behind the idea that we should wait until it — as a single specification — will be finished before we can embrace its selectors and properties. Instead, we can use them now; there's no reason to wait any longer.

But even with the rapid adoption of CSS3 in contemporary browsers, there will always be differences between browser capabilities. Rather than hacking around these differences we should learn to embrace them.

It doesn't have to look the same

ONE PRECONCEPTION THAT OFTEN PREVENTS US and our clients from making the most of emerging technologies such as HTML5 and CSS3 is that websites should look and be experienced exactly the same in every browser.

Dan Cederholm answers the question "Do websites need to look exactly the same in every browser?" [1] with an emphatic "No!" He's right, too.

When we use a highly capable browser such as Safari 5, we see a design that's appropriate for that browser. If our browser has the capability to display `text-shadow`, we'll see Dan's design as he intended.

If a user has a less capable browser, such as Camino, they won't see a shadow. That's OK, because Dan's design doesn't look broken and they won't know they're missing something.

---

[1] http://dowebsitesneedtolookexactlythesameineverybrowser.com

What about 'experience'? Dan's penchant for very long domain names answers that question too — "Do websites need to be experienced exactly the same in every browser?" [1] [2]

Hover your mouse over "Do websites need to be experienced exactly the same in every browser?" and the experience you'll have will depend on the capabilities of the browser you're using. This is the cornerstone of the hardboiled approach.

Of course they don't.

Dan may have a talent for choosing catchy domains but he wasn't the first person to raise the issue.

> "[W]e need to step back from our endless battle to make it look the same across all platforms. We can't make our site look the same on a PDA as a 21" monitor, we can't make our site 'the same' for someone on a speaking browser, and although things are improving there are still differences in support and implementation of various W3C standards. Let go, it[']s not going to look the same." [3]

Rachel Andrew wrote that in 2002. Why are we still having that same conversation today? Of course, some people still think that websites need to look and be experienced exactly the same in every browser, but those people probably still print their e-mails.

[1] http://dowebsitesneedtobeexperiencedexactlythesameineverybrowser.com
[2] http://hardboiledwebdesign.com/v/c4-4
[3] http://edgeofmyseat.com/blog/it-doesnt-have-to-look-the-same

Many organisations maintain matrices that determine which browsers their sites 'support'. While some base support on commonly used browsers, others like Yahoo! grade browsers according to capabilities.

> "Graded Browser Support is a QA philosophy, not a report card on the quality of popular browsers. It's designed to provide guidance for QA teams about how best to use their limited testing resources (and to frontend engineers about how to sanely cross-check work across a finite set of browsers)." [1]

Yahoo! Graded Browser Support, February 2010

	Windows XP	Windows 7	Mac OS x 10.5	Mac OS x 10.6
Firefox 3	A-grade			
Firefox 3.6	A-grade	A-grade		A-grade
Google Chrome 4	A-grade			
Internet Explorer 8	A-grade	A-grade		
Internet Explorer 7	A-grade			
Internet Explorer 6	A-grade			
Safari 4			A-grade	A-grade

Although we may not agree with what Yahoo! considers A, C or X-grade browsers, they understand that the look, feel or experience of using a website doesn't need to be the same in every browser.

> "Support does not mean that everybody gets the same thing. Expecting two users using different browser software to have an identical experience fails to embrace or acknowledge the heterogeneous essence of the Web. In fact, requiring the same experience for all users creates an artificial barrier to participation." [2]

---

[1] http://yuiblog.com/blog/2010/02/16/gbs-update-2010q1
[2] http://developer.yahoo.com/yui/articles/gbs

Yahoo! understands that a website looking or being experienced the same in every browser is not a matter of opinion. It's not something anyone can dictate. Web browsers have different capabilities and so websites can't look or be experienced the same in every one. Period.

Learn to live with that. Of course, we could spend time bulking up our pages with presentational markup, extra images and JavaScript workarounds. This is precisely what we've been doing for years and it's often what our bosses and customers expect — but we're not living in the past. We should make the realities of today's wide-ranging browser landscape clear to them. We could limit a design to a lowest common denominator browser, but when our users carry smartphones or iPads, will they really expect their experience of a website to be the same on those as in Internet Explorer 6 — a browser released in 2001?

It's time for everybody to move on.

> "There are over 10,000 browser brands, versions, and configurations and that number is growing. [...] No two browsers have an identical implementation." [1]

Yahoo! gets it, and so do many savvy web designers and developers.

Responsive design

The idea that websites need not look the same in every browser isn't new. John Allsopp explained this in his seminal A List Apart article, 'The Dao of Web Design' way back in 2000.

---

[1] http://developer.yahoo.com/yui/articles/gbs

"The control which designers know in the print medium, and often desire in the web medium, is simply a function of the limitation of the printed page. We should embrace the fact that the web doesn't have the same constraints, and design for this flexibility. But first, we must 'accept the ebb and flow of things'." [1]

Many smart web designers and developers are already promoting the benefits of website designs and experiences that are tailored to respond to the shape, size and capabilities of browsers. Ethan Marcotte calls this "responsive design" [2] and his ideas have already inspired some of the world's best designers. You'll be seeing their inspired designs and the responsive techniques Ethan describes in use later in this book

Browser makers serve their own priorities

Designs cannot look the same in all browsers because no two browsers are alike. No two browsers are alike because no two browser vendors are alike. Each one has its own revenue streams, its own priorities, its own release schedules. Each one implements the parts of CSS that meet its agenda and in order of its priorities.

Five years of browser releases 2006–2011

	2006	2007	2008	2009	2010
Firefox	2.0		3.0	3.5	3.6
Google Chrome			1.0	2.0/3.0	5.0/6.0
Internet Explorer	7		8		9
Opera	9.0/9.1	9.2	9.5/9.6	10.0/10.1	10.6
Safari	2.0.4	3.0	3.1	4.0	5.0

---

[1] http://alistapart.com/articles/dao
[2] http://alistapart.com/articles/responsive-web-design

To expect browser vendors to release their products to meet anyone's priorities but their own would be folly. Bosses and customers might want a website to look and be experienced exactly the same, but we must remind them — politely but firmly — that a browser's capabilities are a browser maker's business, not a web designer's.

The facts of life

Some organisations have quality assurance teams or marketing department staff who are dedicated to ensuring that their websites remain pixel-perfect across every browser in their matrix. For them, experience and pixel-perfection are indistinguishable from a brand and so differences between browsers are seen as imperfections.

The efforts of these teams should now be directed away from cross-browser perfection and on to ensuring that brand values and a great experience are maintained and tailored for every capability of device. This change might not come easily but it will come.

We should reassure bosses and customers that — when we adopt the hardboiled approach — differences between browsers will enhance a brand because we can precisely tailor experiences. We can inform them that differences are opportunities for us to demonstrate our creativity and therefore should be embraced.

When we shift focus from looking backwards to looking forwards, invest time in design instead of in lengthy workarounds for less capable browsers, our bosses and customers will see real improvements in brand experience. Here's a true story about a switched-on client.

Designing for CannyBill

My redesign for CannyBill was an open, public process. You can read about my design decisions and see the progress from start to finish on my blog[2]

CannyBill[1] is a software company that sells invoicing solutions. Their technically savvy customers use the latest browsers. When the company asked me to work with them I knew I would need CSS3 selectors and properties to accomplish a design that would make its product stand apart from their competitors'.

During the design process we openly discussed that customers using more capable browsers would see rounded corners, CSS3 gradients and transparencies. Those using less capable browsers would see square edges and flat, solid colours.

CannyBill also accepted that its budget was better spent on designing experiences from the best browsers down, instead of on hacks and workarounds to make its website look the same in every browser.

---

[1] http://cannybill.com
[2] http://stuffandnonsense.co.uk/s/1308

Given the choice between hacking and the diminishing returns that would bring, and designing features that add real value, any sensible client will choose the latter. So why do we so often hear designers and developers say:

> *"My customers won't let me use progressive CSS because it's not supported by IE"*

or

> *"I will have to wait until IE6 diminishes and Internet Explorer renders CSS the same as other browsers".*

This is an issue that can easily be resolved if we handle it correctly. If you think that your clients won't allow you to adopt the top down, hardboiled approach try this.

Explain that designing from the top down ensures that everybody will see and experience a website in a way that's appropriately crafted and responsive to the capabilities of their browser. Most importantly, no one will be left out.

Ask clients outright,

> *"Would you prefer me to spend my time hacking around issues for older browsers like Internet Explorer 6 or spend it instead on making the website look the best that it can on better desktop browsers, as well as on a whole host of mobile browsers?"*

I'm confident you'll be surprised by their answer.

You should be so lucky

Not everyone gets lucky enough to work with a client as savvy as CannyBill. But no matter what type of organisations you work for, there are ways to explain the differences between browsers that will help everyone to understand.

I'm lucky that I get to work with clients who are switched on technically and who appreciate that time and their money are better spent on creating tailored and responsive designs, rather than on workarounds to attempt cross-browser pixel perfection. But not all clients are the same.

Some are too busy running their businesses to pay attention to changes in technology. Others care or know little about the changing capabilities of browsers. How can we help them to understand that websites needn't and can't look or be experienced the same in every browser?

If clients raise the thorny issue that a design looks different in an alternative browser, never be defensive. Explain that designing a range of tailored experiences will be better for everyone. This helps clients understand the positive impact of browser differences rather than seeing them as imperfections.

If you work within a traditional institution — perhaps a large business, government department or in education — how can you sell the idea that your organisation's website should be tailored, responsive and hardboiled?

Explaining these issues is less difficult now than it was just a few years ago. Back then, most people experienced the Web through a PC on their desk so the differences between browsers were hard to grasp. Today it's a whole lot easier, as more people regularly browse the web using a mobile device in the form of a smartphone, iPad or an iPod Touch and so more readily understand that browsing is a different experience across devices and platforms:

Worldwide mobile browser usage, January – June 2010[1]

	Opera	iPhone	Nokia	iPod Touch	Blackberry	Android
January	25.53%	21.52%	18.53%	11.6%	9.85%	4.54%
February	25%	22.51%	16.99%	11.41%	10.67%	5.35%
March	26.1%	20.56%	16.45%	9.57%	12.31%	5.84%
April	26.14%	20.18%	15.52%	9.21%	13.67%	6.18%
May	26.68%	19.97%	14.69%	9.09%	13.78%	6.3%
June	26.35%	18.05%	15.84%	8.69%	14.41%	6.69%

[1] http://gs.statcounter.com/#mobile_browser-ww-monthly-201001-201006

I often find it useful to point to the myriad of mobile devices. With so many people carrying mobile web-enabled devices, bosses and customers already know about different browsing experiences. This fact, along with common sense, will strengthen any argument that websites should now be tailored and responsive instead of looking the same.

Breaking it up

The reality is that the web has changed, and our work and our clients' expectations must move beyond the one-size-fits-all approach we have laboured over for so long if we're to make the most of what it has to offer. No two browsers are the same, so to make the most from emerging technologies such as HTML5 and CSS3, we need to banish the notion that websites should look and be experienced exactly the same in every browser.

Perpetuating this idea will continue to cost us and our bosses and customers time and money on expensive hacks and workarounds instead of tailored experiences. It also prevents us from moving forward and embracing change.

To help make change possible, we should explain that browser differences are not imperfections but are instead opportunities to enhance a brand experience by making websites more responsive.

No. 5

Browsers don't limit creativity

THERE ARE PLENTY OF WAYS to get web designers and developers riled up, but none better than starting a conversation about the browser we all love to hate. You know what I'm talking about — Internet Explorer 6.

> *"The problem is IE6. Outdated but still widely used, especially in the developing world, its inaccurate and incomplete CSS support forces web designers and developers to spend expensive hours on workarounds ranging from hacks, to IE6-only styles served via conditional comments, to JavaScript."* [1]

Boy, do we like to complain. We bitch about Microsoft's decision to leave its browser rotting for years. Then we moan about the time we spend writing remedial styles and patches for its rendering bugs.

If we're still going strong, we complain about private users who don't upgrade or about IT departments whose policies keep their users shackled to Internet Explorer 6. Then we scheme about how to persuade users to switch by designing elaborate upgrade messages, or worse, we attempt to trick them into upgrading. All this bitching and moaning does no good because it's neither a web designer's job nor responsibility to get people to switch to a different browser.

Is there an echo in here?

We've been here before, of course, with Netscape 4, then Internet Explorer 5 and now Internet Explorer 6. All were ground-breaking browsers when they were released and each did as much as any browser can to move the web forward.

---

[1] http://zeldman.com/2009/05/21/a-new-answer-to-the-ie6-question

Arguments over whether it is 'safe' to drop 'support' for Internet Explorer
6 today are simply echoes of the discussions we had about Netscape 4 and
Internet Explorer 5. As Dan Cederholm wrote,

> "IE5/Win's support of CSS2 is far from perfect, yet it is possible to
> get things looking close to other standards-aware browsers. But that
> consistency doesn't happen without added time, frustration and
> necessary hacks and workarounds. [...] Can you imagine just not having
> to worry about the poor support for CSS that adds a significant amount of
> time to the development process?"

And.

> "You could also imagine sending IE5/Win a basic set of CSS rules
> that does everything but layout [...] a basic stylesheet that all devices
> (including handhelds) could render that's devoid of anything too
> complicated. IE5/Win is capable of complex CSS — but it comes at a price
> that we're all well aware of." [1]

Dan wrote this in 2004. Now substitute 2004's IE5 for today's Internet Explorer
6 and tell me why we're still agonising over the same issues? Complaining
that old browsers hold back the web isn't the way forward. Neither is moaning
about why people still use them. Instead we need to find mature and creative
ways to tackle the issue.

Do older browsers hold back the web?

In his article 'Calling time on IE6', .net Magazine's Craig Grannell draws an
inevitable conclusion.

> "Like Netscape 4 in 2000, IE6 is perceived to be holding back the web.
> How much longer [will] we prop up this ageing browser[?]" [2]

[1] http://simplebits.com/notebook/2004/12/17/ie5
[2] http://www.netmag.co.uk/zine/discover-culture/calling-time-on-ie6

But we don't have to "prop up" an ageing browser by continuing to labour to make a site look the same in Internet Explorer 6, 7 or any other browser.
We only have ourselves to blame if we let older or less capable browsers hold back the web. It's our outdated thinking that's in danger of letting that happen — not, as the past can show us, any one particular browser.

.net's 'Bring Down IE6' campaign[2] is right about one thing though:

> "*Microsoft is encouraging companies and developers to move on from IE6, designers need to unite, and we all need to move on.*"[1]

Instead of following their suggestion — to add a campaign logo to our websites, to "[e]ducate your colleagues, users and clients", or "[p]rovide an upgrade notice for IE6 users" — we should recognise the fact that there have always been and always will be some browsers that are older or less capable than others. We must also accept that there will always be differences in how browsers render our designs, and then design around them. Lee Munroe puts it very well,

> "*[R]ather than campaigning to get people to upgrade their browser, shouldn't we just deal with it [...]?*"[2]

The issue isn't always as simple as old versus new browsers. Take the open source Camino browser — "developed with a focus on providing the best possible experience for Mac OS X users"[3] — it has a loyal following. Camino shares Firefox's Gecko rendering engine but, unlike Firefox users, Camino fans upgrading to its latest version (2.0 at the time of writing) won't enjoy many CSS3 selectors, properties and web fonts because Camino uses an older version of Gecko.

---

[1] http://bringdownie6.com
[2] http://leemunroe.com/ie6-design-help
[3] http://caminobrowser.org

Upgrading a browser won't guarantee support for new features. Should we encourage Camino 2 users to upgrade? Wait. They just did. The problem isn't Camino or its users — it's how we handle the issue of browsers with different capabilities.

We can't complain about browser makers not innovating either. The developers at Opera worked hard to give their browser some of the best support for new technologies. But even their latest version (10.6 at the time of writing) lacks support for some CSS3 properties.

Microsoft too — after years of letting Internet Explorer stagnate — has made great leaps and Internet Explorer 9 is a world-class browser it should be proud of. But Internet Explorer 9 hasn't got the same CSS3 support as WebKit- or Gecko-based browsers. Should we wait until it has? Or should we accept that there are differences even between contemporary browsers, design around them, then move on?

How to cope with older browsers

One size rarely fits all and no single approach will work for every designer, developer, client or project. So what are our options for coping with older or less capable browsers? How can we best support them and their users?

Supporting a browser needn't mean making a design look the same. On the opposite side of the coin, not supporting a browser shouldn't mean that a website's content will be inaccessible. Support should be a sliding scale. Jeremy Keith wrote about this in his 'IE6 Equation'.

> *"[M]ethods for dealing with IE6 demonstrate that there's no one single answer that works for everyone. [...] There's no shortage of blog posts, articles and even entire websites discussing when to drop support for IE6. But very few of them take the time to define what they mean by "support." This isn't a binary issue. There is no Boolean answer. Instead, there's a sliding scale of support[.]"* [1]

How should we tackle support for older or less capable browsers?

Make our websites look exactly the same

This is precisely what we've done, unchallenged, for years and it's what many of us and our clients believe is the norm. This approach carries a cost, often hidden, in time spent on hacks and workarounds. Whether we explicitly charge for making websites look the same or not, somebody always pays.

Write a remedial stylesheet

Developing for standards-competent browsers first, then testing and rectifying problems caused by Internet Explorer has been an approach favoured by many of us. Conditional comments make it trivial to serve different versions of Internet Explorer their own remedial styles. This approach has few pitfalls, as long as we bear in mind that we must keep our markup lean, mean and hardboiled and that websites needn't and shouldn't look the same in every browser.

---

[1] http://24ways.org/2008/the-ie6-equation

Use JavaScript to boost CSS support

Libraries such as jQuery are powerful and popular because they make it easier to create JavaScript interactivity, transitions and animations. There are few downsides; in fact, many leading developers have advocated using JavaScript to add CSS support to older browsers so that we can get the most from new selectors and properties. As Eric Meyer wrote:

> *"There are two primary benefits [to using JavaScript]. The first is obvious: we can stop waiting around for browser makers to give us what we want, thanks to their efforts on JavaScript engines, and start using the advanced CSS we've been hearing about for years. The second is that the process of finding out which parts of the spec work in the real world, and which fall down, will be greatly accelerated."* [1]

Devote no development or testing time to older browsers

Few of our clients will accept a broken-looking page that reflects badly on their brand. Still, that hasn't stopped Amazon and YouTube from publicly announcing an end to their support for Internet Explorer 6.

> *"We would like to inform you that as of the end of March 2010, we will no longer develop Seller Account pages to be compliant with Internet Explorer 6. This decision allows us to use all modern web development technologies and create an up-to-date user experience."* [2]

37Signals is a company that's in touch with its audience and it understands that people who use their products will most likely use a contemporary browser.

[1] http://meyerweb.com/eric/thoughts/2008/10/22/javascript-will-save-us-all
[2] http://amazonsellercommunity.com/forums/thread.jspa?threadID=182907&tstart=0

"The Internet Explorer 6 browser was released back in 2001, and Internet Explorer 7, the replacement, was released nearly two years ago in 2006. Modern web browsers such as IE 7, Firefox, and Safari provide significantly better online experiences. Since IE 6 usage has finally dipped below a small minority threshold of our customers, it's time to finally move beyond IE 6." [1]

For 37Signals, continuing to develop its web applications means stopping support for Internet Explorer 6 altogether. That browser and others like it simply cannot render the experience that 37Signals aims to deliver. Although I can appreciate that position, altogether stopping support for a browser will often result in a design that looks broken at best, or is inaccessible at worst, for a significant proportion of web users. I think Yahoo! gets it right:

"In the first 10 years of professional web development, back in the early '90s, browser support was binary: Do you — or don't you — support a given browser? When the answer was "No", user access to the site was often actively prevented. In the years following IE5's release in 1998, professional web designers and developers have become accustomed to asking at the outset of any new undertaking, "Do I have to support Netscape 4.x browsers for this project?" By contrast, in modern web development we must support all browsers. Choosing to exclude a segment of users is inappropriate [...]." [2]

We don't have to abandon users or exclude them by using browser sniffing to block access. With a little creative thinking and the knowledge that all browsers, especially older ones, needn't see the same design, we can find better, more inclusive ways.

[1] http://37signals.blogs.com/products/2008/07/basecamp-phasin.html
[2] http://developer.yahoo.com/yui/articles/gbs

Creating our own problems

We often create problems with the way we handle the issue of older or less capable browsers. I know of plenty of designers and developers who make rods for their own backs because they:

- wrongly assume that clients expect cross-browser pixel-precision
- don't frame conversations in ways that matter to a business's bottom-line
- show static Photoshop design visuals and set unrealistic expectations

We often assume that a client will demand cross-browser pixel-perfection even when we don't ask outright. I can't count the number of times I've heard something like this.

> *"If any client I have every* [sic] *dealt with agreed to using this strategy to deal with ie6, I'd check myself into the local hospital as I would have probably lost my marbles."* [1]

Four years ago you'd have found me in the next padded room, but now? Sure, some clients have specific browser support needs — but all of them? I don't buy it.

Our clients often make the wrong assumptions too. Sometimes they demand cross-browser pixel-perfection because their preconceptions about the web tell them it's the norm, not because their business needs depend on it. Our job isn't to re-educate them but to ensure that their demands are based on real needs, facts and statistics. I always find it useful to ask, "Is that request based on empirical evidence or your personal opinion?" Try this yourself and I bet you'll be amazed at how easily demands for cross-browser pixel-perfection melt away.

---

[1] http://stuffandnonsense.co.uk/blog/about/universal_internet_explorer_6_css/#r731

The problem with analytics

Whereas in the past, older or less capable browsers largely prevented us from working with emerging technologies, our statistics should show now that usage of those browsers has declined sharply — at least in the developed world — and especially as people more regularly use smartphones and other mobile devices. On the other hand, the basis on which we make design and technology decisions has changed very little.

Traditionally, we look to statistics to tell us about the browsers people are using today, but it's just as important to use those same statistics to predict what browsers people will use in three, six or maybe nine months' time. To help our clients understand that the hardboiled design approach will pay real dividends, we should ask them:

> *"What's been the month-on-month growth in smartphone usage on your site? What percentage of Android, iPhone and iPad users will you have in a year's time?"*

Questions like these help to strengthen the argument that our time will be better spent on designing the best experiences for the best browsers as they turn attention away from older or less capable browsers and towards future browser use. My experience has been that many clients appreciate this forward-looking approach because it takes into account their future as well as their current business needs. Instead of telling clients what can't be done, give them options on how much of their budget should be spent on handling older and less capable browsers. Here's another true story.

Another real client conversation

The aim of my redesign for *New Internationalist* was to improve visual layout and readability through better typography, and provide an easier path for their readers to important calls to action including subscribing to the magazine.

When I redesigned *New Internationalist*[1], the campaign for social justice magazine, its team and I talked openly about browser support and I asked them to make a decision about how to cope with older browsers, in particular Internet Explorer 6.

---

[1] http://newint.org

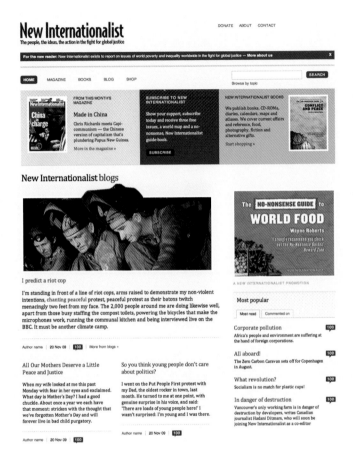

You can read a full account of my redesign for *New Internationalist* across several articles on And All That Malarkey[1], starting with 'Help me to redesign *New Internationalist*[2] and ending with 'A top-down look at the *New Internationalist* redesign[3].

I gave them three options:

- spend three days writing remedial styles to make Internet Explorer 6 look as close as technically possible to other browsers
- spend one day implementing and testing a JavaScript solution for Internet Explorer 6, then two days on polishing the design for better browsers
- spend ten minutes implementing a simple typography stylesheet for Internet Explorer 6 that would give us three days designing for better browsers

[1] http://stuffandnonsense.co.uk/blog/category/design
[2] http://stuffandnonsense.co.uk/blog/about/help_me_to_redesign_new_internationalist
[3] http://stuffandnonsense.co.uk/blog/about/a_top_down_look_at_the_new_internationalist_redesign

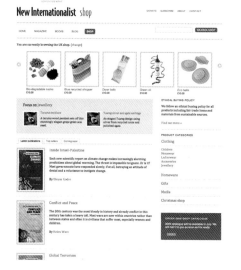

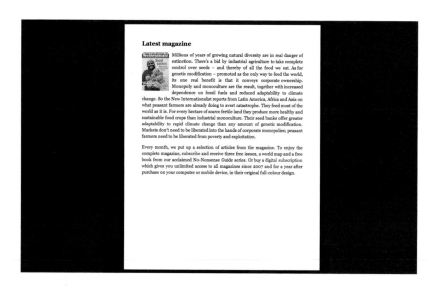

New Internationalist's article pages and archives use a typographic stylesheet that emphasises readability over visual layout. This approach is similar to the Reader feature introduced by Apple into Safari 5.

New Internationalist decided to spend one day ensuring that only their store pages were as consistent as possible in Internet Explorer 6 — their store is a major source of revenue — but they also appreciated that some differences in the design would be inevitable.

On other sections of *New Internationalist* we agreed to implement a typography stylesheet for Internet Explorer 6 — one that maximises readability, but removes layout. This compromise allowed us to spend more time fine-tuning the design for better, newer browsers.

Confidently explaining the issues and their options, and focusing attention on business objectives, help clients like *New Internationalist* to make smart decisions. They will most likely choose to invest time and money on looking forwards rather than backwards.

Being confident, though, can be tough. Not everyone feels comfortable going out on a limb when they fear that a project or even their job might be on the line. Remember, though: our clients aren't paying us just to show up. They're paying for our knowledge and experience, and for us to lead them in the right direction — that's precisely what we should do.

The contract killer

Managing expectations involves explaining what browser support means and how we will approach the business of designing and testing. For most of us this process should begin with the contract we issue.

I've thumbed through enough contracts to fill a filing cabinet. I've signed more than I can remember — many of them so complicated that I should've hired a lawyer (or a detective) to make sense of their jargon. After spending weeks searching for a simple contract, I decided to write my own and I published it online for anyone to use. My first killer contract, in 2009, had this to say about older browsers.

> *"We will test all our markup and CSS in current versions of all major browsers including those made by Apple, Microsoft, Mozilla and Opera. We will also test to ensure that pages will display visually in a 'similar', albeit not necessarily an identical way, in Microsoft Internet Explorer 6 for Windows as this browser is now past it's* [sic] *sell-by date."* [1]

It might come as a surprise, but from the first day that clause was in my contract, no client ever questioned that a website will look different in older or less capable browsers. Since I first wrote that contract, the browser landscape has dramatically changed with the release of Apple's iOS devices, Android and Internet Explorer 9. Internet Explorer 6 has also become less of an issue, so I broadened my browser support clause to take these new circumstances into account. My contract now reads.

> *"The landscape of web browsers and devices changes regularly and our approach is to look forward, not back. With that in mind we will test all our markup and CSS in current versions of all major desktop browsers to ensure that we make the most from them. Users of older or less capable browsers or devices will experience a design that is appropriate to the capabilities of their software. For people using Microsoft Internet Explorer 6, this means a universal, typographically focussed* [sic] *design but no layout."* [2]

These changes are subtle, but they're forward looking and take into account the improvements that all browsers makers have made to their software.

[1] http://24ways.org/2008/contract-killer
[2] http://stuffandnonsense.co.uk/blog/about/contract_killer_the_next_hit

Breaking it up

There are plenty of us who are afraid that being clear from the outset that designs might not look exactly the same in every browser could lose us work to a competitor — one who is less open about their process.

I've experienced precisely the opposite and found that stressing the positive benefits of a forward-looking approach prevents uncomfortable discussions, and demonstrates that as designers and developers we're in touch with the reality of today's web and can help a client's business to benefit from it.

How different is different?

WHEN WE SAY "websites don't need to look the same in every browser," what does this mean for people who pay for or use the websites we make?

First, let's clear something up — different should never mean 'looks broken'. It shouldn't mean 'looks ugly and uncared for' either. If columns drop, content areas overlap or pages become inaccessible, it's simply not acceptable.

How different is different? That will depend on the technologies we choose and the capabilities of browsers receiving them. Sometimes the differences will be minor, other times they will be more noticeable and in some cases our users might see a completely different design — one that has been tailored to the capabilities of their browser.

In the past some people have looked at differences between browsers as imperfections. So we've been forced to compromise by bulking up our markup or using JavaScript. We've been taking this approach for years, kicking our code like a dog to accomplish the same visual design across browsers.

Whereas in the past, unchallenged progressive enhancement meant approaching design from the least capable browser first — providing a functional if dull design — we should now be designing from the top down, for the best browsers first.

Are we already hardboiled?

You might be surprised, but we're already working the hardboiled way when we build font stacks in CSS. We design from the top down, starting with our ideal typeface, then fall back to a series of considered alternatives.

Extending this approach to the major parts of our designs liberates our creativity and allows us to use any and all technologies to create designs that are appropriately tailored to any browser's capabilities. Now let's turn our attention to designing these tailored experiences.

Modernizr

We don't need to carry a gun to be a hardboiled web designer. We won't be bumping anyone off — unless our clients start being bunnies. What we do need is a pocketful of tools to make hardboiled web design practical.

One such tool is Modernizr[1], an open source JavaScript library that enables us to serve appropriate and responsive designs that are tailored to the capabilities of a browser. Instead of enabling CSS3 properties in less capable browsers, Modernizr uses feature detection to test a browser's capabilities to render them. This makes Modernizr an essential part of a web professional's toolkit and the foundation for hardboiled web design.

When we embed Modernizr into our pages, the script detects whether the current browser supports CSS3 features including:

@font-face	border-image	border-radius
box-shadow	Canvas	CSS Animations
CSS Columns	CSS Gradients	CSS Reflections
CSS 2D and 3D Transforms	CSS Transitions	HSLa colour
Multiple backgrounds	opacity	RGBa colour

Keeping one principle of progressive enhancement in mind — that when using any script it's important to consider instances when JavaScript might not be available — to ensure basic styling for non-JavaScript enabled browsers, add the class `no-js` to the HTML element:

```
<html class="no-js">
```

When JavaScript is available, the Modernizr script runs and replaces `no-js` with `js`. Modernizr helps us to 'grade' browsers, not by sniffing their user-agent strings but by performing a series of feature tests. It adds classes to the HTML element based on a browser's abilities.

---

[1] http://modernizr.com

```
<html class="js canvas canvastext geolocation rgba hsla multiplebgs
borderimage borderradius boxshadow opacity cssanimations csscolumns
cssgradients cssreflections csstransforms csstransforms3d
csstransitions video audio localstorage sessionstorage webworkers
applicationcache fontface">
```

When a browser lacks support for a property or feature, Modernizr adds a no-prefix to each class.

```
<html class="js no-canvas no-canvastext no-geolocation no-rgba no-
hsla no-multiplebgs no-borderimage no-borderradius no-boxshadow
no-opacity no-cssanimations no-csscolumns no-cssgradients no-
cssreflections no-csstransforms no-csstransforms3d no-csstransitions
no-video no-audio no-localstorage no-sessionstorage no-webworkers
no-applicationcache no-fontface">
```

With these attributes, we can take advantage of support for CSS3 properties in browsers that support them and decide how to tailor a design for browsers that don't. Take this example of multiple background images. We might start by declaring basic styles that are understood by even the least capable browsers, in this case a single background image applied to a section element.

```
section { background-image : url(section.png); }
```

Alternatively, when we are using Modernizr and it detects that a browser lacks support for multiple background images we can make use of its no- prefix:

```
.no-multiplebgs section { background-image : url(section.png); }
```

For browsers that are capable of rendering more than one background image on a single element, we can serve multiple background images via a more specific Modernizr-powered descendant selector:

```
.multiplebgs section {
background-image : url(section-left.png), url(section-right.png);
}
```

Viewed in Internet Explorer 9 which supports RGBa and box-shadow.

RGBa colour values will make shadows look more natural in most contemporary browsers including Internet Explorer 9. But older versions of Internet Explorer lack support for either RGBA and box-shadow. Learn about RGBa colour and box-shadow in chapter 12.

Viewed in Internet Explorer 8 which has no support for RGBa or box-shadow.

Browsers that can render CSS3 shadows will also likely support RGBa. For those that don't, consider adding thicker, solid right and bottom borders that hint at three dimensions.

This hardboiled card was designed by Peter Fransen (http://www.flickr.com/photos/30162209@N02/4258313050)

404

YOU DUMB MUG!

YOU CAN LOOK ALL YOU WANT, BUT
WHAT YOU'RE LOOKING FOR JUST
AIN'T THERE. DID YOU CLICK A LINK
THAT BUMPED OFF? MAYBE THAT
PAGE IS HOT? EITHER WAY, DON'T
BE A BUNNY.

This page will look its best in browsers that support embedded web fonts. But not every contemporary browser has implemented them. Learn about working with web fonts in Part 3.

Viewed in Safari 5 which supports embedded web fonts.

404

YOU DUMB MUG!

You can look all you want,
but what you're looking for
just ain't here. Did you click
a link that I bumped off?
Maybe that page is hot?
Either way, don't be a bunny.

For browsers without @font-face support, we can design alternative type treatments, perhaps by changing font size, weight and letter-spacing.

Viewed in Camino 2 which has no support for web fonts.

Most contemporary browsers support CSS transforms to translate (move), scale, rotate and skew an element in two dimensions, but they've not been implemented in all browsers. Learn about CSS3 transforms in chapter 16.

Viewed in Chrome 5 which supports CSS3 transforms.

THE NO. 1 LADY BOYS'
DETECTIVE AGENCY

COLE HENLEY ESQ.

SHADES & STACHES
DETECTIVE AGENCY

Command F Detective Services
We can find anyone

The Fat Man

PRIVATE INVESTIGATION

$30 A DAY PLUS EXPENSES
BY APPOINTMENT ONLY.

Dial: M for Murder

PRIVATE INVESTIGATOR
EXTRAORDINAIRE

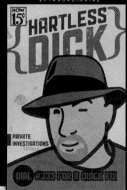

NOW 15¢

HARTLESS DICK

PRIVATE
INVESTIGATIONS

DIAL #333 FOR A QUICK FIX

NICK JEFFERIES
PRIVATE EYE WA6-0086

ELEMENTARY
— MY DEAR WATSON —

PRIVATE INVESTIGATORS

DON'T CALL US. WE'LL FIND YOU

SHOES CLUES
Finding The Footprints They Leave

SMOKE

P.I.
555 – 4763

Fat Man: Dennis Kardys http://flickr.com/photos/14716132@N08/426068131/
Shoes Clues: Paul Randall http://flickr.com/photos/pauldrandall/4253819966/
Hartless Dick: Brian Hart http://flickr.com/photos/51035716156@N01/4249742119
Smoke: Stephen Hay http://flickr.com/photos/stephenhay/4252645548

For browsers without support for CSS3 transforms, arrange elements using CSS positioning instead to provide a simpler, alternative design.

Viewed in Internet Explorer 9 which has no support for CSS3 transforms.

Viewed in Firefox 3.6 which
supports CSS3 columns

CSS3 columns will be added and removed automatically when a browser or device's width changes. But not all the latest browsers have implemented CSS3 columns. Learn about them in chapter 19.

Hardest boiled

Contract Killer by Andy Clarke

Sometimes you let the madness get to you, sometimes you don't. Sometimes the only way to get through the day is to blaze with a crazy anger that tells everyone within earshot that they should stay the hell out of your way. Today was one of those days.

I went as far as the front door and fired up a smoke, drawing deep. The cold winter air on my face and the feeling of smoke filling my lungs made me feel human again.

That was as far as I could get. The reflection that stared back at me in the window told me that I looked like hell. I sneered back in it's face, took another deep drag and flicked the butt outside.

From behind me Letsy said, "Mal…", but she knew better than anyone not to say any more. There was no need, I knew what had to be done.

My guts were a tight little ball under my belt because Letsy wasn't the only one who had remembered. What I had to do had been a fire in my gut. It was a fire that had been burning me up from the inside and there wasn't a Goddamn thing I could do about it. I twisted my fists into hard knots and…

Latest Hardboiled

The Ultimate Package by Simon Collison

I shook the rain from my coat and threw it towards the stand as I walked into the room. Nobody said a word, but I could feel their eyes fixed on me. After seconds like felt like hours, Phil swallowed hard and said slowly…

Pumpkin Soup by Owen Gregory

From the first moment I saw her I knew the dame was trouble. She was a beauty, a goddess who could have any man who could walk. Behind those deep brown eyes I knew a fire was burning that only I could put out…

The Big Break by Gregory Wood

It was one of those nights when the sky came down and smothered the world. The wind howled and the cold rain stung my face as I stumbled, blind drunk and stupid towards the cliff edge…

For browsers that don't support CSS3 columns, improve the readability of written copy by reducing the measure.

Viewed in Opera 10.6 which has no support for CSS3 columns.

Hardest boiled

Contract Killer by Andy Clarke

Sometimes you let the madness get to you, sometimes you don't. Sometimes the only way to get through the day is to blaze with a crazy anger that tells everyone within earshot that they should stay the hell out of your way. Today was one of those days.

I went as far as the front door and fired up a smoke, drawing deep. The cold winter air on my face and the feeling of smoke filling my lungs made me feel human again.

That was as far as I could get. The reflection that stared back at me in the window told me that I looked like hell. I sneered back in it's face, took another deep drag and flicked the butt outside.

From behind me Letsy said, "Mal...", but she knew better than anyone not to say any more. There was no need, I knew what had to be done.

My guts were a tight little ball under my belt because Letsy wasn't the only one who had remembered. What I had to do had been a fire in my gut. It was a fire that had been burning me up from the inside and there wasn't a Goddamn thing I could do about it. I twisted my fists into hard knots and...

Latest Hardboiled

The Ultimate Package by Simon Collison

I shook the rain from my coat and threw it towards the stand as I walked into the room. Nobody said a word, but I could feel their eyes fixed on me. After seconds like felt like hours, Phil swallowed hard and said slowly...

Pumpkin Soup by Owen Gregory

From the first moment I saw her I knew the dame was trouble. She was a beauty, a goddess who could have any man who could walk. Behind those deep brown eyes I knew a fire was burning that only I could put out...

The Big Break by Gregory Wood

It was one of those nights when the sky came down and smothered the world. The wind howled and the cold rain stung my face as I stumbled, blind drunk and stupid towards the cliff edge...

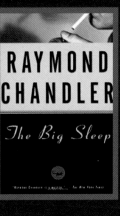

RAYMOND CHANDLER

The Big Sleep

The Long Goodbye by Raymond Chandler

"Philip Marlowe remains the quintessential urban private eye" —Los Angeles Times

Add to basket

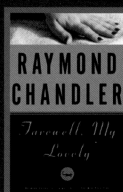

RAYMOND CHANDLER

Farewell, My Lovely

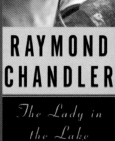

RAYMOND CHANDLER

The Lady in the Lake

RAYMOND CHANDLER

The Simple Art of Murder

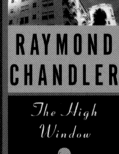

RAYMOND CHANDLER

The High Window

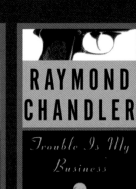

RAYMOND CHANDLER

Trouble Is My Business

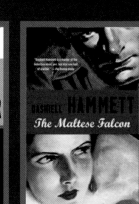

DASHIELL HAMMETT

The Maltese Falcon

For browsers without support for three-dimensional CSS3 transforms, we can float the front and back of each item so that they fit neatly side-by-side.

Viewed in Internet Explorer 9 which has no support for three-dimensional CSS3 transforms.

The Big Sleep by Raymond Chandler

"His thin, claw-like hands were folded loosely on the rug, purple-nailed. A few locks of dry white hair clung to his scalp, like wild flowers fighting for life on a bare rock"

Add to basket

The Long Goodbye by Raymond Chandler

"Philip Marlowe remains the quintessential urban private eye" — Los Angeles Times

Add to basket

Farewell, My Lovely by Raymond Chandler

"Raymond Chandler was one of the finest prose writers of the twentieth century" — Literary Review

Add to basket

The Lady in the Lake by Raymond Chandler

"Raymond Chandler is a master" — New York Times

Add to basket

Viewed in Safari on iOS
(portrait).

Take advantage of iOS devices' ability to switch layouts using media queries and make a design responsive to the orientation of a device. For example, this design works best in portrait.

We can also optimise a design so that it works best when the orientation is landscape without needing to change our HTML.

Viewed in Safari on iOS (landscape).

Serving a typography stylesheet to IE6

When I noticed that use of Internet Explorer 6 was declining sharply on my client projects and was almost non-existent on my own websites, it became clear that spending time and money on hacks and workarounds was yielding diminishing returns.

When I asked why people visited my websites I learned that most came for content and that means type and typography. I designed a stylesheet that focuses primarily on typography and has no layout styles (the area where Internet Explorer 6 has most problems).

I began to serve the same 'Universal Internet Explorer 6 CSS stylesheet' on every website (give or take a little branding or a touch of customisation). This paid dividends because it offers Internet Explorer 6 users a crafted, well-presented experience of what they come for — my content.

Universal Internet Explorer 6 CSS is hosted on Google Code[1] so that you can serve it for your projects. To employ Universal Internet Explorer 6 CSS, first hide all other stylesheets from Internet Explorer 6 and earlier.

```
<!--[if ! lte IE 6]><!-->
<link rel="stylesheet" href="main.css" media="screen, projection">
<!--<![endif]-->
```

Then supply the Universal Internet Explorer 6 CSS stylesheet to Internet Explorer 6 and earlier versions.

```
<!--[if lte IE 6]>
<link rel="stylesheet" href="http://universal-ie6-css.googlecode.com
/files/ie6.0.3.css" media="screen, projection">
<![endif]-->
```

Reaction to the Universal Internet Explorer 6 CSS stylesheet was mixed with some commenters appreciating both its practical advantages and its hardboiled attitude.

> *"You're a mad, beautiful genius. I'd use that in a heartbeat."* [2]

Who do you think you're calling beautiful?

---

[1] http://code.google.com/p/universal-ie6-css
[2] http://stuffandnonsense.co.uk/blog/about/universal_internet_explorer_6_css/#r702

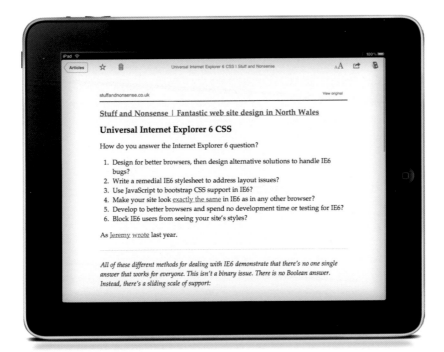

Instapaper[2] is one of the most popular and talked about apps for iOS devices including the iPhone and iPad. Instapaper converts and saves articles into a simple format that emphasises readability.

Others were less enthusiastic.

> *"Andy Clarke states that by simplifying the layout and concentrating on beautiful typography, you put the focus on content:*
>
> *'[...] Content that is almost always written words and that means type.'*
>
> *Almost always written words? What Internet are you using? [...] [W]hat if your content is not text? What if you're an artist and want to show off your work in a way that grabs the attention of the viewer?"* [1]

Well, if you're an artist and you show off your work in a highly visual fashion, or you run an online store where the majority of your paying customers use Internet Explorer 6, a universal typography-based stylesheet won't be appropriate — so don't use one. I think that Jeffrey Zeldman gave the most balanced response when he said:

[1] http://lessfussdesign.com/blog/2009/06/universal-ie6-css-no-thanks
[2] http://instapaper.com

*"No hammer fits all nails, and no solution, however elegant, will work
for every situation. But if we're open minded, Andy's proposal may work
in more situations than we at first suspect. Where it works, it's what
business folk call a 'win, win:' the visitor has a good reading experience,
and client and developer are spared tedium and expense."* [1]

What does browser testing mean today?

Designing experiences that are tailored to browser capabilities raises the
question, "What does browser testing mean today?"

For many of us, browser testing has meant ensuring that a design looks
the same in different browser makes and versions. Not simply that branding
and look and feel appear consistent — or that a design does not look 'broken'
— but that a design looks identical to the nearest pixel.

That approach may have been relevant in the past, but the browser
landscape has changed beyond all recognition in recent years. Internet
Explorer may statistically still be the most widely used browser, but now it
lives inside a broader ecosystem of browsers. Today's browsers, with their
wide-ranging capabilities on computers, gaming machines, media players and
smartphones, plus the rapid development and adoption of new CSS and HTML
standards means we must now adopt a different approach to browser testing.

Perpetuating the idea that websites should look and be experienced
exactly the same is foolhardy and counterproductive. Our time and our clients'
budgets are better spent developing tailored and appropriate experiences, so
what will browser testing mean in today's brave new world?

- Ensuring that content and functionality are accessible
- That designs never look broken
- That an experience is appropriate to the capabilities of hardware or software.

---

[1] http://zeldman.com/2009/05/21/a-new-answer-to-the-ie6-question

Browser version market share top ten January 2010[1]

Browser version	Market share
Internet Explorer 8	22.37%
Internet Explorer 6	20.00%
Firefox 3.5	17.08%
Internet Explorer 7	14.53%
Firefox 3.0	5.24%
Chrome 3.0	3.85%
Safari 4.0	3.57%
Opera 10.x	1.65%
Chrome 4.0	1.24%
Firefox 3.6	1.15%

This approach is creatively liberating. It stimulates us to design to the edges of what is possible in latest browsers and gives us the freedom to create appropriate alternatives. When our clients are satisfied, their end-users certainly won't be disappointed either. That's because people don't find a website that they like, then open up another browser to check that it looks the same. Ignorance, as the poet said, is bliss.

Breaking it up

If we're to create the exciting websites that advances in technology make possible, we must change the way we think about what we design. Will this reality mean we have to take a different approach to design? It already has.

Will creating tailored experiences — ones that get the best from the best browsers and are then matched to the capabilities of others — mean that we have to work harder at design? Yes it will, but we should relish those challenges, not shy away from them. One thing is certain. Living in the past is not an option.

[1] http://netmarketshare.com/browser-market-share.aspx?qprid=2

Presenting designs the hardboiled way

FOR YEARS, I WORKED THE SAME WAY AS MANY DESIGNERS
I KNOW — sketching ideas, making mood boards and
then designing static visuals in Photoshop or Fireworks.
I spent countless hours replicating every rounded box,
shadow, form element and line of type. I then presented
these images to clients to receive their feedback and
gain approval.

Changes took hours longer. I moved layouts pixel-by-pixel, adjusted dozens
of lines of type and even changed the labels on form fields. When clients
signed off a design, I took a deep breath and replicated everything using HTML
and CSS.

There's nothing wrong with the process of designing the look, feel and
layout of a website using a traditional graphics editor like Photoshop, but
there are fundamental problems with using static images to demonstrate an
interactive website design.

I can't hear you over the static

Static images work just fine for conveying look-and-feel but, by definition,
they're an ineffective tool for presenting dynamic content because they fail to
demonstrate even the most rudimentary behaviours and interactions.

Presenting designs as static images sets false expectations and reinforces
old-fashioned ideas such as websites should look the same in every browser.
Today, when websites should be responsive to different browser capabilities,
static visuals all too easily tie a website to a single design. When we should
be making the most of today's technologies, presenting a single design as
a static visual limits our potential to develop tailored experiences, because
clients will then expect their sites to look exactly the same across all browsers
and devices. It therefore limits us to using only a fraction of the creative
capabilities of new technologies such as CSS3.

I looked for a way to solve this problem and realised that the answer was staring me squarely in the face. We're designing web pages, not photographs of web pages, so we should stop presenting designs as static mock-ups and find a way to use hardboiled HTML and CSS instead.

This isn't only important for presenting the mechanics of liquid layouts, link hover states and how users fill in form fields. It's essential for demonstrating more complex interface features such as CSS3 transitions and animations, and most importantly giving us the freedom to use them in place of older, less optimised methods.

Demonstrating type and typography

Over the years we've learned that making text resizable is a fundamental part of accessible design, particularly as Internet Explorer fails to resize text set in pixels. But how can we demonstrate text resizing using a static visual? Should we create a different image for every size increase?

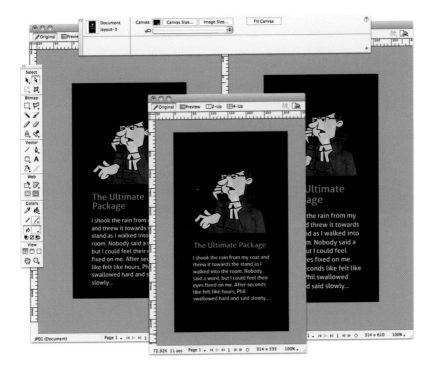

Would creating several images of different text sizes be a sensible use of our time and resources? We would have to demonstrate how boxes move, leading changes and how headings look when they wrap onto multiple lines.

What about font stacks? Should we create separate images to show Aller, Arial and a generic sans-serif?

Should mocking up designs using every font in our stack be part of our design process? How much more complicated will our approval process become if we do? I bet that most clients will point to the primary design and say "I just want it like that!"

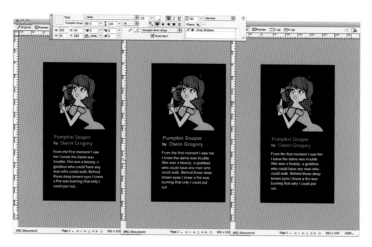

Demonstrating liquid layouts

Even though websites today should be flexible and responsive, fixed pixel-based width designs remain more common than those using percentages. Why is that? I'd bet my PI badge on the reason being that our bosses or customers sign off on fixed-width static visuals.

Demonstrating interactive page elements, transitions and animations

Clients and their users have come to expect that even the simplest websites will be interactive and respond to a 'touch', so a typical website design will likely include:

- hover, active and focus states on text hyperlinks, plain or otherwise styled
- hover, active and focus states on form inputs and buttons
- changes in state on form submissions, help and error messages
- dynamic effects and behaviours created using JavaScript

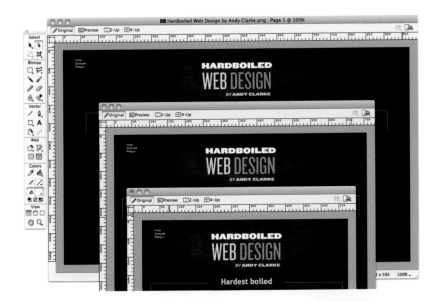

How can we even attempt to demonstrate liquid designs on a fixed-width canvas? Should we make several images for different browser widths?

Demonstrating link hover states is possible by making separate images, but presenting CSS3 transitions and animations would be much more difficult and time-consuming. How could we present even a simple transition between two colours or an element that changes size, rotation or fading opacity?

Should we storyboard every animation, produce a twenty-page flip book? In every case, demonstrating the possibilities offered by emerging CSS is challenging at best and in many situations impossible through the medium of a static image.

Even more challenging and problematic than the inability of a static image to effectively demonstrate a modern day, responsive and interactive design are the false expectations that using static images set in our clients' minds.

It would be possible to produce several 'onion skin' images for each stage of a transformation, but there is nothing quite like experiencing the real thing.

Reinforcing old-fashioned notions

Tools like Photoshop can be invaluable during the creative phase of a project but they aren't the best tools for demonstrating modern website design. Static visuals can't demonstrate the differences between how browsers of varying capabilities will render a design, so our clients will naturally expect that finished web pages will look identical in all browsers. They'll carry on believing that differences between browsers are deviations from the design they signed off.

Static visuals reinforce the notion that websites can and should look the same in every browser. The more time we spend on presenting details like rounded corners or drop-shadows in Photoshop, the more our clients will naturally assume they'll appear in the finished website, regardless of any browser's capability to render them. You can't blame clients for this — we just set the bar.

Is this Photoshop visual a blueprint from which every design element must be reproduced, down to the last detail and in every browser? Or is it an impression of a website's look and feel?

Ultimately the expectations we set add time and money to a project as we'll be forced to use presentational HTML, CSS hacks or JavaScript workarounds, diminishing the integrity of what we produce and reducing its ability to adapt to changing conditions.

How can we demonstrate designs in a way that sets more realistic expectations and at the same time encourages our clients to accept the benefits of different, tailored designs? One solution is to demonstrate designs using HTML and CSS in a browser.

Whether you're a designer who understands HTML and CSS or not — whether you work alone or in a team — demonstrating designs in a browser will mean changes for you and the people you work for. It'll require changes to the way we design, how designers and developers work together and how organisations structure their workflows. These changes may not come easily, but they will pay dividends — improving efficiency, reducing waste and helping everyone involved to make better, more informed decisions. If this sounds good and hardboiled, how can you get started?

Don't scratch that itch

If you're fluent in HTML and CSS — even if you're not, don't skip this part — presenting designs in HTML and CSS won't take much of a change. You can carry on using your preferred design tools, whatever they may be.

After you've crafted a design and you're satisfied it's ready to show, resist the urge to present it as a static image. Take a deep breath and spend a few hours translating it into HTML and CSS. A few hours is all it should take (you can work quickly because, at this stage, HTML and CSS needn't be production-ready). Any extra time spent now will be saved later, because you've already begun working with markup and CSS and so will produce fewer visuals to demonstrate different facets of your designs. Use a framework such as Blueprint[1] or 960 Grid System[2] if that helps, although I've found that using my own set of framework files results in cleaner, more flexible code that can be used for the finished site.

---

[1] http://blueprintcss.org
[2] http://960.gs

Simon Collison's Ultimate Package

In a series of articles about his 'Process Toolbox", Simon Collison explained how he built his own 'Ultimate Package' of files and conventions and how they help him begin each project.

> *"Think of it as a bumper compendium of cascading and connected CSS files, naming conventions, modules, plugins and library scripts that ensure any project led or worked on by any member(s) of a team will stay on convention, and be simpler for anyone else to step into and work with at any time."* [2]

As a starting point for his projects, Simon developed a set of foundation HTML templates. Each includes pre-linked style sheets and JavaScript library files including the latest versions of jQuery and other commonly used plugins.

In addition to jQuery, I've added Ethan Marcotte's image resizing script[1], Modernizr and Selectivizr[2] to my version of Simon's Ultimate Package.

```
<script src="jquery-1.4.min.js"></script>
<script src="imgsizer.js"></script>
<script src="modernizr.js"></script>
<!--[if lt IE 9]>
  <script src="DOMAssistant-2.0.min.js"></script>
  <script src="selectivizr.js"></script>
<![endif]-->
```

Simon's templates also contain patterns for common page layouts, starting with headers, navigation, content areas and footers. He also includes reusable HTML fragments for forms, lists, tables and other elements.

Working with his own conventions for naming elements and attributes helps Simon write HTML faster and when we're building our own packages, it's important to keep conventions simple, memorable and most importantly flexible enough to utilise on any project. You'll learn about how to base naming conventions on existing patterns including microformats and WAI-ARIA roles in the next section.

As Simon often collaborates with other designers and developers, his Ultimate Package contains a standard set of imported CSS style sheets. He gives each collaborator their own 'scratch' CSS file — a sandbox for them to add their own styles. To set up a scratch system, first import two style sheets: screen.css and scratch.css.

---

[1] http://unstoppablerobotninja.com/entry/fluid-images
[2] http://selectivizr.com

```
@import url(screen.css);
@import url(scratch.css);
```

scratch.css overrides rules in the screen style sheet using the cascade. Into scratch.css, import other style sheets, one for each collaborator.

```
@import url(scratch-andy.css);
@import url(scratch-geri.css);
```

When everyone's work is complete, move rules from their scratch style sheet into screen.css. You'll see how effective this set-up can be when you experiment with the files from the 'It's Hardboiled' example site.

Ultimate Package files can also include fixes for common Internet Explorer layout bugs, quarantined into their own dedicated style sheets for each version and served using conditional comments.

```
<!--[if IE 6]>
    <link rel="stylesheet" href="ie6.css" media="screen, projection">
<![endif]-->
<!--[if IE 7]>
    <link rel="stylesheet" href="ie7.css" media="screen, projection">
<![endif]-->
<!--[if IE 8]>
    <link rel="stylesheet" href="ie8.css" media="screen, projection">
<![endif]-->
<!--[if IE 9]>
    <link rel="stylesheet" href="ie9.css" media="screen, projection">
<![endif]-->
```

Building an Ultimate Package will dramatically reduce repetition and make transition from Photoshop to a working prototype ready to be presented in a web browser easier and faster.

Although Simon didn't share his files, Tim Murtaugh has done just that and published his own set of HTML5 and CSS templates that jumpstart web development[3]

HTML5 Boilerplate[4] is a "professional badass's base HTML/CSS/JS template for a fast, robust and future-proof site" by Paul Irish and Divya Manian.

[1] http://colly.com/comments/the_process_toolbox_part_one_backbonen
[2] http://colly.com/comments/the_process_toolbox_part_seven_convention
[3] http://html5reset.org
[4] http://html5boilerplate.com

Make the most of your time

If you're concerned that spending time writing HTML and CSS before a client has seen and approved a visual design could be a waste of time and effort, don't worry. The savings we'll make across the entire duration of a project will far outweigh the time we take initially. After all, we'll be working with HTML and CSS at some point — we're just spending time on them earlier rather than later in the process.

We save time in other areas too. Whereas traditionally we might mock up a large number of page designs in Photoshop, now we need only a minimal set to help with creative direction. These images need only indicate look-and-feel, so we can give those countless hours spent on replicating form elements, tables and type the big kiss off.

By not duplicating work — styling elements in both Photoshop and CSS — the design process gets faster and you'll soon notice a huge boost in productivity. The time we save can be spent fine-tuning a design and on making it more responsive. Switching to demonstrating designs in a browser will be easier for designers who are fluent in HTML and CSS, but what about those who use external developers to write HTML and CSS for them?

Less can mean more

If you concentrate only on visual design and hand images to an external developer, it could be more difficult to adapt to a new workflow. Nevertheless, the benefits of presenting designs in a browser remain tangible.

Hold off producing a stack of static images and make designs for just one or two key pages instead — pages that illustrate a creative direction. Before you present these designs, ask a developer to implement them in HTML and CSS before demonstrating them to a client. At first this might seem like we're showing less, but presenting a smaller selection of designs in HTML and CSS gives clients a far better overall impression than a stack of images ever can. Clients can interact with designs more closely, make better decisions and provide more accurate and appropriate feedback.

After gathering comments, provide developers with a detailed set of instructions for the remaining pages, not as Photoshop images but as sketches and written notes. This will save time and money, and avoid costly repetition.

Partner up

What if you work for an organisation which has separate design and development teams, and design is viewed as creative work and development as technical? If that's the case, how can you demonstrate designs in a browser?

Partnering designers and developers to produce designs ready for presenting in a browser needn't take a major organisational shift and it will pay real dividends. By working more closely together, designers appreciate the complexities of implementing their designs. On the flip side, developers can explain the complexities of working with HTML and CSS and get better, earlier feedback on how a design should look when implemented.

Problems that often cause friction can be averted and when working together, developers can ask questions such as

"How much line-height should I apply to these headings?"

or

"If this layout is liquid, how do you want the navigation to wrap at smaller window sizes?"

This breaks the costly back-and-forth, trial and error approval cycle that frequently adds complexity, time and money to a project.

Presenting designs in a browser

When we demonstrate a design to a client using HTML and CSS, we don't need anything more than a browser — often their browser, any browser. Before a presentation, look over designs in the latest browsers — I start with Safari and Google Chrome, before moving on through Firefox, Opera and finally on to Internet Explorer 9.

Even these excellent contemporary browsers have varying capabilities, so we're not looking for cross-browser pixel-perfection. Instead, we're testing to ensure there are no layout problems during the demonstration. It might be prudent to test for layout bugs in Internet Explorer 7 or 8 too, depending on what we know about the client's browsing environment.

When working remotely, upload all necessary files to a server and talk your clients through each part of a design. I prefer to present in person, starting with the best browsers, then progressively less capable ones.

Walk and talk a client through each design and, with every browser, explain why aspects of the design differ and how the design can be tailored to a browser's capabilities. Make clients aware that these differences should be seen as opportunities to be creative — to craft better user experiences.

To help clients understand that differences are not imperfections, use an alternative device such as a smartphone or iPad. These devices will help to reinforce that the web has moved beyond a one-size-fits-all approach. By demonstrating designs in a browser we set more realistic expectations, and clients can make informed decisions about how much time we should spend on harmonising aspects of a design between browsers.

Give them options. Are rounded corners really that important? If not, we can spend time on crafting tailored experiences that will add real value to their bottom line. In my experience, clients appreciate the opportunity to participate more effectively and they feel more involved in the design process. Presenting designs in a browser also makes asking for sign-off easier too. Even the best Photoshop visual leaves questions unanswered and I've heard first-hand from my clients that they feel more confident in signing off after seeing a working web page, because what they see feels more real, more complete.

The implications of writing code earlier

We've come to accept that writing HTML and CSS comes after visual design has been approved and that this is the natural order. So if we write HTML and CSS earlier, what will be the implications of a client asking for changes? Will we need to rewrite our HTML and CSS, and could this outweigh the advantages of demonstrating designs in a browser?

If a design has been built on solid foundations — research, planning and information architecture — changes are often minor. Major rewrites will usually be unnecessary and even when they're required, they can be achieved more easily and quickly using HTML and CSS than Photoshop. I often keep a client on hand so they can make instant decisions and give immediate approval.

If a design needs to go back to the drawing board, creating new graphics, HTML and CSS will be unavoidable. That's just a fact of life — not every project will be as smooth as we'd like. But unlike static visuals that will most likely be thrown away with each change of creative direction, many HTML elements and CSS properties can be used again on the next concept, and the next. Navigation HTML and CSS can be reused, as can content. Even switching from a two-column to a three-column layout can be trivial.

Breaking it up

It's clear that the web has moved away from the desktop and onto a variety of devices. Browsers have wide-ranging capabilities so we can and should be making use of emerging technologies such as HTML5 and CSS3. That's why the way we present designs needs to adapt to meet these realities.

No single approach will work for every designer or developer. No solution will work for every client or every project. It's up to us to discover what works best for our individual circumstances. Whether or not we continue to sketch ideas using traditional graphics tools, how we demonstrate designs has a huge impact on our clients' experience of them.

Static design visuals are simply not up to the challenges we face today. They aren't the best medium for presenting tailored, responsive designs — that's why we should find better ways that enable our work to move forward. Having honest discussions about the consequences of design decisions will help clients to more readily accept new technologies and will shift their focus from looking backwards to looking forwards.

HARDBOILED HTML

Fit and lean HTML makes the web a better place for everyone. The trouble is, our pages are often built on less than optimal markup. Divisions, classes and identifiers are perfectly valid HTML, so what's the problem? Unless you're obsessive about keeping your markup in shape, it can all too easily become flabby. But, never fear, there's a better way. In **Hardboiled HTML**, you'll learn about HTML5 — the latest version of HTML that brings with it new semantic elements. You'll also discover microformats — simple markup patterns for making data machine-readable — and investigate WAI-ARIA Roles. All of these will reduce your reliance on presentational elements and attributes. Get ready, it's time to make your HTML *hardboiled*.

Destination HTML5

COFFEE, GMAIL, AND TWITTER @replies are part of my
morning ritual. I look at photos on Flickr, then check
screenshots uploaded to Dribbble too. Then I read RSS
feeds using Google Reader and see where friends checked
into on Gowalla. These sites don't have pages in the
traditional sense. They're web applications that behave
more like desktop software.

Web applications have become extremely powerful and complex in recent
years, but the markup languages we use to build them have stayed pretty much
the same as they were in the early days of the web. HTML and the stricter and
XML-infused XHTML are tools designed to make web pages, not applications.
That's where HTML5 comes in but, first, a little history.

Mark Pilgrim has written a
thoroughly readable history
of HTML5[4]

After publishing HTML 4.01, the W3C shut down its HTML Working Group.
HTML was done. The future — or so it thought — wasn't HTML, it was XML.
Then, in 2004, the W3C held a workshop attended by several of the big browser
makers. On their minds was how a document language could be used for
making web applications.

Mozilla and Opera responded with their recommendations[1] but the W3C
ignored them.

> "At present, W3C does not intend to put any resources into [...] extensions
> to HTML and CSS for Web Applications"[2]

Like it or not, in the real world it is browser makers, not the W3C, who are
the big cheeses. When the W3C refused outright to take up their suggestions,
several of these companies took their ideas outside of the W3C. They formed
the Web Hypertext Applications Technology Working Group (WHATWG)[3],

[1] http://www.w3.org/2004/04/webapps-cdf-ws/papers/opera.html
[2] http://www.w3.org/2004/04/webapps-cdf-ws/summary
[3] http://www.whatwg.org/
[4] http://diveintohtml5.org/past.html

a "loose, unofficial, and open collaboration of web browser manufacturers and interested parties" [1] that includes Apple, Google, Mozilla and Opera. Only Microsoft was originally absent from the group. WHATWG called its specification 'Web Applications 1.0'.

Meanwhile, back at the W3C, work continued on what the W3C saw as a future document language, XHTML 2. Its goals were ambitious and revolutionary, but were also ignored by the big gun browser makers and, without their support, XHTML 2 was doomed. As Mark Pilgrim astutely observed, "The ones that win are the ones that ship." [2]

Currently, Web Applications 1.0 is worked on by two groups, WHATWG (outside the W3C) and by the re-chartered W3C HTML Working Group which adopted it and renamed it HTML5.

In the web standards business, browser makers hold the cards. Those players at WHATWG threw their weight behind HTML5, quickly developing the specification and implementing many parts of it in their browsers. The result? Much of HTML5 is ready to use today. What? HTML5 is finished? You thought it wouldn't be ready until 2022?

HTML5 editor Ian Hickson has outlined a timetable for HTML5 — finalised in 2011 with a final 'proposed recommendation' (after building test suites) in 2022. Some HTML5 structural elements are still evolving and there are still aspects of the specification that browser makers haven't implemented, but most browsers — including Internet Explorer 9 — already have strong support for HTML5.

Are we going to wait until 2022 and the W3C's official stamp of approval before we start using HTML5? Good luck with that. If we do wait, we'll miss out on making a generation of exciting and innovative websites and applications.

I can hear you asking, "What happens when the specification changes? Will I need to rework my HTML?" The short answer is yes. But we do that anyway. No HTML stays frozen forever, and rewriting and relearning markup as HTML5 evolves will just become part of our normal development process.

[1] http://www.whatwg.org/news/start
[2] http://diveintohtml5.org/past.html

HTML5 builds on how we already work with markup — it isn't a new markup language: it's the same markup we're already used to, but with powerful features built on top. If you're familiar with HTML 4.01 or XHTML 1.0 already, learning HTML5 won't be difficult, so let's get started.

Get Shorty

I don't think I've ever actually written out a Document Type Declaration or doctype. I've cut-and-pasted one more times than I can remember, but usually I let my HTML editor insert one for me.

HTML5's doctype is short and simple. No version number, no language, no URI:

```
<!DOCTYPE html>
```

HTML5's doctype is case-insensitive too, so we can write it as `<!doctype html>`, `<!DOCTYPE html>` or even `<!Doctype HTML>`.

Doctypes weren't intended to be read by humans, and not even browsers really need them, except to 'switch doctype' between their quirks and standards modes. In fact, we could leave out a doctype altogether and our documents would still be valid HTML5.

The doctype isn't the only thing that's got shorter in HTML5: character encoding has too. Here's a `meta` element for a document written in HTML 4.01:

```
<meta http-equiv="Content-Type" content="text/html; charset=UTF-8">
```

This is shortened in HTML5 to just:

```
<meta charset="UTF-8">
```

We now needn't specify a type value of `text/css` on every link to every style sheet. We can simply write:

```
<link rel="stylesheet" href="main.css">
```

Because browsers don't need it, we can forget `text/javascript` applied to scripts too, and simply write:

```
<script src="modernizr-1.5.js"></script>
```

HTML5 isn't fussy about how we write our markup either. Whether we like lower case, upper case or mixed case HTML elements, we can use our preferred style in HTML5. If we learned to write XHTML 1.0-style lower case elements, that's fine in HTML5 too. Whether we self-close images or not, or use quote marks around our attributes or not, HTML5 won't mind. Neither will browsers, so we can carry on writing HTML in whatever style we prefer.

New elements in HTML5

HTML5 introduced several new elements that improve the structure of our pages. If we've been writing standards-based markup using best practices, our documents will be full of divisions — what the HTML 4.01 specification describes as a "mechanism for adding structure" [1] — that group together related content.

```
<div class="branding">[…]</div>
<div class="nav-main">[…]</div>
<div class="content">
    <div class="content-main">[…]</div>
    <div class="content-sub">[…]</div>
</div>
<div class="footer">[…]</div>
```

[1] http://www.w3.org/TR/REC-html40/struct/global.html#edef-DIV

Any semantic meaning in these attributes is largely implicit and they aren't machine-readable so, in practice, user agents will treat `content-main` no differently than they would `you-dumb-mug`. Adding presentational `id` and `class` attributes simply to build a visual layout dilutes any tenuous meaning even further.

We can now replace some of our divisions with more semantically precise structural elements to help reduce our reliance on divisions and presentational `id` and `class` attributes. As a result, our markup will be fitter, leaner and less tied to a single visual layout or design.

Future browsers will also use these new HTML5 elements to add extra levels of functionality (for example, an automated table of contents and pagination). Future generations of assistive technologies will help people to navigate a page or application more easily, making markup hacks such as 'skip' links a thing of the past.

In 2005, Google surveyed over three billion web pages' to find out what `id` and `class` attributes web designers most commonly use to name HTML elements. Their findings became the names of HTML5 structural elements and many are already widely supported in contemporary browsers. They include:

- `section`
- `header`
- `article`
- `footer`
- `aside`
- `nav`

This list isn't exhaustive because this book isn't intended to be a HTML5 reference. (I've added my suggestions for some further HTML5 reading at the end of this chapter.)

' http://code.google.com/webstats/2005-12/classes.html

Section

Pick apart the structure of a typical web page and we'll find divisions. These elements group related areas of content and help us build a visual layout using CSS. Take this example from the 'It's Hardboiled' archives page, written in either HTML 4.01 or XHTML 1.0:

```
<div class="content">
    <div class="content-uk">[…]</div>
    <div class="content-usa">[…]</div>
    <div class="content-world">[…]</div>
</div>
```

This markup pattern is perfectly valid, but even though we understand that the divisions represent sections of a page, browsers make no distinction between them and render them as anonymous block-level containers.

HTML5's section element groups content not into generic containers but into explicit, semantic sections. Think of them as distinct and possibly self-contained parts of a document. In the next example, sections contain stories from different regions — UK, USA and world. All stories from each region are directly related. Notice that because each section should be able to stand alone, we'll include a descriptive heading in each one.

If necessary we could add id attributes to each section to make them individually addressable and style each differently using CSS:

```
<section id="content-uk">
    <h1>Stories from the UK</h1>
</section>

<section id="content-usa">
    <h1>Stories from the USA</h1>
</section>

<section id="content-world">
    <h1>Stories from around the world</h1>
</section>
```

Let's continue building our HTML5 document by adding articles.

Article

When we write for a blog or online magazine or news site, we publish articles. In HTML5 an `article` is just like an individual story, in that it should be understandable outside of the context of a page. That might sound similar to a `section`, but there's a big difference. Whereas an `article` represents a story that can stand apart, a `section` is a self-contained part of the page and could contain several related `articles`.

One way to check if `article` is the most appropriate element is to see if an article's content makes sense on its own; For example, would it make sense on its own when viewed in an RSS reader like Reeder for the iPad.

If you're still confused about the difference between HTML5 `section` and `article`, HTML5 Doctor Bruce Lawson explains more in his 'HTML5 articles and sections: what's the difference?' [1]

If you're lucky enough to own an iPad, the Reeder application is one of the most enjoyable ways to read articles from your RSS feeds. In Reeder, content is isolated and shown without branding, layout, navigation or other articles that might give it context.

Let's carry on building up the outline of the 'It's Hardboiled' archives page by adding three articles to each of the sections:

---

[1] http://brucelawson.co.uk/2010/html5-articles-and-sections-whats-the-difference

```
<section id="content-uk">
    <h1>Stories from the UK</h1>
    <article>[…]</article>
    <article>[…]</article>
    <article>[…]</article>
</section>

<section id="content-usa">
    <h1>Stories from the USA</h1>
    <article>[…]</article>
    <article>[…]</article>
    <article>[…]</article>
</section>

<section id="content-world">
    <h1>Stories from around the world</h1>
    <article>[…]</article>
    <article>[…]</article>
    <article>[…]</article>
</section>
```

Sections can contain articles, and guess what? An `article` element can contain `sections` too! What, you thought learning new HTML elements was going to come without a little head scratching? To help clear that up — the `article`/`section` confusion, not your dandruff — this next `article` has three `sections`, each about a famous fiction writer:

To help us understand when to use each HTML5 element, the HTML5 Doctors have prepared their handy 'Easily Confused HTML5 Element Flowchart of Enlightment'.[1]

```
<article>
    <section id="raymond-chandler">[…]</section>
    <section id="dashiell-hammett">[…]</section>
    <section id="mickey-spillane">[…]</section>
</article>
```

[1] http://html5doctor.com/wp-content/uploads/HTML5Doctor-sectioning-flowchart.pdf

Header

In HTML5, a page's branding area or its masthead can be described with the
new header element. These headers traditionally appear at the top of a page,
although we could position a header on the side, at the bottom or anywhere
we choose. We'll replace that classified banner division with a much more
appropriate header element:

```
<header>
    <h1>It's Hardboiled</h1>
</header>
```

To find out more about hgroup,
consult the HTML5 Doctor[1].

This page needs to tell its readers it means business, so let's include a suitably
hardboiled strapline using a second-level heading. Because we don't want this
second heading to affect the document's outline structure, we can group both
headings inside an hgroup:

```
<header>
    <hgroup>
        <h1>It's Hardboiled</h1>
        <h2>Don't sugar-coat the truth</h2>
    </hgroup>
</header>
```

Check your document outlines
using tools such as Geoffrey
Sneddon's 'HTML 5 Outliner'[2]

When we combine headings of different levels inside an hgroup in this way,
only the first heading — not always an h1 — will be included in the
document outline.

We can also add a header to any section or article: we're not limited to
using just one header on a page. This means we can use a header in several
different ways — as the masthead or branding for a entire page, to introduce
sections and articles or a combination of all of the above.

In this next example, we'll add one 'Hardboiled authors' header to describe
the article, followed by another in each of the sections:

---

[1] http://html5doctor.com/the-hgroup-element.
[2] http://gsnedders.html5.org/outliner

```
<article>
    <header>
        <h1>Hardboiled authors</h1>
    </header>
    <section id="raymond-chandler">
        <header>
            <h1>Raymond Chandler</h1>
        </header>
    </section>
    <section id="dashiell-hammett">
        <header>
            <h1>Dashiell Hammett</h1>
        </header>
    </section>
    <section id="mickey-spillane">
        <header>
            <h1>Mickey Spillane</h1>
        </header>
    </section>
</article>
```

The HTML5 specification describes the header element as a container for "a group of introductory or navigational aids" [1] leaving us free to include a search form, and the time and date that a page, section or article was written or updated.

Footer

In an amazing turn of events (or was it simply coincidence?) some of the results of my 2004 non-scientific survey of element names [2] were the same as Google's. We both found that the most common name web designers gave to the foot area of a page — the one that typically contains contact and copyright information — was 'footer'. In a typical HTML 4.01 or XHTML 1.0 document, this footer will be marked up using a division, perhaps with an attribute value of 'footer' applied to it:

[1] http://www.whatwg.org/specs/web-apps/current-work/multipage/sections.html#the-header-element
[2] http://www.stuffandnonsense.co.uk/blog/about/whats_in_a_name

```
<div class="footer">
[…]
</div>
```

Using HTML5, we can replace that anonymous division with a more
appropriate footer element:

```
<footer>
    <h3>It's Hardboiled</h3>
    <p>Licensed with Creative Commons Attribution 2.5.</p>
</footer>
```

Contrary to its name, we needn't position a footer at the bottom of a page,
section or article. In fact we can place one anywhere inside its containing
element. Like header, we can use footer to define 'meta' information for
any section or article too. Inside an article, a footer might contain
information about the author, or the date and time it was published. A section
footer could include when it was updated or new articles added:

```
<section id="mickey-spillane">
    <header>
        <h1>Mickey Spillane</h1>
    </header>
    <footer>
        <p>Published by Andy Clarke on November 20th, 2010</p>
    </footer>
</section>
```

Aside

Mickey Spillane was a prolific fiction writer and if we were writing an article
about his life and work, our biography might include related information
about one of my favourite books, *My Gun Is Quick*. Conversely, if we were
writing a review of that book, we might want to include a biography of its
author. Surprisingly, in HTML 4.01 and XHTML 1.0 there's no way to define any
relationship between these types of content.

HTML5 defines the relationship using the `aside` element and despite its name, `aside` needn't be visually positioned in a sidebar.

We can use `aside` to describe content that's related to — but not essential for understanding — an `article`. Let's start writing that biographical `article` of Mickey Spillane. We'll include a `header` containing the title, and a `footer` containing the author's name and the `article`'s publication date for good measure.

```
<article>
    <header>
        <h1>Mickey Spillane'</h1>
    </header>
    <footer>
        <p>Published by Andy Clarke on November 20th, 2010</p>
    </footer>
    <p>Frank Morrison Spillane, better known as Mickey Spillane… </p>
</article>
```

Sweet, just like I take my coffee. Now let's add an `aside` that contains related information about *My Gun Is Quick*.

```
<article>
    <header>
        <h1>Mickey Spillane</h1>
    </header>
    <footer>
        <p>Published by Andy Clarke on November 20th, 2010</p>
    </footer>
    <p>Frank Morrison Spillane, better known as Mickey Spillane… </p>
    <aside>
        <h2>My Gun Is Quick</h2>
        <p>Mickey Spillane's second novel featuring private
        investigator Mike Hammer.</p>
    </aside>
</article>
```

Perhaps our page contains information about other fiction writers? This
content would be less strictly related to our biography, so we'll place that `aside`
outside of the `article` . In this case, we should also wrap both the `article` and
`aside` inside a `section` element to make it explicit that the two are related.

```
<section>
    <article>
        <header>
            <h1>Mickey Spillane</h1>
        </header>
        <footer>
            <p>Published by Andy Clarke on November 20th, 2010</p>
        </footer>

        <p>Frank Morrison Spillane, better known as Mickey Spillane,
        was an author of crime novels, many featuring his detective
        character Mike Hammer. More than 225 million copies of his
        books have been sold internationally.</p>

        <aside>
            <h2>My Gun Is Quick</h2>
            <p>Mickey Spillane's second novel featuring private
            investigator Mike Hammer.</p>
        </aside>
    </article>

    <aside>
        <h2>Other crime fiction writers</h2>
        <ul>
            <li>Raymond Chandler</li>
            <li>Dashiell Hammett</li>
            <li>Jonathan Latimer</li>
        </ul>
    </aside>
</section>
```

Nav

Readers shouldn't need to hire a detective to help them find something on a website — that's what navigation's for. When we're building pages in HTML 4.01 or XHTML 1.0, navigation might look something like this.

```
<div class="nav-main">
    <ul>
        <li><a href="about.html">What is Hardboiled?</a></li>
        <li><a href="archives.html">Archives</a></li>
        <li><a href="authors.html">Hardboiled authors</a></li>
        <li><a href="store.html">Classic Hardboiled</a></li>
    </ul>
</div>
```

We've become accustomed to marking up navigation using lists but, the trouble is, we mark up other things using lists too. How the hell is a browser supposed to know the difference between a list of links and a list of people we owe money to?

HTML5 introduced the nav element for one or more "major navigation blocks"[1] on a page. Not all links, or even groups of links, are major navigation blocks, so we should reserve nav for the primary ways that people navigate.

Navigation will likely include lists of links to your most important pages in the page's header, a sidebar, or possibly in the page footer. Next, we'll replace the anonymous division with a meaningful nav element.

```
<nav>
    <ul>
        <li><a href="about.html">What is Hardboiled?</a></li>
        <li><a href="archives.html">Archives</a></li>
        <li><a href="authors.html">Hardboiled authors</a></li>
        <li><a href="store.html">Classic Hardboiled</a></li>
    </ul>
</nav>
```

[1] http://dev.w3.org/html5/spec/Overview.html#the-nav-element

When our visitors use search to find content, add a search form inside your nav. If we've included 'skip links', these could also be considered as major navigation blocks for people who use assistive technologies.

Figure

Like all private dicks, I appreciate a good figure. This has got me into hot water on more than one occasion. In printed media, images, charts and diagrams are often paired with written captions. In the past, we've struggled to find the most appropriate semantic elements for captioning because neither HTML 4.01 nor XHTML 1.0 have elements designed for that purpose. You've likely experimented with divisions or even definition lists to create 'pairs' of images and descriptions.

```
<dl class="figure">
    <dt><img src="jury.jpg" alt="I, The Jury"></dt>
    <dd>I, The Jury by Mickey Spillane</dd>
</dl>
```

HTML5 addresses this problem by introducing figure and figcaption elements to associate captions with images, charts, diagrams and even code examples.

```
<figure>
    <img src="jury.jpg" alt="I, The Jury">
    <figcaption>I, The Jury by Mickey Spillane</figcaption>
</figure>
```

When we need to caption a group of elements we can nest multiple images, charts or diagrams and label them with a single figcaption.

```
<figure>
    <img src="jury.jpg" alt="I, The Jury">
    <img src="gun.jpg" alt="My Gun is Quick">
    <img src="vengeance.jpg" alt="Vengeance Is Mine!">
    <figcaption>Books by Mickey Spillane</figcaption>
</figure>
```

HTML5 dates and times

You might imagine that writing a date in HTML would be as simple as.

```
<footer>
    <p>Published by Andy Clarke on 06/05/2010</p>
</footer>
```

Unfortunately, software finds it hard to know that this string of numbers is a date. People, on the other hand, are far more intuitive, but sometimes even we have different interpretations of the same numbers depending on where we live. Coming from the UK, I read those numbers as the sixth (day) of May (month) in the year 2010, but if you live in the United States, you'll probably read the date as June 5th, 2010.

HTML5 offers a solution with a `time` element that's readable by people — 6 May 2010; May 6th, 2010; next Thursday — and formatted for parsers.

```
<time>May 6th 2010</time>
```

The `time` element is made from two versions of a date or date/time. The first is a human readable, natural language date; the second is a `datetime` attribute with a machine-readable, ISO-formatted date: `YYYY-MM-DDThh:mm:ss`. That's year–month–day — followed by time in hours, minutes and seconds (if we need to be that precise):

```
<time datetime="2010-05-06">May 6th 2010</time>
```

When we need to say explicitly that a date or time refer to the publication date of an `article`, we can also add an optional `pubdate` attribute:

```
<time datetime="2010-05-06" pubdate>6 May 2010</time>
```

By bringing together both an ISO-formatted time-stamp and a date set out in natural language, we've implemented a format that is readable by both people and machines.

Styling HTML5 elements

We can already use HTML5 structural elements and style them with CSS in all modern web browsers. And don't worry about Internet Explorer 6, 7 or 8 — there are JavaScript workarounds including Modernizr and Remy Sharp's HTML5 Shiv[1] that enable us to style HTML5 elements in those browsers too.

We can style HTML5 elements using CSS just as we do those in HTML 4.01 or XHTML 1.0 in every contemporary browser, including Safari 5, Firefox 3.6, Google Chrome 6, Opera 10.6 and Internet Explorer 9. It's not all plain sailing though, as some browsers natively render HTML5 elements as text-level (previously called 'inline') rather than block-level elements. Don't worry, there's a simple fix that will suit our needs for now. Just set them to display as blocks in our style sheets.

HTML5 Doctor Bruce Lawson explains 'Supporting IE with Conditional Comments' on Opera's Developer Community[3]

```
section, article, aside, header, footer, nav, figure {
display : block; }
```

Modernizr[4] not only creates DOM elements for HTML5 but also tests a browser's ability to run HTML5 video, audio and other features. When we use Modernizr, we won't have to use Remy Sharp's HTML5Shiv too.

Older browsers — in particular Internet Explorer 6, 7 and 8 — need a little help from a JavaScript enabler from Remy Sharp: HTML5Shiv[2]. This tiny script creates elements in Internet Explorer's DOM so we can style them using CSS. HTML5Shiv won't run in non-Microsoft browsers, so it's a good idea to serve it via conditional comments to prevent people who use other browsers from downloading the script unnecessarily:

```
<!--[if lt IE 9]>
<script src="http://html5shiv.googlecode.com/svn/trunk/html5.js">
</script>
<![endif]-->
```

Forms in HTML5

What website or application would be complete with a form or two? Love building them or hate styling them, the web without forms would be like a private eye's night out without a voluptuous redhead. Since the W3C closed the book on HTML 4.01, and XHTML 1.0 introduced no new form fields, we've had to make do with only a tiny selection of input types.

[1] http://remysharp.com/2009/01/07/html5-enabling-script/
[2] http:code.google.com/p/html5shiv
[3] http://dev.opera.com/articles/view/supporting-ie-with-conditional-comments
[4] http://modernizr.com
[5] http://www.miketaylr.com/code/input-type-attr.html

HTML5 introduces more than a dozen new `input` types and attributes that make implementing complicated controls and functions — like sliders, date pickers and client-side validation — a breeze. HTML5's new form elements include `email`, `url`, `tel` and `search`.

Michael Taylor provides a comprehensive HTML5 inputs and attribute support test[5]

We can start using these today as they work in every browser, even ancient ones: these `input` types degrade to simple text fields when a browser doesn't understand them.

E-mail

Lift the floorboards covering most web forms and we'll likely uncover a field asking for an e-mail address. Contact forms, comment forms, registration forms and sign-ups all demand an e-mail address for their grubby little databases. HTML 4.01 and XHTML 1.0 didn't have a dedicated e-mail field type so we were forced to use:

```
<input type="text">
```

HTML5 puts that right with an `input` type dedicated to `email` addresses:

```
<input type="email">
```

Did I mention that you can use this `input` type now? Most desktop browsers won't do anything special with `email` yet, but in the future all kinds of interesting functionality will be possible, including checking that a form submission includes a valid e-mail address that contains an @ symbol and is properly constructed.

What desktop browser makers will implement in the future is just an educated guess, but one clue might lie in how Apple's iOS handles this field today. Tap into an `email` field type today and Safari brings up a software keyboard that places an @ symbol and a dot prominently at the foot of the keyboard.

Using a software keyboard may not be ideal but, unlike hardware keyboards, they can adapt to the job at hand. Here, the iPad's keyboard includes a set of keys to make entering an e-mail address easier.

URLs

It's strange that the authors of HTML and XHTML didn't implement an `input` type dedicated to entering a website address. HTML5's authors fixed this with `url`:

When we add `url`, desktop browsers might one day autocomplete from our browsing history. Apple's iOS software keyboard already adapts by adding a prominent slash, a dot and a '.com' key.

```
<input type="url">
```

Telephone

If we use the `tel` input type (not to be confused with the 'tel' value we'll learn about in the next chapter), iOS automatically pulls up a numbers-only keypad.

```
<input type="tel">
```

Search

In HTML 4.01 and XHTML 1.0 an `input` with a type of `text` was the only option, but HTML5 added a `search` dedicated `input` type:

```
<input type="search">
```

Native date pickers

As a designer and not a developer, implementing the sort of date pickers we find on airline, car rental and hotel sites always puts me behind the eight-ball. JavaScript frameworks made adding them less painful and now HTML5 has native date pickers.

time for hours, minutes, and seconds (10:10:00)

date for a year, month and day (2010-11-20)

week from 1–53

month for a year and a month but no day (2010-11)

datetime for a year, month and day plus hours, minutes, seconds and a time zone (2010-11-20T10:00:00+00)

datetime-local, as datetime but no time zone (2010-11-20T10:00:00)

The date and time inputs shown above are from Opera 10.60's rendering. In the future, let's hope browser makers will make their own implementations look less like they've been attacked with a hatchet, or give designers some way to style them using CSS.

Placeholder text

`label` text isn't required for accessibility when the purpose of a form is simple and the text can be substituted with a title or an explicitly titled button.

Damn those troublesome form labels. I bet I'm not the only one who sometimes wants to provide a visual cue for how to use a form element without showing label text. HTML5 includes a `placeholder` attribute that adds placeholder text to any `input` that is either empty or not in focus. Browsers that don't support `placeholder` will safely ignore it by leaving the `input` blank.

```
<input type="search" placeholder="Search this site">
```

An input containing a placeholder can be used instead of label text and, when used correctly, can remove clutter from an interface design. Focusing on the search input removes the placeholder text faster than a bartender takes bills from my billfold.

Search this site

Search this site

Autofocus

Like millions of others, when I do a search on Google my cursor automatically focuses on its search field. Unlike millions of others, you and I notice these small enhancements. In the past, we were forced to use a script to do this, but HTML5 has added the `autofocus` attribute to tell a browser to do the hard work for us. Browsers that don't support `autofocus` will ignore it:

```
<input type="search" autofocus>
```

Auto-complete

HTML5 has also standardised `autocomplete`, so we can dictate which form inputs will be pre-filled with information from a visitor's previous form submissions:

```
<input type="text" name="name" autocomplete="on">
```

Use `autocomplete` wisely, though, as some fields are best left alone, in particular anything that relates to credit cards or other financial information:

```
<input type="text" name="credit-card" autocomplete="off">
```

List and datalist

Often, one of the best ways to help a visitor complete a form is to suggest an answer to a question or to give them options. The HTML5 `list` attribute, including a `datalist`, combines the convenience of a select with a visitor's own ability to enter text.

Imagine that we wanted to ask someone who their favourite detective is. To help them along, we could suggest a few hardboiled heroes in a `datalist`, then associate that `list` with a text `input` using the `list` attribute:

```
<input type="text" list="detectives">
<datalist id="detectives">
    <option value="Mike Hammer">Mike Hammer</option>
    <option value="Sam Spade">Sam Spade</option>
    <option value="Philip Marlowe">Philip Marlowe</option>
</datalist>
```

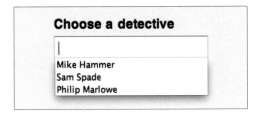

A visitor can type in their own favourite, or they can choose from the options available in the `datalist`. Any browser that doesn't support `list` and `datalist` will ignore them and display a normal text input field instead.

Client-side validation

Writing form validation scripts is one of my least favourite jobs. JavaScript libraries like jQuery make that job easier but I bet that even the most hardcore JavaScript nerds don't actually enjoy implementing these scripts. Wouldn't it be better if a browser handled form validation for us? The good news is that HTML5 includes simple features that make client-side form validation a breeze.

Required

HTML5 added the `required` attribute which will prevent a browser from submitting any form data until all required fields (`text`, `email`, `url`, etc.) have been completed correctly:

```
<input type="email" required>
```

Opera implemented HTML5 form validation in version 9 and Firefox, Safari and Google Chrome have also started implementing these features (although they're not all available in public releases at the time of writing).

Min and max

Limiting quantities with `min` and `max` attributes

Perhaps you sell books online and your site has a minimum order quantity, or, like me, you run training courses and limit the maximum number of places available. HTML5 includes the `min` and `max` attributes to allow us to specify upper and lower limits for the data.

```
<input type="number" id="book" min="1">
<input type="number" id="course" max="6">
```

It's worth knowing that currently `min` and `max` attributes don't work with the `required` attribute in any browser. In fact, we can't use `required` with a number input at all.

Breaking it up

HTML5 has brought markup into the web application age and there's far more to the new specification than just the elements I've covered in this book. There are new ways to embed video and audio files, and play them without needing browser plugins, plus new ways to enable interaction with web pages and applications offline. How far you go with HTML5 will depend entirely upon your specific work and the needs of the people that you work for. One thing's for sure, HTML5 is here to stay and if we're to stay ahead of the curve we should be working with as much of it as possible.

Want to do your own HTML5 detective work?

Books about HTML5 are starting to flood the shelves, so if you're excited about HTML5 and are keen to learn more, I recommended starting with either *Introducing HTML 5* by Bruce Lawson and Remy Sharp[1] or *HTML5 For Web Designers* by Jeremy Keith[2]. You can also keep up with changes to the specification and learn more about how to use HTML5 in your work today from these excellent sites:

WHATWG: The Web Hypertext Application Technology Working Group

http://whatwg.org

W3C HTML Working Group: The home of HTML5 at the W3C

http://w3.org/html/wg

HTML5 Doctor: A community resource run by HTML5 enthusiasts

http://html5doctor.com

HTML5 Demos and examples: Remy Sharp, creator of the HTML5Shiv explores what is possible

http://html5demos.com

Dive into HTML5: A free-to-read online book by Mark Pilgrim that is essential HTML5 reading

http://diveintohtml5.org

---

[1] http://introducinghtml5.com
[2] http://books.alistapart.com/product/html5-for-web-designers

Hardboiled microformats

I*F* Y*OU* C*ARE* about making every HTML element and attribute count, and want to make semantics go further, you'll soon be getting excited about microformats. Microformats are HTML-based patterns for marking up specific types of information — such as contact details, calendar entries, reviews and syndicated content like blog entries — so that they become machine-readable as well as human-readable. I think that Brian Suda explained their purpose best:

> *"Microformats are all about representing semantic information encoded within a web page, allowing that information to be leveraged in ways that were possibly never conceived by the original publisher."* [1]

In practice, when we use microformats to mark up information in our websites, we make that content more usable for our visitors.

For example, when we use hCard to mark up contact information, our users can more easily extract that content and import it into their address books. If we mark up events using hCalendar, people can subscribe to calendars or even add those events to their diaries in just a few clicks. Best of all, to give people this added functionality, all we need to do is add a set of standard `class` attribute values to our HTML. That really is all there is to it.

Microformats have been developed around existing standards (attributes added to the elements that describe our content), so the only thing we need to know to start using them is how to write HTML. But what makes microformats hardboiled?

---

[1] http://sitepoint.com/article/microformats-meaning-markup

View source on any website and we'll see a mass of id and class attributes used to bind CSS styles to those elements. I would hope that the values that you choose are descriptive of the content; for example, using a value like 'tagline' instead of a presentational value like 'bold-heading'. Even so, the values that we commonly choose add little real value to our content and are of no use to our users.

When we follow 'microformatted' patterns, we can largely give presentational id and class attributes a concrete overcoat, because microformats bring with them more class attributes than you can hang a raincoat on.

Microformats is a subject that's too wide to cover fully within the scope of this book. I hope that you'll want to find out more and there's no better place to start than *Microformats Made Simple* by Emily P. Lewis (New Riders, 2009).

Focusing on content

Let's start by thinking about content — not just the content that we publish, but about the wide variety of content we read on the web every day. There's plenty of it and it comes in all shapes and sizes, from blog entries, news articles and product information, to events and reviews. With such a variety of content, semantics become ever more important, but it's been difficult for markup languages to keep pace. As long ago as 1998, the W3C had its vision for a future 'Semantic Web',

> "[M]ost information on the Web is designed for human consumption, and [...] the structure of the data is not evident to a robot browsing the web. [...] [T]he Semantic Web approach instead develops languages for expressing information in a machine processable form." [1]

---

[1] http://w3.org/DesignIssues/Semantic.html

The Semantic Web is still a pipe dream, but microformats now enable a similar distribution of information in a way that puts people — instead of machines — first. As the microformats community outlines on its website:

> *"Designed for humans first and machines second, microformats are a set of simple, open data formats built upon existing and widely adopted standards. Instead of throwing away what works today, microformats intend to solve simpler problems first by adapting to current behaviours and usage patterns (e.g. XHTML, blogging)."* [1]

Microformats aren't complicated to use or to learn. They have no grand vision for the future of the web, and they're designed to solve some of the problems that we and the people who use our content face every day. They're built around three principles:

1. to solve a specific problem, such as how to help people add contact information to an address book more easily
2. to be modular, so we can embed one microformat inside another; for example, a venue's contact information inside an event or review
3. to build on existing standards; for example, the hCard microformat is based on the vCard standard.

You'll soon see how using microformats will help to make your HTML leaner, fitter and less tied to just one design or layout — in short, hardboiled. We'll start by investigating some of the most widely adopted microformats.

---

[1] http://microformats.org/about

Link-based microformats

If you're familiar with links to external files in the head of an HTML document, you'll recognise this as a link to an external CSS style sheet:

```
<link rel="stylesheet" href="screen.css" media="screen">
```

This attribute defines the relationship between an HTML document and the link's destination. This relationship is one of a style sheet. We're used to taking a similar approach when linking to RSS or Atom feeds:

```
<link rel="alternate" type="application/rss+xml" href="articles.rss">
```

We can also define a relationship to a favicon or even an apple-touch-icon — one that's been designed for the home screens of Apple's iOS devices:

```
<link rel="shortcut icon" href="favicon.jpg" type="image/gif">
<link rel="shortcut icon" href="favicon.png" type="image/png">
<link rel="apple-touch-icon" href="iphonetouch.jpg">
```

All link-based microformats apply this idea to describe other relationships between documents.

Rel-license

Linking to a licence is one of the most common uses of link-based microformats. When we use rel-license, we say explicitly that "this link points to a licence for this content."

```
<a href="http://creativecommons.org/licenses/by/2.5/" ↵
rel="license">Creative Commons Attribution 2.5</a>
```

You're probably thinking that any dumb mug can link to a licence using a microformat and you'd be right on the money. After all, one of the principles of microformats is that they should have a low barrier to entry — in this case really low. But the benefits can be huge, especially now that Google has added a 'usage rights' option to its advanced search[1].

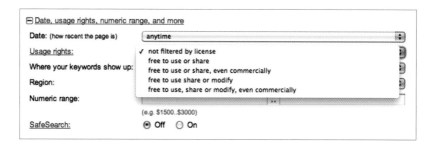

There are other search engines apart from Google. You knew that right? Yahoo! has added its own search[2] of `rel-license` content that finds content across the web published under a Creative Commons licence.

What's `rel-license` got to do with being hardboiled? Well, in the past, if we wanted to style a licence link differently to other links on a page — perhaps by adding a small icon — we would have added a `class` to that link.

```
<a href="http://creativecommons.org/licenses/by/2.5/" rel="license" ↵
class="license"> Creative Commons Attribution 2.5</a>
```

Now, we've no need for that extra `class` because we can style the link in exactly the same way by using a CSS attribute selector.

```
a[rel="license"] {
padding-left : 20px;
background : transparent url(cc.png) no-repeat 0 0;
}
```

[1] http://www.google.com/advanced_search
[2] http://search.yahoo.com/cc

By using a microformat, we've immediately made our HTML more hardboiled by eliminating a presentational attribute that offered nothing of value to us or our users.

Rel-tag

The last few years have seen an explosion in tag-based services, two of the best known being Flickr[1] and delicious[2]. Both are also great examples of high-traffic sites that have adopted microformats.

rel-tag is nothing more complicated than a hyperlink containing a rel attribute with a value of tag added. The URL must contain the word 'tag' and finish with the tag itself, in this case, 'hardboiled.'

```
<a href="http://www.amazon.com/tag/hardboiled/" ↵
rel="tag">Hardboiled</a>
```

In that example, rel-tag makes it explicit that we're labelling the Amazon.com destination page by tagging it with 'hardboiled.'

Jeremy Keith's podcasting site Huffduffer[3] makes great use of rel-tag to help its users find related products, bookmarks, photos and videos. If you're a Firefox user and have the Operator extension installed[4], visit Huffduffer and watch the toolbar light up like a Christmas tree.

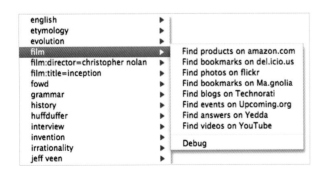

Simply by adding rel-tag to his hyperlinks, and pointing to a 'tag space' on Amazon, delicious, Flickr and YouTube, Jeremy enables other people, such as the developers of the Operator toolbar, to give extra functionality to users from his HTML content.

[1] http://flickr.com
[2] http://delicious.com
[3] http://huffduffer.com
[4] https://addons.mozilla.org/firefox/4106

HTML5 link relationships

HTML5 includes several more link relationships that enable us to define the meaning of links to other pages.

archives	A collection of past content; for example, a news site's or blog's archives
author	The author of the content; for example, their biography or contact information on the same site or another.
bookmark	A complete page or an HTML5 section element.
external	A link destination on an external site.
nofollow	First adopted by Google in an attempt to combat spam comments, this attribute makes it explicit that a link is not an endorsement of the destination.
search	A dedicated search page or a search interface.
sidebar	Specifies that a link's destination should load into a browser's sidebar panel (if it has one) and not into the browser window.

Although there's some overlap between HTML5 link relationships and both microformats and WAI-ARIA roles, don't let that put you off using them. They all add deeper semantics and provide hooks for us to style links using CSS.

hCard: People, places and organisation's

Wouldn't it be cool if, when we find a person's contact information online, we could add them into an address book in just a couple of clicks? Guess what: if they publish contact information using the hCard microformat, we can. Take a close look at the following paragraph:

> Andy Clarke (Malarkey) is a web designer and wannabe detective based in the United Kingdom. He runs a small agency called Stuff and Nonsense, writes books and speaks at conferences. If you'd like to hire Andy, you can e-mail him at dropadime@hardboiledwebdesign.com or call him on 01745 851 848.

That paragraph is chock-full of information and you shouldn't need to be a detective to spot my full name, nickname, place of work, e-mail address and work telephone number.

Markup languages have a limited vocabulary and even HTML5 — with an expanded set of elements — can't adequately convey all the meaning in this content. Headings and paragraphs, sections and articles — they're no trouble — but what about elements that describe a person's contact information? Where are they? Nowhere, but hCard[1] is a microformat that adds that missing meaning to a person's or an organisation's contact information.

[1] http://microformats.org/wiki/hcard

Building on vCard

If you use an address book on your computer or smartphone, you'll already be familiar with seeing this structured information because most address books use a standard called vCard. Open a vCard in a text editor and you'll find structured information, including: a name (FN for 'formatted name'); organisation (ORG); address (ADR); telephone (TEL); e-mail address (EMAIL), and more. The hCard microformat's attribute values — the 'h' comes from HTML — are based on a one-to-one relationship with vCard.

vCard information inside Apple's Address Book has a structured data format. Because the hCard microformat uses the same values as `class` attributes, developers have made tools that convert hCards to vCards.

The best way to learn hCard is to make a card. You could head over to the hCard creator on the Microformats website[1] — if you want a hatchet man to do your dirty work for you. If you do, you'll wonder what is so damned hardboiled about microformats when you see the mass of `div` and `span` elements that the hCard creator spits at you. What's so revolutionary about this?

---

[1] http://microformats.org/code/hcard/creator

```
<div class="vcard">
    <span class="fn">Andy Clarke</span>
    <div class="org">Stuff and Nonsense</div>
    <a class="email" href="mailto:dropadime@hardboiledwebdesign. ↵
    com">dropadime@hardboiledwebdesign.com</a>
    <div class="adr">
        <span class="country-name">United Kingdom</span>
    </div>
    <div class="tel">01745 851848</div>
</div>
```

It's true that on first impression, the sheer quantity of microformat attribute values looks excessive, but those values are important because they enable our content to be more easily extracted and used by other applications. Keeping that in mind, let's go back and review that earlier block of text. We'll add `class` attribute values from hCard to make my details more meaningful, starting with applying a `class` of `vcard` to the paragraph as it's the 'root' element of this microformat.

```
<p class="vcard"><span class="fn n"><span class="given-
name">Andy</span><span class="family-name"> Clarke </span>(<span
class="nickname">Malarkey</span>)</span> is a web designer
and wannabe detective based in the <span class="adr"><span
class="country-name">United Kingdom</span></span>. He runs a
small agency called <span class="org">Stuff and Nonsense</span>,
writes books and speaks at conferences. If you would like to hire
Andy, you can e-mail him at <a class="email" href="dropadime@
hardboiledwebdesign.com">dropadime@hardboiledwebdesign.com</a> or
call him on <span class="tel">01745 851848</span>.</p>
```

Remember back to when you learned that `html` is the root element of an HTML or XHTML document? Microformats need their own root element to tell an application that a microformat is present and then to extract information from its structure. For hCard, we identify that root element by adding the `class` attribute `vcard`.

Names

Now let's dig deeper by looking at the values that make up an hCard, which ones are required and how to structure them. We'll start by describing a person's name — there are two types of name formats we can choose from:

1. a complete, formatted version
2. a structured name including prefixes, middle names and suffixes, etc.

Formatted name

When we present a person's name as it would appear on a nameplate on their office door or business card, we can roll up several values including a prefix, their `given-name`, `middle-name`, `family-name` and suffix into a single string. To do this, we need only apply a single value of `fn` — this is the only required value in hCard — to an element and we're done.

```
<span class="fn">Nick Jefferies</span>
```

Structured name

Now we'll structure a name, separating the parts of that name into individual elements. We'll add another value of `n` as this indicates to a parser that the name is comprised of several parts. The parts we'll use for this detective's hCard are his `given-name` (Nick) and his `family-name` (Jefferies).

```
<span class="fn n">
    <span class="given-name">Nick</span>
    <span class="family-name">Jefferies</span>
</span>
```

If Nick Jefferies' hCard business card includes an `honorific-prefix` (Mr, Mrs, Sir, Professor, etc.) or, more likely, his `nickname` (Sawbuck), we can include those too.

```
<span class="honorific-prefix">Mr. </span>
<span class="nickname">"Sawbuck"</span>
```

Mr Nick (Sawbuck) Jefferies' structured name, with all of its separate components, now looks like this.

```
<span class="fn n">
    <span class="honorific-prefix">Mr. </span>
    <span class="given-name">Nick </span>
    <span class="nickname">"Sawbuck" </span>
    <span class="family-name">Jefferies</span>
</span>
```

All that remains for us to do is to enclose Nick's structured name in the most appropriate root HTML element — in this case a division, although it could just as easily be a list, paragraph, section, article or footer if one of those is more appropriate — and apply the class attribute value vcard to that.

```
<div class="vcard">
    <span class="fn n">
        <span class="honorific-prefix">Mr. </span>
        <span class="given-name">Nick </span>
        <span class="nickname">"Sawbuck" </span>
        <span class="family-name">Jefferies</span>
    </span>
</div>
```

URLs

Today's address book entries wouldn't be much use without at least one website address, so it shouldn't come as a surprise to find out that hCard includes a value for a url. The most obvious way to add URL to an hCard is something like this:

```
<span class="url">http://hardboiledwebdesign.com</span>
```

While this works fine as a valid hCard property, it isn't exactly user-friendly because the address isn't a link. To fix this, we can combine a person's formatted name and a link to their website into one element. You remember:

```
<span class="fn">Nick Jefferies</span>
```

Replace this span with an anchor, then apply both fn and url values to that.

```
<a class="fn url" href="http://hardboiledwebdesign.com"> ↵
Nick Jefferies</a>
```

Organisations

There are two ways that hCards can to relate to an organisation: first, an hCard for the organisation itself; and second, one of its employee's hCards. Organisations and individuals have similar contact information — names, addresses, contact methods — so how can we differentiate the two? The answer is to set both fn and org (meaning organisation) on the same element:

```
<div class="vcard">
    <span class="fn org">The No. 1 Lady Boys' Detective Agency</span>
</div>
```

When we create an hCard for an employee, we can add their organisation's name, their job title and, finally, their role:

```
<div class="vcard">
    <span class="fn n">
        <span class="given-name">Cole</span>
        <span class="nickname">Henley</span>
        <span class="honorific-suffix">Esq.</span>
    </span>
    <span class="org">The No. 1 Lady Boys' Detective Agency</span>,
    <span class="title">House dick</span>,
    <span class="role">Sleuth</span>
</div>
```

When we need an employee's organisation's logo embedded in their hCard, add an image and apply the `class` attribute value of `logo`.

```
<img src="logo.png" class="logo">
```

Addresses

Tracked the guy down? Know where he lives or works? Now add that information to his hCard. Because hCard and vCard values have a one-to-one relationship, hCard uses the `adr` property to describe addresses, along with the child values `street-address`, `locality`, `region`, `postal-code` and `country-name`:

```
<div class="adr">
    <span class="street-address">221b Baker Street</span>,
    <span class="locality">London</span>,
    <span class="postal-code">NW1 6XE</span>,
    <span class="country-name">United Kingdom</span>
</div>
```

At this point you could be wondering "Why use a division? What's wrong with an HTML `address` element?" Despite what you may infer from its name, `address` should only be used for marking up contact information from the author of a specific page or block of content. `address` was — rather confusingly — never designed solely to describe physical addresses. Don't take my word for it; here it is from the horse's mouth at WHATWG:

> "The address element represents the contact information for its nearest article or body element ancestor. [...] The address element must not be used to represent arbitrary addresses (e.g. postal addresses), unless those addresses are in fact the relevant contact information." [1]

---

[1] http://www.whatwg.org/specs/web-apps/current-work/multipage/sections.html#the-address-element

Need more than one address?

What if someone has more than one address? Unless you run an agency from home like I do, you'll have both a home and a work address. Not to worry, we can include both in an hCard by using a type value: in this next example, 'work'. Other adr types include home, postal for a postal address and parcel for deliveries.

```
<div class="adr">
    <div class="type">Work</div>:
    <span class="street-address">221b Baker Street</span>
    <span class="locality">London</span>,
    <span class="postal-code">NW1 6XE</span>,
    <span class="country-name">United Kingdom</span>
</div>
```

If a work address is the same as a delivery address, we can combine multiple values and even specify which address is preferred using the pref value.

```
<div class="type parcel pref">Work</div>
```

Phone numbers

I still prefer to talk on the phone. I guess I'm old-fashioned like that. Lucky for me, then, that including a phone number (or two, or three) in an hCard is a piece of cake. We simply use the tel value:

```
<div class="tel">01745 851848</div>
```

Most people have more than one number — at home, in their office and, of course, a mobile. We can add telephone number types including home, work, fax, cell, and even pager if you still carry one of those.

```
<div class="tel">
    <span class="type">Work</span>
    <span class="value">01745 851848</span>
</div>

<div class="tel">
    <span class="type">Fax</span>
    <span class="value">01745 851848</span>
</div>
```

E-mail

You shouldn't be surprised to learn that to add e-mail addresses to an hCard we use the email class:

```
<a href="mailto:dropadime@hardboiledwebdesign.com" class="email"> ↵
Drop me a dime</a>
```

If an hCard includes more than one e-mail address, we can specify which of them is preferred using pref.

```
<a href="mailto:dropadime@hardboiledwebdesign.com" class="email ↵
pref">Drop me a dime</a>
```

IM and Skype

Each of the hCard values we've seen has a one-to-one relationship with vCard values, but some of the communication technologies we use today weren't around when the vCard standard was drafted. For these more modern methods, we reuse the URL value; for example, instant messaging:

```
<a href="aim:goim?screenname=itshardboiled" class="url"> ↵
iChat with me</a>
```

We can take the same approach with Skype usernames:

```
<a href="callto:itshardboiled" class="url">Skype with me</a>
```

Birthdays and the value-title design pattern

Now let's move on to learn about dates and date formats; after all, no self-respecting address book entry would be complete without a birthday. We can't leave it up to Facebook to remind us about our friends' birthdays. vCard has a property for a birthday — it's called BDAY — and because hCard takes its values directly from vCard, the hCard equivalent is bday. We can apply bday to an HTML5 time element when we're including a birthday in an hCard.
Here's mine:

```
<time datetime="1965-11-20" class="bday">November 20th, 1965</time>
```

Unfortunately, that's not the whole story, because to make this date understandable by microformats parsers we also need another value-title element, together with a title. We'll use a span containing a single empty space to avoid our ISO-formatted time-stamp appearing as a 'tooltip' in some browsers.

```
<time datetime="1965-11-20" class="bday">
<span class="value-title" title="1965-11-20"> </span>
November 20th, 1965</time>
```

Why the duplication? You'd be right to wonder and you're in good company. For the past few years, microformats parsers, including browser extensions, have relied on time-stamps marked up using `value-title`.

Future software will no doubt extract time-stamps natively from HTML5's `time` element and `datetime` attribute, but currently there are no tools that do this. To future-proof our markup and ensure compatibility with today's software, we should present our time-stamps as both `datetime` and `value-title`.

Marking up the 'It's Hardboiled' authors page

There's no better way to understand the nuances of hCard than to work with them. We'll build a series of nine hCards for the 'It's Hardboiled' authors page. Each detective's business card uses slightly different hCard values.

```
<div class="vcard">
<h3 class="org">
The No. 1 Lady Boys' Detective Agency
</h3>
<p class="fn n">
<span class="given-name">Cole</span>
<span class="family-name">Henley</span>
<span class="honorific-suffixes">Esq.</span>
</p>
</div>
```

```
<div class="vcard">
<h3 class="fn org">
Shades & Staches Detective Agency
</h3>
<p class="role">
Private investigator extraordinaire
</p>
</div>
```

```
<div class="vcard">
<h3 class="fn org">
Command F Detective Services
</h3>
<p>We can find <em>anyone</em></p>
</div>
```

```
<div class="vcard">
<h3 class="fn">The Fat Man</h3>
<p class="role">Private Investigator</p>
<p>$50 a day plus expenses.
By appointment only</p>
<p>Dial: M for Murder</p>
</div>
```

```
<div class="vcard">
<h3 class="fn org">Nick Jefferies</h3>
<p>
<span class="role">Private eye</span>
<span class="postal-code">WA6-0089</span>
</p>
</div>
```

```
<div class="vcard">
<h3 class="fn org">
Elementary My Dear Watson</h3>
<p class="role">Private Investigator</p>
<p>Don't call us, we'll find you</p>
</div>
```

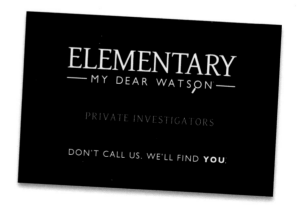

hCalendar: Events

You might prefer to find a stooge to build your calendars for you. In that case, head over to the Microformats website's own hCalendar Creator[2].

Think for a moment about the event information that you see around the web every day. You'll find details about conferences, sporting events, concerts and movie showings. Do you think it would be cool if we could add these events to our calendar applications in just a couple of clicks? Guess what? If an event has been published using the hCalendar microformat, we can!

Sometimes event information appears structured — perhaps on a service like Yahoo!'s Upcoming[1] — or in a list of show times for a movie at a local cinema. Other times it might appear in natural language. On my blog I might write, "Last Monday I saw Paul Weller in concert at the Royal Albert Hall in London." You don't have to look hard to find event information online, but the HTML used to mark up this information varies enormously from site to site. This is how that Paul Weller concert was marked up on Ticketmaster:

```html
<td>
    <span class="tableListing-date">Tue 24/05/10<br>19:30</span>
</td>
<td>
    <span class="tableListing-venue">
        <a href="#">Royal Albert Hall</a> London,  GB
    </span>
</td>
<td>
    <span class="tableListing-act">
        <a href="#">Paul Weller</a>
    </span>
</td>
```

Seetickets published the same event using different HTML:

```html
<td><a href="#">PAUL WELLER</a></td>
<td><a href="#">Royal Albert Hall</a></td>
<td><a href="#">London</a></td>
<td>TUE</td>
<td><a href="#">24/05/10</a></td>
<td>19:30</td>
```

[1] http://upcoming.yahoo.com/
[2] http://microformats.org/code/hcalendar/creator

People can easily understand this contains an event, but there's nothing in that HTML to help a machine. This makes events a perfect problem for a microformat to solve.

Given that microformats reuse building blocks from existing standards, it shouldn't come as much of surprise to learn that hCalendar — the event microformat — has been developed to mirror the iCalendar standard used in calendar software such as Microsoft's Outlook, Apple's iCal and others in HTML.

A calendar event will most likely contain:

- name or summary
- type of event
- description
- start and end dates and times
- location
- URL pointing to the event page or site
- venue contact information

We'll build an hCalendar for a single event, starting by specifying the root element for the event using the vevent attribute value:

```
<article class="vevent">
    <h1>The Maltese Falcon</h1>
</article>
```

In hCalendar the name of an event is, somewhat confusingly, summary and not, as we might expect, 'name' or 'title'. Why? Because hCalendar values come directly from iCalendar. Apply the summary value to the most appropriate titling element; in this case, a heading:

```
<h1 class="summary">The Maltese Falcon</h1>
```

Next, we'll add a description by applying the `description` value to an appropriate HTML element; in our case, it's a paragraph:

```
<p class="description">A special showing of the remastered
mystery that kicked off the film noir genre of the 1940s.</p>
```

If our description contains more than just a single paragraph, we can group headings, paragraphs, lists or any other elements inside a division or `section` and apply `description` to that. We mustn't include more than one `description` per event as that would be invalid.

```
<section class="description">
    <p>A special showing of the remastered mystery that kicked off
    the film noir genre of the 1940s.</p>

    <p>Private detectives Sam Spade and Miles Archer are hired by a
    woman to follow a man called Thursby.</p>
</section>
```

Letting people know where an event will take place involves nothing more than applying the `location` value to an element, in this case a text-level `span` wrapped around the venue's name:

```
<p>Showing at <span class="location"> ↵
The Scala Cinema and Art  Centre</span></p>
```

If the event has a website, we'll use the same `url` value as we did when building an hCard:

```
<a href="http://scalaprestatyn.co.uk" class="url"> ↵
The Scala Cinema website</a>
```

Our event microformat is almost complete, but it's still missing a start date to tell people when to show up. To make this date both human- and machine-readable, once again combine microformats' `value-title` pattern with HTML5's `time` and `datetime`:

```
<time datetime="2010-11-20T19:30">
<span class="value-title" title="2010-11-20T19:30"> </span>
November 20th, 2010 at 7:30pm</time>
```

To make it explicit that this is a start date, we'll also need to add a dtstart
class attribute value to the time element:

```
<time datetime="2010-11-20T19:30" class="dtstart">
<span class="value-title" title="2010-11-20T19:30"> </span>
November 20th, 2010 at 7:30pm</time>
```

As our event runs for just one evening and finishes at 10pm, we can add that
end date and time to our hCalendar by applying the dtend value to a second
time element.

```
<time datetime="2010-11-20T22:00" class="dtend">
<span class="value-title" title="2010-11-20T22:00"> </span>
10pm</time>
```

Mixing events and contacts

Microformats are designed to be modular and embeddable, so we can easily
include a contact's hCard in an event, anywhere inside that event's root
element. We should be explicit in stating that the contact is for this event so,
to do this, apply a second value of contact after the vcard class:

```
<div class="vcard contact">
    <span class="fn org">The Scala Cinema and Art Centre</span>
</div>
```

Managing multiple events and contacts

While a single event implies that it's part of a calendar, when we mark up a series of events — for example sporting fixtures or concert dates — we should explicitly declare that series of events using the `vcalendar` value on the most appropriate HTML element. For this series of movie show times, that's a `table`:

```
<table class="vcalendar">
    <tr>
        <th scope="col">Movie name</th>
        <th scope="col">Date and time</th>
        <th scope="col">Screen</th>
    </tr>

    <tr>
        <th scope="row" class="summary">The Maltese Falcon</th>
        <td><time datetime="2010-11-20T19:30" class="dtstart">
        <span class="value-title" title="2010-11-20T19:30"> </span>
        November 20th, 2010 at 7:30pm</time></td>
        <td class="location">Scala Screen 1</td>
    </tr>

    <tr>
        <th scope="row" class="summary">The Big Sleep</th>
        <td><time datetime="2010-11-21T19:30" class="dtstart">
        <span class="value-title" title="2010-11-21T19:30"> </span>
        November 21st, 2010 at 7:30pm</time></td>
        <td class="location">Scala Screen 2</td>
    </tr>

    <tr>
        <th scope="row" class="summary">Who Framed Roger Rabbit?</th>
        <td><time datetime="2010-11-22T19:30" class="dtstart">
        <span class="value-title" title="2010-11-22T19:30"> </span>
        November 22nd, 2010 at 7:30pm</time></td>
        <td class="location">Scala Screen 3</td>
    </tr>
</table>
```

I really hope that tickets to the showing of *Who Framed Roger Rabbit?* — the best detective movie ever made — aren't sold out. If they are, it would be useful if the cinema were able to let me know that on its website in advance by using the status value:

```
<tr>
    <th scope="row" class="summary">Who Framed Roger Rabbit?</th>
    <td><time datetime="2010-11-22T19:30" class="dtstart">
    <span class="value-title" title="2010-11-22T19:30"> </span>
    November 22nd, 2010 at 7:30pm</time></td>
    <td class="status">Seats available</td>
</tr>
```

Exporting hCalendar events

Now that you've learned how to write hCalendar events, it's time to see how other people can use them. Because hCalendar is based on the iCalendar standard, anyone can download event information straight into their calendars, and there are several tools that perform hCalendar to iCalendar conversions.

You can use Brian Suda's open source X2V[1], which will happily convert hCalendar information to the iCalendar format and make an .ics file available to download and then import it into users' calendar applications. To offer this service to users, simply add a link to Brian's X2V: one that contains the URL of a page that contains a single vevent or a series in hCalendar[2].

```
<a href="http://suda.co.uk/projects/microformats/hcard/get-contact.↵
php?uri=http://hardboiledwebdesign.com/events/">Download calendar</a>
```

Tails Export and Operator extensions for Firefox both generate .ics files from hCalendars and make exporting hCalendar events easy in that browser.

---

[1] http://suda.co.uk/projects/X2V
[2] http://suda.co.uk/projects/microformats/hcard/get-contact.php?uri=http://hardboiledwebdesign.com/events/

hReview: Reviews of events, products and people

The Microformats website includes a handy tool to take most of the effort out of writing hReviews[1].

I hope that you've enjoyed what you've read so far and, if you have, that you'll write a glowing review because hReview, a draft stage microformat that's stable enough to use today, is coming next.

If we listen to almost any conversation or read almost any article, we'll find people expressing opinions about almost anything — everyone has to have an opinion! If we search the web, we'll find plenty of reviews, but it's rare to find a place where opinions are collected or aggregated in any meaningful way — a place where we can gauge collective opinion. We could turn to sites like Amazon which encourage reviews, but we wouldn't gain access to potentially hundreds or thousands of other reviews of the same product or service published on other sites.

Our brains are adept at recognising all kinds of reviews wherever we see them.

> *"Last week I rented the DVD of the 1941 movie* The Maltese Falcon *starring Humphrey Bogart as Sam Spade. It remains one of my favourite movies and I give it a big thumbs up."*

> *"Movie:* The Maltese Falcon. *Rating: 10/10"*

> *"I had pretty low expectations of* Who Framed Roger Rabbit? *but I'm giving it five stars."*

Computers are less able to recognise the delicate nuances of language. To them, the information in each of these reviews is nothing more than a string of characters. hReview addresses this by providing a rich semantic schema for review content — one that's built on the lessons learned from established microformats such as hCard and hCalendar.

As with the other microformats, an hReview comprises elements contained within a root element. This time that's `hreview` and we can apply that value to any appropriate HTML element, in this case an `article`.

```
<article class="hreview">
    <h1>A review of Who Framed Roger Rabbit?</h1>
</article>
```

---

[1] http://microformats.org/code/hreview/creator

Reviews describe and rate all kinds of products, services and more. Because a machine won't know the difference between a movie, book, or restaurant review, we should indicate the `type` of review by choosing from the several types, including: `product`; `business`; `event`; `person`; `place`; `website`; and `url`.

```
<article class="hreview">
    <span class="type">event</span>
</article>
```

Writing an hReview will take less time than you might think, because hReview reuses values you should recognise from both hCard and hCalendar. First, we'll title our review using the `item` value. This value is required in hReview, so make sure you don't leave it out.

```
<h1 class="item">A review of Who Framed Roger Rabbit?</h1>
```

An `item` has three sub-properties, but only the formatted name, `fn`, is absolutely required. As sub-values must be contained inside another element, we can wrap a `strong` element around the item's name:

```
<h1 class="item">
A review of <strong class="fn">Who Framed Roger Rabbit?</strong>
</h1>
```

A review wouldn't be much use without an opinion and for this we'll use the `description` value. If a review is short, apply this to one element, perhaps a list or, in this case, a paragraph:

```
<p class="description">How much do I know about show business?
Only that there is no business like it, no business I know.</p>
```

If the description covers more than one paragraph or includes other HTML elements, group them all into a containing element and apply the `description` value to that:

```
<div class="description">
    <p>How much do I know about show business? Only that there is no
    business like it, no business I know.</p>

    <p>A classic movie has to work on several different levels and
    animated action movie 'Who Framed Roger Rabbit?' scores on all
    of them. It's a fantastic children's movie with characters like
    Roger, the Weasels and Benny the Cab for them to enjoy. It also
    plays perfectly as a detective story for adults. And who will
    ever forget Jessica Rabbit?</p>
</div>
```

Our `description` includes words that will make useful links to tagged content elsewhere on the web — perhaps products on Amazon, photos on Flickr or YouTube videos. First add those links, then define the link relationship as a tag using `rel-tag`:

```
<p>A classic <a href="/tag/movie/" rel="tag">movie</a> has to
work on several different levels and <a href="/tag/animated/"
rel="tag">animated</a> action movie 'Who Framed Roger Rabbit?' scores
on all of them. It's a fantastic children's movie with characters
like Roger, the Weasels and Benny the Cab for them to enjoy. It also
plays perfectly as a <a href="/tag/detective/" rel="tag">detective</
a> story for adults. And who will ever forget Jessica Rabbit?</p>
```

Mixing reviews and contacts

As it's not essential to know who wrote a review, hReview doesn't require us to include a name, but we may choose to add one because a person's identity can greatly enhance the credibility of a review.

We should always use hCard to describe a reviewer, so to state explicitly that the hCard belongs to the person writing the review, apply a second value of `reviewer` after the `vcard` class. We can include as much contact information as we want, but here we'll only add the reviewer's name:

```
<span class="vcard reviewer">
    <span class="fn">Andy Clarke</span>
</span>
```

If our review contains a link to a reviewer's biography or even their own website, we can make that link relationship explicit by adding an HTML5 `author` relationship:

```
<span class="vcard reviewer">
    <a href="http://hardboiledwebdesign.com" class="fn" ↵
    rel="author">Andy Clarke</a>
</span>
```

A movie isn't going to change over time but a restaurant or hotel certainly could. A musician can have an off night, so the date of a review can have a huge impact on its relevance. Cast your mind back to when you learned about HTML5's `time` and `datetime` features, as well as the microformat `value-title` pattern. We'll use both a machine-readable time-stamp and a human-readable date, then we'll add the `dtreviewed` value:

```
<time datetime="2010-11-20" class="dtreviewed">
    <span class="value-title" title="2010-11-20"> </span>
    November 20th, 2010
</time>
```

Who's already using hReview?

Although the hReview microformat is still at the draft stage, this hasn't stopped plenty of big name websites from using it to publish their own reviews:

Online retailer **Zappos.com** uses hReview on its landing and brand pages.
http://www.zappos.com/

Yahoo! UK Movie Reviews has implemented hReview on all its reviews.
http://uk.movies.yahoo.com/movie-reviews/

Corkd, for wine enthusiasts, uses hReview on all of its member-created tasting notes.

The New York Times has implemented hReview on its travel section venue pages covering hotels, restaurants, shopping, nightlife and attractions.
http://travel.nytimes.com/travel/guides/

hAtom: Defining syndicated content

Next, you'll learn about hAtom, a microformat that's been designed for publishing syndicated content such as news articles, blog posts and podcasts. So far, all of the microformats we've covered have been designed to solve common, real-world problems, so you could be forgiven for wondering, "What's the problem hAtom aims to solve?" After all, millions of people publish content every day and there are lots of ways to subscribe to it.

RSS is a common tool that's used for subscription-based services, blogs and other regularly updated content. It was once just for hardened geeks, but RSS is now in the mainstream thanks to browser makers and mainstream publishers such as the BBC.

We commonly think that RSS is one technology, but in fact it's several largely incompatible technologies, including RSS (Rich Site Summary, or Really Simple Syndication), RDF (Resource Description Framework) and Atom. Because microformats reuse widely adopted standards, hAtom is based on Atom. Unlike RSS that has become a de facto standard, Atom is an IETF (Internet Engineering Task Force) standard. hAtom takes only what it needs from Atom — a minimal set of elements — to develop a microformat that's easy to learn and provides syndication of content straight from HTML, without the need for separate RSS or Atom feeds. I'm sure you'll now agree that this is a problem that's well worth solving.

Inside hAtom

While hAtom is based on Atom, there's a difference. Both Atom feeds and hAtom can be used for a series of entries, but hAtom is better suited for a single blog entry. Let's write an hAtom blog entry. As the microformats community suggests, we should start by using "the most accurately precise semantic XHTML building block for each object etc.[1]" Here's our initial HTML, which starts with a heading followed by a paragraph:

```
<h1>Explorer wanted in double margin murders</h1>
<p>Police found another body floating in the early hours
of the morning.</p>
```

Now that we know how to use an HTML5 `article` element for stand-alone entries, we'll group those elements inside an `article` and turn it into an hAtom entry by adding a `class` attribute value of `hentry`. This is the root element for each individual hAtom entry:

```
<article class="hentry">
    <h1>Explorer wanted in double margin murders</h1>
    <p>Police found another body floating in the early hours
    of the morning.</p>
</article>
```

---

[1] http://microformats.org/wiki/semantic-xhtml-design-principles

Every valid hAtom entry must contain an `entry-title`, `published` and `updated` dates and some information about its `author`. We can include some other optional properties such as summary extract and a bookmark link to a permanent URL if we need to. First, let's apply the required `entry-title` value to our main heading:

```
<h1 class="entry-title">Explorer wanted in double margin murders</h1>
```

When we need to say explicitly that a date or time refer to a publication date, use HTML5's `pubdate` attribute combined with hAtom's `published` value:

```
<time datetime="2010-11-20" pubdate class="published">
    <span class="value-title" title="2010-11-20"> </span>
    November 20th, 2010
</time>
```

If an `article` is updated after the published date, we should change the `published` value to one of `updated`:

```
<time datetime="2010-11-20" pubdate class="updated">
    <span class="value-title" title="2010-11-20"> </span>
    November 20th, 2010
</time>
```

Our final required value for an hAtom entry is its `author`. You should be familiar with hCards by now, so to state explicitly that this hCard belongs to the person writing the entry, apply a second value of `author` after the `vcard` class:

```
<address class="vcard author">
    <a href="http://hardboiledwebdesign.com" class="fn url">
        Andy Clarke
    </a>
</address>
```

W... wh... what's with that `address` element?

The `address` element wasn't intended to describe physical addresses but it is absolutely the right element to use for an author's contact information. We'll define the link relationship as one of an `author`. If this link points to a different website, we'll mark that relationship as `external`:

```
<address class="vcard author">
    <a href="http://hardboiledwebdesign.com" class="fn url" ↵
    rel="author external">Andy Clarke</a>
</address>
```

Some authors often like to split blog entries across more than one page; for example, we might have summaries on our home page or in our archives, then present the full entry on its own page. hAtom can define a short segment of an `article` as an `entry-summary`. For our example, we'll use a single paragraph:

```
<p class="entry-summary">Police found another body floating in the
early hours of the morning.</p>
```

For a longer summary, one that consists of several elements, group them together in a `section` and then apply `entry-summary`:

```
<section class="entry-summary">
    <p>Police found another body floating in the early hours of the
    morning.</p>

    <p>Sources within the police department have confirmed that this
    latest case bears all the hallmarks of the recent double margin
    murders. The perp, dubbed "the Explorer", is still at large.</p>
</section>
```

When an `entry-summary` appears on a different page, it's important to include a permanent link to the full article. To make it clear that the link destination is related to the `entry-summary`, add a `rel` attribute with a value of `bookmark`:

```
<a href="http://hardboiledwebdesign.com/a/explorer-wanted.html" ↵
rel="bookmark">Permalink</a>
```

Managing multiple hAtom entries

So far, we've been working with a single hAtom entry, but many websites have lists of related articles on their home and archives pages. These hAtom entries combined are known as an `hfeed`. To assemble a feed, all we need is an an appropriate parent element and for this we'll use an HTML5 `section`. As a `section` should make sense when taken out of the context of a page, we'll also give it a descriptive heading:

```
<section class="hfeed">
    <h1>Hardboiled archives</h1>
    <article class="hentry">
      [...]
    </article>
    <article class="hentry">
      [...]
    </article>
</section>
```

Exporting hAtom entries

Several developers have made tools for exporting hAtom content. Optimus' will process all of the microformats on a page. To make sure that Optimus only transforms hAtom entries, specify `format=rss` in your link to it:

```
<a href="http://microformatique.com/optimus/?= ↵
http://hardboiledwebdesign.com&format=rss">Subscribe</a>
```

---

[1] http://microformatique.com/optimus/

Breaking it up

Microformats supercharge your HTML by allowing others to capitalise on the rich meaning that they add to your content. They make it simple for users to extract contact information, events, reviews and more, and to subscribe to updated content with minimum effort. But these possibilities are just the start. For web designers and developers, microformats offer a way to break away from the presentational ways we have written HTML in the past, and to liberate our documents by making them more flexible, adaptable and hardboiled.

Want to do your own microformats detective work?

I hope you've become as excited about microformats as I am and want to find out more. There are more microformats than it is possible to cover within the scope of this book, but I've given you a good overview of the most important ones, and you can find out more at:

Microformats: The home of the Microformats community

http://microformats.org

Twitter: Follow Microformats updates on Twitter

http://twitter.com/microformats

Cheat sheet: Grab Brian Suda's handy microformats cheat sheet

http://suda.co.uk/projects/microformats/cheatsheet/

Why-Oh WAI-ARIA roles

YOU'VE ALREADY LEARNED HOW HTML5 and microformats have brought HTML into the web application age. You might not have heard that there's another specification that has different but complementary goals. That specification is WAI-ARIA, the Accessible Rich Internet Applications Suite[1], which has been created as a stopgap solution to make web applications more accessible.

WAI-ARIA aims to make dynamic web content processed by technologies such as Ajax easier to use by people who use assistive technologies — that is, until web browsers and assistive technologies have better support for HTML5. As accessibility specialist John Foliot describes:

> *"ARIA has always been considered a bridging solution [...] [It] was designed to be a retrofitting solution (for HTML4/XHTML1 [...])."* [2]

So, will HTML5 make WAI-ARIA redundant? Probably not, at least not for a while because even when there's more complete support for HTML5, there will still be roles and properties in WAI-ARIA that are not matched by HTML5.

WAI-ARIA includes:

- roles for widgets such as a navigation menus, sliders and progress meters
- properties that define dynamically updated sections of a page
- ways to enable keyboard navigation
- roles to describe the structure of a page, including headings, regions, and tables (grids)

---

[1] http://www.w3.org/TR/wai-aria
[2] http://lists.w3.org/Archives/Public/public-html/2010Apr/0049.html

All this sounds great, but what makes WAI-ARIA hardboiled? As well as providing valuable help to people who rely on assistive technologies, web designers and developers can use WAI-ARIA roles to help us reduce our reliance on presentational id and class attributes. After all, why would we add a class of banner to an HTML element just for the purpose of styling, when we can do away with the class altogether and use a CSS attribute selector to bind styles to a WAI-ARIA role?

WAI-ARIA landmark roles

To make proper use of WAI-ARIA, users need both a browser and an assistive technology that understands it. Firefox, Safari, Google Chrome and Opera all offer some level of support. WAI-ARIA landmark roles are also supported by the Jaws 10 screen reader, and other assistive technologies will no doubt follow its lead.

WAI-ARIA includes a set of navigation landmark roles, which help people with disabilities identify common sections of a page or web application and navigate around them using assistive technologies. These roles can be used in combination with either HTML 4.01, XHTML 1.0 or HTML5 elements to maximise their semantics.

We'll be covering several specific WAI-ARIA roles that offer us the opportunity to hard boil our HTML and CSS by making it less necessary to pack our markup with class and id attributes. These WAI-ARIA roles include banner, complementary, contentinfo, main, navigation and search.

To add a WAI-ARIA role, we simply apply the role attribute to any appropriate element. For example, when we're marking up a branding area or masthead, apply a role of banner. If we're writing HTML 4.01 or XHTML 1.0, our markup would look like this:

```
<div role="banner">
    <h1>It's Hardboiled</h1>
</div>
```

Using HTML5's `header` element would look like this:

```
<header role="banner">
    <h1>It's Hardboiled</h1>
</header>
```

Banner

In HTML5, the `header` element can be used for the branding or masthead area, and it often appears at the top of a page. The WAI-ARIA `banner` role helps people who use assistive-technologies recognise this `header` and distinguish it from others on the page.

But unlike a plain HTML5 `header` element — which can be used as many times as we need inside multiple `section` and `article` elements — we can use a `header` with the role of `banner` just the once.

Complementary

The WAI-ARIA `complementary` role is similar in function to HTML5's `aside` element. It delineates content that is somehow related to and supports other content, although it doesn't have to be either contained by or visually linked to that content. If we're writing an article about the hardboiled author Mickey Spillane, we could apply the `complementary` role to an `aside` about his famous book *My Gun Is Quick.*

```
<aside role="complementary">
    <h2>My Gun Is Quick</h2>
    <p>Mickey Spillane's second novel featuring Mike Hammer.</p>
</aside>
```

Contentinfo

WAI-ARIA defines the `contentinfo` role as a "perceivable region that contains information about the parent document." [1] Does that sound like a HTML5 `footer` to you? Me too.

It's true that the `contentinfo` role has a lot in common with HTML5's `footer` element and this helps to illustrate that there are overlaps (and in some cases conflicts) between WAI-ARIA's goals and those of HTML5. Should this stop us embracing WAI-ARIA? I don't think so, and neither does Jeremy Keith:

> "[T]here's no reason not to start using ARIA roles today: browsers, libraries and screenreaders already offer a good level of support and it's only going to get better. If we start adding ARIA roles to our websites — and in our CMS themes —then if the HTML5 community stays true to its stated principal [sic] of paving the cowpaths, the pragmatic here-and-now solution should triumph." [2]

Let's continue developing the 'It's Hardboiled' archives page by adding the `contentinfo` role to the main page `footer`.

```
<footer role="contentinfo">
    <h3>It's Hardboiled</h3>
    <p>A fictitious demonstration, designed by Andy Clarke.</p>
</footer>
```

Just like the `banner` role and unlike HTML5's plain `footer` element, we can only use a `footer` with the role of `contentinfo` once on each page.

Main

'Skip to content' links form one of the most commonly used web accessibility techniques, intended to help people who rely on assistive technologies to skip past repetitive blocks of navigation. WAI-ARIA's `main` role aims to eliminate the need for skip links because it helps assistive technology users navigate straight to a page's main content.

Where we apply the `main` role depends entirely on our content, and on the 'It's Hardboiled' archives page we're developing, we might choose to add it to the HTML5 `section` that contains the latest, most important news.

```
<section id="content-world">[…]</section>
<section id="content-latest" role="main">[…]</section>
<section id="content-local">[…]</section>
```

If we're developing a page that contains just one story, we should add the `main` role to an `article` element.

```
<article role="main">
    <header><h1>Mickey Spillane</h1></header>
    <p>Frank Morrison Spillane, better known as Mickey Spillane, was
    an author of crime novels, many featuring his detective character
    Mike Hammer. More than 225 million copies of his books have been
    sold internationally, including my personal favourite, 'My Gun Is
    Quick'.</p>
</article>
```

Navigation

WAI-ARIA's `navigation` role is similar in function to HTML5's `nav` element as it's intended to describe the major navigation blocks in a page or web application. We'll apply the role even though `navigation` and `nav` serve the same purpose to give the widest possible support until browsers and assistive technologies have fully implemented HTML5.

```
<nav role="navigation">
    <ul>
        <li><a href="about.html">What is Hardboiled?</a></li>
        <li><a href="archives.html">Archives</a></li>
        <li><a href="authors.html">Hardboiled authors</a></li>
        <li><a href="store.html">Classic Hardboiled</a></li>
    </ul>
</nav>
```

On many sites, searching is the primary way that people navigate to content. In HTML5, it's therefore perfectly acceptable to embed a search form inside a nav element, but the same isn't true of an element given WAI-ARIA's navigation role. Why? That's because WAI-ARIA includes its own dedicated role for search.

Search

A page or web application will often contain more than one form, each with a distinct purpose. We might include "add to cart" forms on an online store, feedback forms on a news site and comment forms on a blog. HTML5 includes a dedicated search input, but web browsers and assistive technologies still might find it difficult to distinguish between different types of form.

WAI-ARIA's search role describes a complete search interface — including labels, inputs, buttons and other HTML elements. In the past, when we wanted to style a search form, we gave it a unique id or perhaps a class attribute. Now we can stop adding presentational attributes and use WAI-ARIA's search role and a CSS attribute selector instead:

```
<form method="post" action="results.html" role="search">
    <fieldset>
        <input type="search" title="Search this site">
        <button type="submit">Go</button>
    </fieldset>
</form>
```

Breaking it up

Accessibility matters, not only to those people who rely on our work being readily available through screen readers and other assistive technologies, but for the integrity of the work that we make. WAI-ARIA roles are just one of the ways that we can help improve accessibility. But there's more to them than that. Like microformats, WAI-ARIA roles in HTML allow us to reduce our reliance on presentational elements and attributes, setting our markup free and tying it less to a single design. By binding CSS styles to WAI-ARIA roles instead of attributes which serve only a visual design, our documents become more flexible and better equipped to render in the many different browsers and devices that people now use to access our websites and applications.

That was a breeze

In *Hardboiled HTML*, you learned about HTML5 — the latest incarnation of HTML — and how this new specification has brought with it more precise and better defined semantic elements that make redundant many of the presentational ways that we've worked in the past. HTML5 may be new and some of its features are still being developed and implemented, but the time to start taking advantage of HTML5 is now.

You learned about how microformats build on HTML5, supercharging the meaning of your markup to provide developers with new HTML-based APIs. Microformats' rich semantics and the abundance of `rel` and `class` attributes they provide mean that we no longer need to fill our documents with presentational elements and attributes, and we can use their rich library of values instead.

Finally, you learned that using WAI-ARIA roles not only improves web accessibility for the people who need it most but, in combination with HTML5 and microformats, they can also make our markup leaner, fitter and ready to be styled using the very latest, hardboiled style sheets.

HARDBOILED CSS3

For years, designing for the web has seemed like a constant battle between what we want to achieve and what is technically possible. Designing and developing sites that were in any way cross-browser used to involve a whole host of hacks and compromises, but this has changed.

In **Hardboiled CSS3**, you'll learn about web fonts for better type and typography, how to layer colour with RGBa and how to use opacity. You'll discover how use CSS3 multiple background images and how to make borders rounded and full of images. You'll wind up knowing how to replace many images with CSS3 gradients to make your designs lighter and more flexible. Your world may never be quite the same again.

Working with web fonts

INFORMATION ARCHITECTS Japan's Oliver Reichenstein wrote that "Web Design is 95% Typography"[1]. I'm not 95% sure if that's true, but I do know that web content largely consists of the written word. It's ironic, then, that our options for type and typography on the web have been so limited.

I'm sure we're all familiar with the challenges posed by a limited set of commonly installed fonts and poor typographic controls, and how these have forced us to find workarounds to allow us to get more creative with type.

When we need to use fonts outside of a Mac and PC's core set — those usual suspects like Arial, Georgia, Times, Verdana and others — we make pictures of text or use clever alternatives like Flash, SVG and Canvas. None of these methods are perfect, all of them suffering from accessibility concerns, performance problems and other headaches. Fortunately, the game has changed and we now have a better option allowing us to display real fonts on the web. We call them 'web fonts'.

A short history of web fonts

In the late 1990s, both Netscape and Microsoft released browsers that allowed us to embed fonts into a web page. Given the competition between them, they didn't make it easy. I can remember trying — but mostly failing — to use their incompatible TrueDoc and Embedded Open Type (EOT) formats.

---

[1] http://informationarchitects.jp/the-web-is-all-about-typography-period

Netscape lost the browser war and although Internet Explorer continued to support font embedding, its EOT format was never implemented by other browser makers or widely used by web designers. For a decade web fonts stalled, so we resorted to elaborate image replacement techniques and other hacks like sIFR[1] and Cufón[2] when we needed non-standard typefaces in our designs.

It wasn't until ten years later — ten years, dammit! — that Apple's Safari 3.1 became the first browser that supported embedding fonts in TrueType and OpenType formats (but not EOT). Mozilla followed and so did Opera. Web fonts moved forward at the W3C too, and the CSS3 Fonts Module contains standard specifications for `@font-face` and the WOFF (Web Open Font Format) format[2].

Why web fonts matter

Web fonts offer a way to use more varied fonts. With almost all contemporary browsers now supporting web fonts, we can largely guarantee that people will experience our type designs as we intend them to.

Web fonts are simple to implement and when we use them our text stays accessible, selectable and search engine friendly. (Actually, that's not quite true. Comic Sans makes your pages invisible to Google.*)

To embed a web font we need three things:

1. a font file, in a format that browsers will understand. We can use any copyrighted or free to use font.

---

[1] http://novemberborn.net/sifr3
[2] http://cufon.shoqolate.com
[2] http://w3.org/TR/css3-fonts
* Disclaimer: Using Comic Sans won't actually make your pages invisible to Google, but it will make me beat you to a pulp.

2. an @font-face declaration at the start of our style sheet. This will define the font-family name, the source of the font file and, finally, its format (TrueType in the following example). A simple declaration looks like this:

```
@font-face {
font-family : "AllerRegular";
src : url("AllerRegular.ttf")
format("truetype");
}
```

3. a font-family property, which applies the embedded font to an element, id, class, child, sibling, attribute, pseudo- or any other CSS selector.

```
h1 { font-family : "AllerRegular" }
```

We'll work through the details of embedded web fonts syntax in just a moment.

Web font formats

There are five font formats widely used on the web — EOT, OpenType, SVG, TrueType and WOFF — each with varied browser support. As of July 2010, browser support for these font formats looks like this, but keep on top of each new browser version because the situation changes all the time.

Web font format support in contemporary browsers as of October 2010

	Firefox 3.6	Google Chrome 6	Internet Explorer 9	Opera 10.6	Safari 5	iOS Safari
EOT			●			
OpenType	●	●	●	●	●	
SVG		●		●		●
TrueType	●	●		●	●	
WOFF	●		●			

This varied browser support means that we should link to more than one font file if we want any degree of consistency between browsers. Still, we mustn't grumble too much, because embedding web fonts is a great deal easier than working with image replacement, sIFR or Cufón. Let's take a look at these font formats in more detail.

TrueType (TTF)

Apple introduced TrueType in the late 1980s as an alternative to Adobe's PostScript Type 1 format. With TrueType, all aspects of a typeface — including its kerning and hinting information — are contained within a single file. This can make some TrueType font files large and impractical to use as web fonts.

OpenType (OTF)

OpenType is an extension of TrueType that offers better control over typography because it provides up to 65,000 different glyphs and has better rendering of complex script typefaces.

Embedded OpenType (EOT)

Designed by Microsoft specifically for embedding web fonts, EOT contains a wrapper for TrueType that makes it more difficult to download, extract and reuse an embedded font. This makes it easier to uphold font licences, or at least that's the theory. Although Microsoft submitted EOT to the W3C in 2007, it has never been part of any standard.

To convert a font into EOT you need either Microsoft's WEFT tool[1] (if you can ever get that to work) or another convertor such as Font Squirrel's online Font Face Generator[2].

Microsoft's WEFT tool creates compressed EOT files that are restricted for use on specific domains. Windows users can also create EOT files using EOTFAST[6]. These files are compressed, but unlike WEFT, they're not restricted. Font Squirrel's EOT files are not compressed, nor are they restricted.

SVG

SVG isn't a font format at all — it's a technology for making scalable vector graphics — but we can include font information inside an SVG document and link to that in the same way we would any other type of font. With SVG, it's possible to shoehorn web fonts onto mobile devices including the iPad.

When SVG is the only option, we can convert fonts to SVG using applications like FontForge[3] or Font Squirrel's Font Face Generator. Web fonts service Typekit also provides an option for serving fonts as SVG. They explained this in 'Typekit now supports fonts for the iPad'[4].

Web Open Font Format (WOFF)

The W3C's Web Fonts Working Group[5] has been working on standardising a web font file format — it's called WOFF (Web Open Font Format).

FontForge[3] and sfnt2woff[7] are suites of tools for compressing TTF and OTF fonts into WOFF files.

WOFF isn't strictly a font format. It's a compressed wrapper for TrueType and OpenType fonts — a 'transfer format' similar to a compressed ZIP file. This makes it small in size and therefore eminently suitable for using on the web. Because WOFF includes ownership information, it's more attractive to font foundries that are concerned about protecting their intellectual properties. WOFF is also great news for web font delivery services like TypeKit who appreciate its smaller file size.

Firefox was the first browser to implement WOFF and now that Microsoft has implemented WOFF in Internet Explorer 9, it looks increasingly likely that the days of serving multiple file formats will soon come to an end.

[1] http://microsoft.com/typography/weft.mspx
[2] http://fontsquirrel.com/fontface/generator
[3] http://fontforge.sourceforge.net
[4] http://blog.typekit.com/2010/04/09/typekit-now-supports-fonts-for-the-ipad
[5] http://w3.org/Fonts/WG
[6] http://eotfast.com
[7] http://people.mozilla.com/~jkew/woff

Finding fonts on Font Squirrel

It's time to start including web fonts in the 'It's Hardboiled' site. We'll head straight to Font Squirrel[1] to select from a set of freely available typefaces. Font Squirrel offers both single format fonts and complete kits that include web fonts in several formats:

- EOT for older versions of Microsoft Internet Explorer
- TrueType, supported by Firefox, Google Chrome, Opera and Safari
- SVG, supported by Google Chrome, Opera and iOS Safari on the iPad
- WOFF, supported by Firefox, Google Chrome 6 and Internet Explorer 9

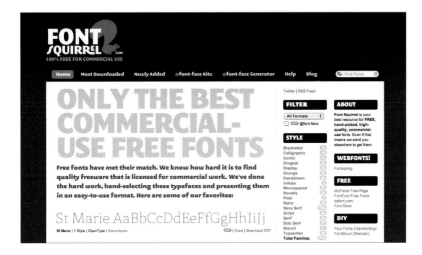

Font Squirrel includes hundreds of free fonts that have been converted for use as web font kits.

We'll download one of Font Squirrel's zipped kits — you can store it locally or upload it to a server — and then embed the fonts in our web pages.

[1] http://fontsquirrel.com

Font Squirrel's @font-face generator takes the pain away from converting font files into the various formats we need for reliable font embedding. Best of all it's free and there's no software to install.

When we already own a font and its licence allows for font embedding, Font Squirrel offers an @font-face generator[1] to convert those fonts into all the formats we need for wide browser support. To use Font Squirrel's @font-face generator, add one or more fonts from your computer and in seconds they will be uploaded and ready for conversion. Font Squirrel's @font-face generator offers two modes.

Easy: Automatically chooses formats for all common browsers.

Expert: We're experts, so choose that mode and select from the advanced options.

We might sometimes choose to leave older browsers, particularly those that run on older hardware, out of the web fonts party.

Choose formats for the browsers we want to target. In our case, these will be EOT, SVG, TrueType (as this works better than OpenType in browsers running on Windows) and WOFF.

We want people who use Windows PCs to see smooth type, so make sure 'Add Hinting' is checked. If we need to stop third parties from reusing a font, check 'WebOnly', which disables desktop use of any font.

Choose your web font options wisely as some will increase the file size of the kit. As some web font files can be large, any savings we can make are always welcome.

Font Options:	☑ Add Hinting	☑ WebOnly™	☐ Keep OT Features*
	Improve Win rendering	Disable desktop use	Ligatures, alt glyphs etc.
	☐ Remove Kerning	☐ Simplify Outlines	☐ Build Cufón File
	Strip kerning Data	Remove extra points (lossy)	Javascript font alternative

Font Squirrel also provides CSS declarations to paste straight into our style sheets and we can choose between several syntax options. We'll choose Paul Irish's modified Bulletproof (Smiley) method. More about that in just a moment.

---

[1] http://fontsquirrel.com/fontface/generator

CSS Formats:	◉ Bulletproof (Smiley)	○ Bulletproof (Original)	○ Mo' Bulletproofer
	Modified Bulletproof	Paul Irish Method	Richard Fink Method
	Avoids local() problems	Safe and compact	Uses double declarations

Finally, we must agree to Font Squirrel's terms and conditions. These make it our responsibility to check that a font's licence allows for linking and embedding. Since we know that the fonts we're converting can legally be used, we'll go ahead and click to 'download the kit'. These fonts, along with a demonstration page and sample CSS, will be sent straight to our downloads folder.

To improve the legibility of type in Firefox, Google Chrome and Safari 5, use the `text-rendering` property supported in those browsers. For example, to add kerning pairs and ligatures to a top-level heading:

```
h1 { text- rendering:
optimizeLegibility; }
```

Find out more about optimising legibility at 'Cross-browser kerning-pairs & ligatures' by Anthony Kolber[1].

Including @font-face in a stylesheet

To link web fonts to our style sheets, the first step is to specify the name of a font and where a browser can find it. We'll link to the Aller TrueType font we downloaded from Font Squirrel:

```
@font-face {
font-family : "AllerRegular";
src : url("AllerRegular.ttf")
format("truetype");
}
```

Place this `@font-face` declaration at the top of a style sheet (or the top of your typography section) so that it's available to any declarations below.

The `font-face` name we choose need not match the font's file name: we can name it anything that makes referencing it in our style sheets easier. This web font should appear first in the font stack:

```
body { font-family : "AllerRegular", Helvetica, Arial, sans-serif; }
```

---

[1] http://aestheticallyloyal.com/public/optimize-legibility

A TrueType font will only work in browsers that support that format. To include the other formats we'll need for wider browser support, add those to the declaration, starting with EOT which is used by older versions of Internet Explorer.

Paul Irish explains in detail how browsers interpret and use @font-face declarations in his article 'Bulletproof @ font-face syntax'.[1]

```
@font-face {
font-family : "AllerRegular";
src : url("AllerRegular.eot");
src : url("AllerRegular.ttf") format("truetype");
}
```

This simple rule should be enough to provide Internet Explorer with its EOT format, while other browsers will use the TrueType format. Internet Explorer should ignore any later values because it doesn't understand the CSS3 `format()` hint. Unfortunately, the reality is somewhat more complicated.

Internet Explorer will stop using EOT while it tries to parse the formats it doesn't understand. The result? Internet Explorer displays no web fonts at all. Fortunately, Paul Irish has devised a method that preserves our sanity by writing all non-EOT formats into a comma-separated list. Paul separates these even further from Internet Explorer by adding a dummy local rule that includes nothing more than a ☺ face.

If you're wondering why the dummy local path in the code examples is a smiley ☺ and want to know the reasons why, read Paul's @font-face gotchas article.[2]

```
@font-face {
font-family : "AllerRegular";
src : url("AllerRegular.eot");
src : local("☺"),
url("AllerRegular.svg#AllerRegular") format("svg"),
url("AllerRegular.ttf") format("truetype"),
url("AllerRegular.woff") format("woff");
}
```

Internet Explorer will now ignore both the ☺ face local rule and the comma-separated string, and will only use EOT. This syntax isn't so much bulletproof as bombproof.

---

[1] http://paulirish.com/2009/bulletproof-font-face-implementation-syntax
[2] http://paulirish.com/2010/font-face-gotchas/#smiley

Web fonts' 404 adventure

I hope that you're not feeling lost among all this talk of web fonts, because now we'll put what you learned to work on a 404 page for 'It's Hardboiled'.

This page uses two web fonts, an image and a splattering of experimental CSS. Don't worry that web fonts or some of the CSS3 properties aren't supported by all browsers. We'll make sure that everyone who finds themselves on this page will get an appropriate experience.

This design doesn't need much markup — two divisions, a heading and a couple of paragraphs:

```
<div class="splatter">
    <div class="content">
        <h1>404</h1>
        <p>You dumb mug!</p>
        <p>You can look all you
        want, but what you're
        looking for just ain't here.</p>
    </div>
</div>
```

Our first job is to add a bloody background image to the outer 'splatter' division. We'll make sure the whole splash will always be visible by setting a minimum height on that division:

```
.splatter {
min-height : 900px;
background : url(blood.png) no-repeat 50% 0;
}
```

We hope that our users never see a 404 page, so it's strange that so many designers use theirs as a playground for experimental techniques and emerging technologies. Don't be a dumb mug — move that CSS3 from your 404 to your home page.

Centre the 'content' division horizontally and make sure that it's only just wide enough for the large heading inside:

```
.content {
width : 280px;
max-width : 280px;
min-width : 280px;
margin : 0 auto;
padding-top : 270px;
text-shadow : 0 1px 2px rgb(0,0,0);
}
```

Want to preview how web fonts look on any website, even one that's not yours? FontFonter[1] is an online tool that does just that.

Now link to two typefaces — ChunkFive and Boycott. We'll use EOT, SVG, TrueType and WOFF formats so that as many people as possible will see the hardboiled design:

```
@font-face {
font-family : "ChunkFive";
src : url("ChunkFive.eot");
src : local("☺"),
url("chunkFive.svg#chunkFive") format("svg"),
url("ChunkFive.ttf") format("truetype"),
url("ChunkFive.woff") format("woff");
}

@font-face {
font-family : "Boycott";
src : url("Boycott.eot");
src : local("☺"),
url("boycott.svg#boycott") format("svg"),
url("Boycott.ttf") format("truetype"),
url("Boycott.woff") format("woff");
}
```

---

[1] http://fontfonter.com

With these links in place, let's style the main heading with ChunkFive and make its colour grey so that it matches the wall behind:

With its mixture of web fonts, images and utter rudeness, this won't be a 404 page that anyone will forget in a hurry.

```
h1 {
font-size : 10em;
font-weight : bold;
text-align: center;
line-height : 1;
font-family : ChunkFive;
color : rgb(224,224,224);
}
```

Next we'll style the two paragraphs using Boycott in grey:

```
p {
color : rgb(224,224,224);
font-family : Boycott;
font-size : 1em;
text-align : center;
}
```

To complete the design for all web font-capable browsers, we'll style the "You Dumb Mug" paragraph. Since this immediately follows the main heading, we don't need to apply a specific id or class attribute; we can target it with just an adjacent sibling selector:

```
h1 + p {
margin : -30px 0 .5em 0;
padding-bottom : .25em;
border-bottom : 1px solid rgb(224,224,224);
font-family : ChunkFive;
font-size : 1.6em;
text-transform : uppercase;
letter-spacing : 3px;
}
```

Designing to browser capabilities with Modernizr

The way we normally make font stacks doesn't need to change when we work with web fonts. We start with a linked web font, then offer a list of system font alternatives. The font stacks for the 'It's Hardboiled' 404 page look like this:

```
h1, h1 + p { font-family : ChunkFive, Helvetica, Arial; }


p { font-family : Boycott, Helvetica, Arial;  }
```

Browsers that are incapable of rendering web fonts will default to the next available font in the stack. But why hand control to a browser when we can use Modernizr to provide the alternatives?

Modernizr detects if a browser is capable of rendering web fonts. When they're not supported, it adds its `no-fontface` class to the `html` element. This allows us to provide alternative styles that go way beyond simple font stacks:

```
.no-fontface .content h1,
.no-fontface .content p,
.no-fontface .content h1 + p {
font-family : Helvetica, Arial, sans-serif;
font-weight : bold;
}

.no-fontface .content p {
line-height : 1.3;
font-size: 16px;
}

.no-fontface .content h1 + p {
margin : -10px 0 .5em 0;
padding-bottom : .5em;
}

.no-fontface .content h1 + p + p {
padding : 0 30px;
}
```

Experimental WebKit properties

WebKit includes several experimental but highly useful properties that can transform the look of our 404 heading. These properties are currently available only in Safari and Google Chrome. We will use two of them: `-webkit-text-stroke` to add a stroke to our text; and `-webkit-text-fill-color` to make our 404 text transparent:

```
h1 {
-webkit-text-fill-color : transparent;
-webkit-text-stroke : 3px rgb(133,29,25);   }
```

Web font services

We should always be cautious when using experimental CSS properties that aren't part of an ongoing standards process.

Even though we can convert fonts into multiple formats and link to them from our websites, we can't just use any typeface we want. Whether we've spent a little time tracking down free fonts or several hundred pounds buying them from a font foundry, we need to check the EULA (End User License Agreement) for each and every font. Ignore the EULA and we'll find ourselves in hot water.

Font designers and the foundries who sell their wares were slow to respond to the demand for web fonts and, just like music in the pre-iTunes era, web fonts needed a service, like iTunes, to make buying and implementing them easier. They needed services that take care of technical issues, licensing and implementation, and the first service to do just that was Typekit.

Typekit[1]

With a growing catalogue of web fonts and support from individual type designers and font foundries including exljbris, TypeTogether and the Suitcase Type Foundry, Typekit is one of the best-known and most established web font delivery services. Typekit works on the principle that using web fonts shouldn't be a struggle. It solved many of the technical challenges of delivering web fonts and combined this with a business model that allows designers to pay for licences, and font designers and foundries to make money every time we choose their fonts.

Typekit was the first web fonts service that made it easy to legally embed real fonts into websites. Other services soon followed, including FontsLive[2] and Fontdeck[3]. These also offer fonts that have been licensed from leading type designers and font foundries.

[1] http://typekit.com
[2] http://fontslive.com
[3] http://fontdeck.com

Typekit uses JavaScript to protect fonts from unauthorised use and this makes linking to web fonts even easier. Instead of juggling `@font-face` declarations, add a Typekit script into any page and then style the web fonts using CSS as you would any font:.

```
<script src="http://use.typekit.com/tallveen.js"></script>
<script>try{Typekit.load();}catch(e){}</script>
```

Google fonts

When services like Typekit proved there was a strong demand for web fonts, it was only a matter of time before Google entered the game with their Google Font API[1]. Google's Font Directory[2] hosts a selection of fonts and Google has worked closely with Typekit to enable their fonts to be used with an open source WebFont Loader.

Using Google's Font API is simple and it provides previews and cut-and-paste code to make it easy to add its web fonts to any website or application. Embedding Google's library of web fonts into pages and applications is simple too. Either download and self-host a font, or link to a copy on Google's servers and let its Font API take care of the rest.

When we embed a Google-hosted font, we simply need to add a style sheet link and replace spaces in the font file names with a + symbol. Then we can style the font using CSS in any way we choose:

```
<link rel="stylesheet" href="http://fonts.googleapis.com/ ↵
css?family=Droid+Sans">

body {
font-family : "Droid Sans";
font-size : .82em;
}
```

---

[1] http://code.google.com/apis/webfonts
[2] http://code.google.com/webfonts

Embedding multiple web fonts is even easier with the Google Font API than it is with multiple CSS declarations. Instead of writing two separate declarations like this:

```
@font-face { font-family : "Droid Sans"; }
@font-face { font-family : "Droid Serif"; }
```

We can combine both fonts into a single call to Google's API by separating their names using a vertical pipe or bar:

```
http://fonts.googleapis.com/css?family=Droid+Sans|Droid+Serif
```

If you still needed convincing that web fonts have arrived and we can use them today in our websites and applications, Google's entry into web fonts proves that the technology has matured. The reliability of Google's server infrastructure can only help to convince more of us to start implementing web fonts and more of our clients to ask for them. As Typekit's founder Jeffrey Veen wrote:

> "Using real fonts on the web is no longer something to look forward to – the technology is ready, the industry has responded, and designers are building sites with them every day."[2]

With the technical aspects of working with web fonts taken care of, we'll cast our net wider and investigate some of the creative ways that designers have used them.

Throughout this book, you'll find 'investigate' sections that highlight some of the amazing work being done by some of the world's top designers. We'll look under the hood too, to investigate the new technologies and ground-breaking techniques they've used.

Want to compare how FontSquirrel, Typekit and Google render web fonts differently? FontSquirrel has prepared a handy comparison at sizes from 10pt to 72pt[1]

[1] http:/fontsquirrel.com/webfont_comparison
[2] http://blog.typekit.com/2010/05/19/typekit-and-google

ALAN RICKMAN

Reagan Ray, Dave Rupert and Trent Walton are the faces of Paravel[1] — a three-man web design and branding agency hailing from Texas. The three amigos love movies and their The Many Faces Of... Alan Rickman[2] site uses web fonts to give their pages a character as memorable as one of Rickman's performances.

For the site's headings, Reagan chose Prociono Regular by Barry Schwartz. This font has been released under a public domain licence, making it legally usable as a web font:

```
@font-face {font-family :"ProcionoRegular";
src : url("Prociono-Regular.eot");
src : local("☺"),
url("Prociono-Regular.svg#Prociono-Regular") format("svg"),
url("Prociono-Regular.ttf") format("truetype"),
url("Prociono-Regular.woff") format("woff"); }
```

Reagan links to the different Prociono Regular font file formats and then applies them to all of his headings (from levels one to six) like this:

```
h1, h2, h3, h4, h5, h6 {
font-family : "ProcionoRegular", Georgia, serif; }
```

Rickmanrolling. If you like The Many Faces Of..., Reagan, Dave and Trent aren't stopping with Alan Rickman and have 'a bit of a thing' for John Cusack too. Check out their League Gothic-infused tribute.[3]

[1] http://paravelinc.com
[2] http://themanyfacesof.com/alan-rickman
[3] http://themanyfacesof.com/john-cusack

Trent Walton often gains inspiration from movies and in his Quoting Lebowski series¹, he mixed web fonts hosted on his own server with those licensed through Typekit. Trent added a dash of CSS and a handful of images to amazing effect.

Trent choose The League of Moveable Type's League Gothic font², an open source remake of the classic Alternate Gothic No.1 and a perfect choice for this design:

```
@font-face {
font-family : "LeagueGothicRegular';
src: url("League_Gothic.eot");
src: local("☺"),
url("League_Gothic.woff") format("woff"),
url("League_Gothic.otf") format("opentype"),
url("League_Gothic.svg#LeagueGothic") format("svg");
}
```

To achieve those curly type details, Trent chose Bistro Script Web by Suitcase Type Foundry³, which he licensed from Typekit's catalogue. Typekit delivered the font formats Trent needed right into his page, leaving him free to style Bistro Script Web by setting `font-size` and `line-height` and making the text lowercase.

```
.itworked {
font-family : "bistro-script-web-1", "bistro-script web-2", cursive;
font-size :  60px;
line-height : 0
text-transform : lowercase;
}
```

Trent has published a write-up about how he achieved his Quoting Lebowski design, including how he used experimental CSS properties such as `text-fill-color` and `background-clip` with text⁴. The result is a striking design that would previously only have been possible using images; this shows the real creative potential of web fonts.

---

¹ http://trentwalton.com/css3/type
² http://theleagueofmoveabletype.com/fonts/7-league-gothic
³ http://suitcasetype.com
⁴ http://trentwalton.com/2010/04/06/css3-background-clip-font-face

Text shadows

Text shadows are an effective tool to add depth, create a letterpress-style feel or simply enhance the legibility of text. The `text-shadow` syntax is easy to learn; here a `text-shadow` declaration is applied to a heading.

```
h2 { text-shadow : 0 2px 3px rgba(0,0,0,.8); }
```

Let's break down those `text-shadow` values.

The first two (`0` and `2px`) are the shadow's horizontal and vertical offsets; the greater the offset, the further away a shadow will appear from the text. The third value (`3px`) is the shadow's blur radius. In this case, the blur radius is small, resulting in a reasonably hard shadow. Finally, we declare the colour and transparency of the shadow. Don't worry If you're not familiar with RGBa colour, as you'll learn about how to use it in the next chapter.

In this example, we'll add just one primary shadow to our text.

The Big Sleep

Next, we'll make a softer shadow by increasing the vertical offset to five pixels and the blur radius to ten pixels.

This primary shadow is softer as we've increased its blur radius from three pixels to ten pixels.

The Long Goodbye

```
h2 { text-shadow : 0 5px 10px rgba(0,0,0,.8); }
```

Text shadows can accept negative as well as positive values, so in this next example we'll change the vertical offset to minus five pixels to move the light source and cast a shadow above the text.

The Lady in the Lake

By changing the horizontal and vertical offsets we can cast a shadow on all sides of our text.

```
h2 { text-shadow : 0 -5px 10px rgba(0,0,0,.8); }
```

Working with multiple text shadows

If our designs demand a more natural looking result, we can layer multiple shadows, separating their sets of values using a comma:

The High Window

There are very few occasions in the physical world where an object will have just one shadow. Add a second or third shadow for a more natural looking result.

```
h2 { text-shadow : 0 2px 3px rgba(0,0,0,.8), 0 10px 30px ↵
rgba(0,0,0,.5);  }
```

We can create three-dimensional text objects by using three shadows. Here, we'll cast one white shadow above the text and two shadows beneath.

Trouble Is My Business

text-shadow can be used to create many different effects and, when combined with web fonts, they reduce our need to use images of text enormously.

```
h2 {
text-shadow :
0 -2px 3px rgba(255,255,255,1),
0 2px 3px rgba(0,0,0,.8),
0 10px 30px rgba(0,0,0,.5);
}
```

David Desandro isn't afraid of putting CSS3 properties to good use in his designs. For this experiment, David combined typefaces licensed from Typekit with three text shadows to create a lens flare effect'.

```
h2 em {
font-size : 240px;
font-weight : 800;
font-style : normal;
text-transform : uppercase;
letter-spacing : 0.1em;
color : rgb(255,255,255);
text-shadow :
0 0 150px rgb(255,255,255),
0 0 60px rgb(255,255,255),
0 0 10px rgb(255,255,255);
}
```

David Desandro[2] article's love to show off the creative possibilities of emerging technologies. His site is a showcase for CSS3 and a must visit for everyone interested in getting the very best from it.

[1] http://desandro.com/articles/the-new-lens-flare
[2] http://desandro.com/

Analog¹ is "a company of friends who make web sites" — their line-up includes typography expert Jon Tan², and it shows. Their site is powerful, but subtle, with exquisite typography that's been enhanced with `text-shadow`.

Analog chose a standard American Typewriter typeface that is lifted from the page background:

```
h2, h3, p, li {
font-weight : 400;
text-shadow: 0 1px 1px #f8fcee;
}
```

Analog is a company of frie... who mak... sites.
It's a co-operative where ...ination, des...nd
engineering thrive; good ... ...k.
...e doing goo...

¹ http://analog.coop
² http://jontangerine.com

Breaking it up

After a decade of promise and frustration, web fonts have arrived. Mature
delivery services such as Typekit, along with APIs from Google, mean that
we no longer have to design with a limited set of typefaces. We can use
(almost) any font we choose. CSS3 makes web fonts easy to apply and style
in contemporary browsers. Although there are (and will likely remain)
differences in the ways that browsers handle type, there are very few reasons
not to be using real fonts in your websites and applications today.

Keen to dig up more dirt on web fonts?

For an in-depth investigation into web fonts, in far more detail than we could
cover in just a single chapter, I cannot recommend Jason Cranford Teague's
Fluid Web Typography[1] highly enough. As for where to license web fonts for use
in your projects, here are a few recommendations to get you started.

exljbris is the font foundry behind some of the most distinctive web fonts.
Best of all, their fonts are free to download and are licensed to use as web
fonts. Their site is a joy to explore and a great place to discover new typefaces.
http://www.josbuivenga.demon.nl

Fontdeck, a partnership between design agency Clearleft and OmniIT, has a
small but growing catalogue of web fonts.
http://fontdeck.com

FontShop has made more than thirty of its most popular fonts available for
font linking in both EOT and WOFF formats. You can buy these fonts from
FontShop and host them on a Typekit account for easier implementation and
better security.
http://fontshop.com/fontlist/n/web_fontfonts

---

[1] http://www.fluidwebtype.info

Fontspring has a growing catalogue of typefaces and many of them are licensed as web fonts. Each Fontspring web font package includes TrueType and EOT files, plus a sample style sheet. Fontspring also encodes TrueType fonts as base-64 to help diminish a flash of unstyled text (FOUT) that occurs in some browsers as a font is downloaded.

http://fontspring.com

The League of Moveable Type is a collection of open source typefaces including my personal favourite — Meredith Mandel's Chunk — and the fabulous League Gothic.

http://theleagueofmoveabletype.com

RGBa and opacity

THERE'S MORE THAN ONE WAY TO DESCRIBE A COLOUR
IN CSS — colour names, hexadecimal values, RGB/RGBa
and HSL/HSLa — but no matter which you choose, the
colour displayed by a computer, smartphone or television
screen is made from a combination of red, green and blue
transmitted light (RGB), these days usually in 24-bit.

In 24-bit RGB, zero indicates no light and 255 indicates the maximum. So when
red, green and blue channels are all zero, the result is black. When they're all
255, the result is white — with a wide gamut of over 16 million colours
in between.

Shaun Chapman's 0to255.
Pick a colour and 0to255 gives
you a range of options from
black to white at intervals
optimised for the web.[1]

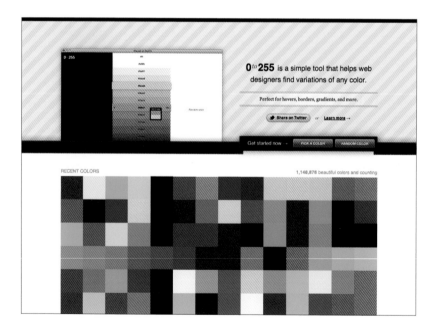

[1] http://0to255.com

Switching to RGB

Open Photoshop and one of the options in the colour picker is the familiar hexadecimal value, where white is defined as #ffffff and black as #000000.

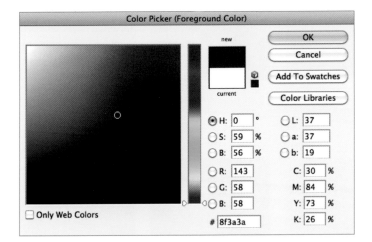

The red background colour I've chosen for the 'action' links on 'It's Hardboiled' is represented in hexadecimal as #8f3a3a.

In CSS, we can also describe that same red colour using RGB, first declaring the colour space and then, in parentheses, the quantities of red, green and blue in values between 0 and 255:

```
a.action { background-color : rgb(143,58,58); }
```

You might be asking, "Why choose RGB over hexadecimal?" There's no technical reason to use RGB colour over hexadecimal — after all, every colour we see on-screen is RGB — but when we're choosing colours for our style sheets, hex values can be tougher to visualise. Pub quiz question: what colour is #003399? Stumped? [A]

When we understand that for each channel, 0 is no colour and 255 is the maximum, RGB becomes a piece of cake to visualise. This is why I've switched to using RGB values in my stylesheets:

A: #003399 is a deep blue.

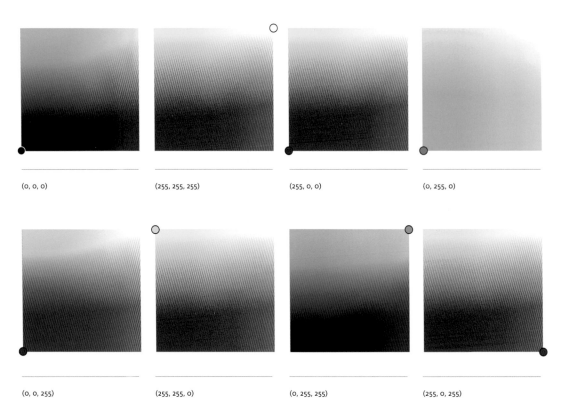

(0, 0, 0)   (255, 255, 255)   (255, 0, 0)   (0, 255, 0)

(0, 0, 255)   (255, 255, 0)   (0, 255, 255)   (255, 0, 255)

Layering colour with RGBa

At art school, subtlety wasn't my style — but then, you probably guessed that already. My friend Ben, on the other hand, made exquisite paintings because he laid on hundreds of thin layers of paint. In CSS, RGBa values help us to layer colour and add depth in a similar way.

RGBa is short for red, green, blue, plus a fourth channel — an alpha channel — which defines the transparency of the resulting colour. This alpha value can range between zero (fully transparent) and one (fully opaque). If you use either Photoshop or Fireworks you'll be used to working with alpha-transparency.

In the 'It's Hardboiled' store, the background colour of the 'action' links will have fifty per cent transparency. We'll add a fourth value, an alpha channel value of .5, to our CSS declaration to turn RGB into RGBa.

Making a layer semi-transparent in Adobe Photoshop.

```
a.action {
background-color : rgba(143,58,58,.5);
color : rgb(255,255,255);
}
```

Our ability to use RGBa to subtly adjust colour transparency levels in this way opens up a world of elegant design possibilities.

RGBa vs. opacity

There's another way we can make elements appear semi-opaque using CSS — it's called the opacity property.

Opacity works in a similar way to how we adjust the transparency of a layer in Photoshop or an object in Fireworks.

In CSS, both RGBa and opacity vary the alpha-channel, but there are subtle differences between them. While RGBa changes the transparency of just one colour on one element, opacity affects an element and all of its children.

To demonstrate this, we'll use those action links from the 'It's Hardboiled' store. We'll replace the RGBa background colour with a solid red and then apply a fifty per cent opacity level:

```
a.action {
opacity : .5
background-color : rgb(143,58,58);
color : rgb(255,255,255);
}
```

Both the anchor and its text are now semi-opaque.

Using RGBa, only the background colour is affected.

Designing to browser capabilities with Modernizr

RGBa and `opacity` are both widely supported in contemporary browsers, including Internet Explorer 9, but how can we make sure that people using less capable browsers won't see a broken design? Should we avoid using these properties altogether? Browsers without support for `opacity` will safely ignore it. RGBa is harmless too, but we should always have a backup plan.

First, let's add a solid red background colour to those 'action' links. Earlier versions of Internet Explorer choke if we use RGB, so we'll use a hexadecimal value instead. Follow that with RGBa for browsers that have implemented it:

```
a.action {
background-color : #8f3a3a;
background-color : rgba(143,58,58,.5);
color : rgb(255,255,255);
}
```

Modernizr tests a browser's capability to render RGBa. It adds a class of no-rgba to the `html` element when it detects a lack of support, so we can target those unfortunate browsers with a specific selector and perhaps apply a tiling, semi-transparent image as a backup:

```
a.action {
opacity : .5
background-color : rgba(143,58,58,.5);
color : rgb(255,255,255);
}
```

```
.no-opacity a.action {
background-color : transparent;
background-image : (tile.png);
}
```

Using images to work around a browser's lack of support for RGBa might sometimes be appropriate, but let's not forget that they add page weight. Whenever possible, stay hardboiled and remember that websites don't need to look exactly the same in every browser.

Opacity gets us out of a tight spot

Let's head back to the 'It's Hardboiled' store. We'll make a grid of eight images that hides this secret.

For this interface, we'll arrange eight images into a grid and then hide their associated descriptions using absolute positioning and opacity.[1]

[1] http://hardboiledwebdesign.com/v/c12-16

To build this interface, we need only a tiny amount of hardboiled HTML — one division with a `class` attribute value of `hlisting`.

Inside this division, we'll add another division for each `item` and give each one a unique `id` so that we can address them all individually:

If you're wondering where the attribute values, `hlisting`, `offer` and `sale` come from, they're part of the hListing draft microformat[1].

```
<div id="items" class="hlisting offer sale group">
    <div class="item" id="f01"></div>
    <div class="item" id="f02"></div>
    <div class="item" id="f03"></div>
    <div class="item" id="f04"></div>
    <div class="item" id="f05"></div>
    <div class="item" id="f06"></div>
    <div class="item" id="f07"></div>
    <div class="item" id="f08"></div>
</div>
```

Now add an image and description division inside each `item`. We'll also need an anchor that points back to the `id` fragment on each parent division.

Make a mental note of this markup pattern as we'll be reusing it several times.

```
<div class="item" id="f01">
    <a href="#f01"><img src="01.jpg" alt=""></a>
    <div class="description">
        <h3 class="fn">
            <a href="fiction.html">The Scarlet Menace</a>
        </h3>
        <ul>
            <li>Volume 1 Number 3</li>
            <li>Issue #3</li>
            <li>May 1933</li>
        </ul>
        <a href="fiction.html" class="action">Add to basket</a>
        <a href="#items"><img src="a-close.png" alt="Close"></a>
    </div>
</div>
```

---

[1] http://microformats.org/wiki/hlisting-proposal

With the hardboiled HTML all set, we'll style the interface, beginning by
setting the outer container width and specifying it as a positioning context
for its absolutely positioned children. We can do this simply by applying CSS
relative positioning (but no horizontal or vertical offsets):

```
.hlisting {
position : relative;
width : 520px;
}
```

We'll float each item, give them a width too, and set margins that will space
them evenly, horizontally and vertically:

```
.item {
float : left;
width : 120px;
margin : 0 10px 10px 0;
}
```

To make this interface load faster, we can use each image twice: once for
the main grid; and again as a background image on each item's description
overlay. To start, scale the inline images down to one hundred pixels — that's
half their size — then add a solid border:

```
.item img {
width : 100px;
border : 10px solid rgb(220,220,220);
}
```

Now it's time to turn our attention to the descriptions. We'll position them
absolutely to the top and left of each item and give them zero (0) opacity. This
makes them completely transparent:

```
.item .description {
position : absolute;
top : 0;
left : 0;
opacity : 0;
}
```

Here's how our finished grid interface should now look. Each of the description divisions is invisible, hidden by opacity.

Targeting with pseudo-class selectors

When we apply a unique `id`, we turn any element into a uniquely addressable fragment of a page. We can even target these fragments from links on the same page. The CSS `:target` pseudo-class selector allows us to change the styles applied to these elements when a user follows a link pointing to them. In this hardboiled interface, the `:target` pseudo-class selector changes the look of interface elements without using JavaScript.

Next, we'll change the styling properties of the description divisions using the :target pseudo-class selector. We'll give them dimensions, padding, and background and border properties and, most importantly, reset their opacity back to fully opaque (1):

```
.item:target .description {
width : 230px;
height : 290px;
padding : 20px 20px 20px 240px;
background-color  :  rgb(57,53,70);
background-repeat : no-repeat;
background-position : 20px 20px;
border  :  10px  solid  rgb(220,220,220);
opacity : 1;
}
```

Why so much padding on the left? We'll place a CSS background image into that space, reusing the same image as we used to form the grid. To apply these background images, use a selector that descends from the id we applied to each item:

```
#f01:target .description {
background-image : url(01.jpg);
}
```

```
#f02:target .description {
background-image : url(02.jpg);
}
```

```
#f03:target .description {
background-image : url(03.jpg);
}
```

[…]

To complete this interface, we need to include a way to hide the description division to reveal the image grid. We can achieve this by providing a link that points back to the outer 'items' container thereby resetting the interface back to its original state:

```
<a href="#items"><img src="a-close.png" alt="Close"></a>
```

We'll use a CSS attribute selector to position that link outside at the top right of the interface:

```
a[href="#items"] {
position : absolute;
top : -20px;
right : -20px;
display : block;
width : 26px;
height : 26px;
}
```

Our JavaScript-free, CSS opacity and :target pseudo-class interface is now complete.[1]

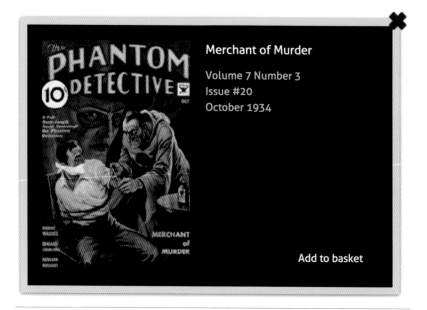

massiveBLUE

Sam Brown puts RGBa to work on his striking portfolio website'.
Dig into Sam's stylesheets and we can see how he subtly blends colours by
changing their transparency.

On portfolio pages, Sam cleverly adjusts background colours to key into
the colours in the work he's displaying. For example, his text takes on shades
of the background colours behind them:

```
body {
color : rgba(255,255,255,.8);
}


h2 abbr {
color :
rgba(255,255,255,.33);
}


h3 { color : rgba(0,0,0,.9); }
```

RGBa isn't just limited to styling text: it can be applied to any element.
Sam uses it to tint borders and other elements with the colour of the
background behind.

```
#content {
border-top: 1px solid
rgba(255,255,255,.33);
}
```

Sam also made his logo semi-transparent, and combined that with RGBa text to create branding that's also tinted by what lies behind it.

' http://massiveblue.com

dribbble dribbble

Dan Cederholm's Dribbble', a "show and tell for designers, developers and other creatives", has a wealth of CSS3 inspiration. Instead of using image-swapping or sprites, Dan changes the appearance of Dribbble's logo on mouse-over using CSS opacity.

```
<div id="logo">
    <a href="/"><img alt="dribbble" src="dribbble.gif"></a>
</div>

#logo a:hover { opacity : .6; }
```

Dan uses the same technique on Dribbble's 404 page, although this time in reverse. The 404 page logo starts at twenty per cent (.2) opacity, then switches to thirty per cent (.3) on hover:

```
<a href="/" id="back"><img src="404-logo.png" alt="dribbble"></a>

#back {
opacity : .2;
transition : .2s
opacity ease;
}

a:hover#back {
opacity : .3;
}
```

Wondering what that transition property is doing, or if Dan's some kind of fakeloo artist? Cool it. All will be revealed when you learn about CSS transitions in chapter 17.

¹ http://dribbble.com

Breaking it up

Designing for a screen doesn't have to mean that designs must appear
two-dimensional. By taking a hardboiled approach and designing for the
capabilities of the best browsers first, CSS RGBa and `opacity` properties give
our designs depth and add richness without us needing to resort to using
image hacks or JavaScript. Of course, these subtle effects won't be visible to
people who use less capable browsers, but you know what? That's OK. We can
cater for those people too by using Modernizr and carefully considering an
appropriate, different design.

CSS3 borders

IT'S ALWAYS BEEN HARD to get overexcited about CSS borders — dotted, dashed, solid, double, and groove, ridge, inset, outset. OK, put your hands in the air those of you who've recently used any of the last four? Ever? Me neither.

The good news is that CSS borders just got exciting again because CSS3 adds new properties that save time, solve common implementation problems and open up a wealth of new creative opportunities. These properties are border-radius to give (almost) any element those rounded corners our clients love so much, and border-image for using images inside our borders. Let's investigate.

Rounding corners with CSS border-radius

You don't have to dig too deep into 'It's Hardboiled' before you'll find rounded corners. I've used them to make irregular shapes, style links so they look like buttons and chamfer the sharp edges off boxes. In the past we used images to create these rounded corners. That meant first carving out images in Photoshop or Fireworks, usually in several colours and radii.

Even for the simplest, fixed-width designs, rounded corners using images were time-consuming to make and a world of pain to update. The HTML we needed to create rounded corners was full of presentational elements and attributes. I guess we've all seen this a million times:

```
<div class="box">
    <div class="box-inner">
    <img scr="fiction.jpg" alt="The Phantom Detective">
    </div>
</div>
```

For fluid designs, it gets worse. A flexible box needs four — that's *four* — presentational elements. We might as well take our HTML outside and shoot it for all the respect we've shown it:

```
<div class="box">
    <div class="box-inner">
        <div class="box-inner-2">
            <div class="box-inner-3">
                <img src="fiction.jpg" alt="The Phantom Detective">
            </div>
        </div>
    </div>
</div>
```

You might not be a markup puritan, but you'll know deep down that when we write HTML that primarily services a visual design, we tie it tightly to one specific layout. We make our HTML less flexible, and less responsive.

Thankfully, we don't need to continue to abuse HTML because CSS `border-radius` makes it easy to add uniform or non-uniform rounded or elliptical corners to almost any element.

Uniform corners

Using CSS `border-radius` we can round every corner of a box uniformly using either percentages based on the size of the box, pixels or ems.

When we use `border-radius` in combination with either background colours or CSS gradients, we can change the appearance of an element with just a few lines of CSS. There's no need to open Photoshop to carve out new images.

PIE (Progressive Internet Explorer) uses an .htc file which, when applied to an element, allows Internet Explorer 7 and 8 to render a number of CSS3 properties, including: `border-radius`; `border-image`; `box-shadow`; multiple background images; and a linear gradient as a background image.[1]

You might be asking, "What about less capable browsers, including Internet Explorer 7 or 8? What will people who use them see?" Browsers that are incapable of rendering the `border-radius` property will safely ignore it and will display square corners. That should be acceptable, because being hardboiled means we never limit a design to the abilities of less capable browsers.

Pushing the right buttons

Maintaining consistency in design is important, but making sets of images in Photoshop or Fireworks and updating them every time we need to change their size or colour can be a struggle. Fortunately, the CSS `border-radius` property just made our jobs a whole lot easier. We'll start by styling links on the 'It's Hardboiled' store to make them look more like buttons. Here's the hardboiled HTML:

```
<a href="store.html" class="action">Add to basket</a>
```

Now transform that link into a faux button. We'll add padding specified in ems to allow its proportions to scale up and down when a user changes the size text in their browser, and a background colour:

```
a.action {
padding : .5em .8em;
background-color : rgb(143,58,58);
}
```

Complete the look by rounding every corner with a uniform, em-based `border-radius` that will also scale along with the text:

```
a.action { border-radius : .8em; }
```

---

[1] http://css3pie.com

Rounding selected corners

If we round every corner of this description box, it will look out of place next to the square-cornered book covers that appear below it.

Fortunately, the CSS `border-radius` property allows us to specify individual radii on each corner:

```
div {
border-top-left-radius : .8em;
border-top-right-radius : .8em;
border-bottom-left-radius : 0;
border-bottom-right-radius : 0;
}
```

The tiniest details matter and there is something 'not quite right' about the rounded corners on the bottom of this box.

By selectively rounding only the top-left and top-right corners, we visually link the book covers to their descriptions.

Making irregular shapes

When you need rounded
corners in a hurry, using
Jacob Bijani's `border-radius`
generator[1] and Paul Irish's
CSS3 Please[2] is a piece of cake.

Rounded corners don't have to be circular and we can use 'twin-radius' values to create ellipses, where the first value sets a horizontal radius and the second a vertical radius. In this next declaration, the same two radii are applied to all four corners.

```
div { border-radius : 30px 60px; }
```

We can also create more complex shapes by specifying twin values individually for each corner.

```
div {
border-top-left-radius : 5px 30px;
border-top-right-radius : 30px 60px;
border-bottom-left-radius : 80px 40px;
border-bottom-right-radius : 40px 100px;
}
```

By selectively styling each corner with different `border-radius` properties, we can create even more complex shapes without using images.

---

[1] http://border-radius.com
[2] http://css3please.com

Specifying individual corners for Firefox

While `border-radius` is widely supported, some older browsers require us to use vendor-specific prefixes. For simple, uniform rounded corners we'll add prefixes for Firefox and older versions of WebKit browsers, followed by the W3C's official syntax, which is supported by Opera, Internet Explorer 9 and Safari 5:

```
div {
-moz-border-radius : .8em;
-webkit-border-radius : .8em;
border-radius : .8em;
}
```

Creating rounded boxes with non-uniform corners is a slightly more complex affair, because Firefox's current implementation is different from the W3C's official syntax.

Corner	W3C official syntax	Mozilla
Top left	`border-top-left-radius`	`-moz-border-radius-topleft`
Top right	`border-top-right-radius`	`-moz-border-radius-topright`
Bottom left	`border-bottom-left-radius`	`-moz-border-radius-bottomleft`
Bottom right	`border-bottom-right-radius`	`-moz-border-radius-bottomright`

I'll place a bet Mozilla will implement the W3C's official syntax in a future release of Firefox. There's also a strong likelihood that it will continue to support its current, non-standard syntax to maintain backwards compatibility.

Shorthand properties

Although vendor-specific prefixes are essential to help browser makers and designers alike, writing longhand `border-radius` declarations with several prefixes is inconvenient:

```
-webkit-border-top-left-radius : 15px;
-webkit-border-top-right-radius : 30px;
-webkit-border-bottom-left-radius : 45px;
-webkit-border-bottom-right-radius : 60px;
-moz-border-radius-topleft : 15px;
-moz-border-radius-topright : 30px;
-moz-border-radius-bottomleft : 45px;
-moz-border-radius-bottomright : 60px;
border-top-left-radius : 15px;
border-top-right-radius : 30px;
border-bottom-left-radius : 45px;
border-bottom-right-radius : 60px;
```

Quite a fistful, I'm sure you'll agree. So it's lucky we can use shorthand values to crush this back to just three lines:

```
-moz-border-radius : 15px 30px 45px 60px;
-webkit-border-radius : 15px 30px 45px 60px;
border-radius : 15px 30px 45px 60px;
```

When we need to combine elliptical corners in a shorthand declaration, we specify all horizontal values before a forward slash and all vertical values after:

```
border-radius : 60px / 15px;
```

For individual radii, the values are set clockwise starting from the top-left, so: top-left; top-right; bottom-right; then bottom-left. When we omit bottom-left, its radius will be the same as top-right. If we omit bottom-right, it will be the same as top-left and so on. To set an elliptical value on each radius individually, you'd use something like this:

```
border-radius: 5px 30px 80px 40px / 30px 60px 40px 100px
```

Translucent box-shadow with RGBa

When we want buttons to stand out, add a subtle shadow by combining CSS `box-shadow` with RGBa. The `box-shadow` syntax is easy to learn as the first and second values apply horizontal and vertical offsets respectively, the third applies blur-radius and finally we set the shadow colour inside parentheses:

```
a.action { box-shadow : 0 1px 3px rgba(0, 0, 0, .8); }
```

Unless it's noon and you're in the middle of a desert, everything you see around you has more than one shadow. To create a more natural three-dimensional result, add a second, softer shadow. This one should have a greater vertical offset, a wider blur-radius and be more transparent. The values for each shadow should be separated using a comma:

```
a.action {
box-shadow : 0 1px 3px rgba(0, 0, 0, .8), 0 3px 9px rgba(0, 0, 0, .2); }
```

For the time being at least, `box-shadow` requires one or more vendor-specific prefixes plus the W3C's official syntax. We'll add vendor prefixes for Mozilla- and WebKit-based browsers (Opera uses the W3C standard):

```
a.action {
-moz-box-shadow : 0 1px 3px rgba(0, 0, 0, .8), 0 3px 9px rgba(0, 0, 0, .2);
-webkit-box-shadow : 0 1px 3px rgba(0, 0, 0, .8), 0 3px 9px rgba(0, 0, 0, .2);
box-shadow : 0 1px 3px rgba(0, 0, 0, .8), 0 3px 9px rgba(0, 0, 0, .2);
}
```

Browsers that don't support `box-shadow` will safely ignore it, but why leave how a design looks to chance when we can use Modernizr? Modernizr tests for `box-shadow` support and adds a class of `boxshadow` to the `html` element for browsers that do, and `no-boxshadow` for those that don't. We can then provide a simpler design to less capable browsers, perhaps by setting thicker border properties that hint at three dimensions.

If we need box shadows in a hurry, John Allsopp has made a `box-shadow` generator[1] that uses sliders to make multiple shadows and outputs CSS ready to paste into our stylesheets.

---

[1] http://www.westciv.com/tools/boxshadows/index.html

The Beercamp party at the SXSW conference in 2010[1] was the perfect way to round off the evening. The site's designers, nclud[2], used border-radius to pour a frothy head onto their design. Despite the complexities of the design, Beercamp's HTML is simple and for the date, nclud chose to use a division and several HTML5 time elements:

```
<div id="date">
  <time class="day_of_week">Monday</time>
  <time class="day">March 15</time>
  <time class="year">Twenty Ten</time>
  <time class="time">Festivities begins at 7:30 PM</time>
</div>
```

nclud focus our attention onto this date by using elliptical corners in a shorthand border-radius declaration:

```
#date {
-moz-border-radius : 140px 75px;
-webkit-border-radius : 140px 75px;
border-radius : 140px 75px;
}
```

The Beercamp site also uses text-shadow, box-shadow and transform properties, so we'll be returning to it later for more inspiration (hic).

[1] http://sxsw.beercamp.com
[2] http://nclud.com

Adding images to borders with CSS border-image

After years of waiting, we're now finally able to use CSS background images inside the border area of a box. The syntax for the `border-image` property can be a little tough to learn, so I'll guide you through it as painlessly as possible.

Let's start by using CSS `border-image` to transform a link into a graduated faux button.

```
<a href="store.html" class="action">Add to basket</a>
```

We'll only need one tiny image which is far smaller than the flexible button we're making. This image is thirty pixels square and contains four uniform rounded corners and a subtle gradient.

The CSS `border-image` property slices up any image into nine parts of a 3×3 grid. To calculate the height and width of each slice, we use slice guides, similar to those we know from Photoshop or Fireworks.

In the next rule, the first value specifies the URL of the image to be sliced, followed by the position of the slice guides. Each slice becomes a component in a border: four corners; four sides between the corners; and the central part of the element. For this image we'll set slice guides ten pixels from each side; the values are applied clockwise from the top (top, right, bottom, left).

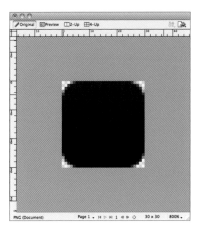
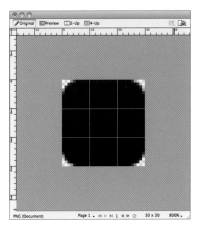

LEFT: The CSS `border-image` property is a powerful tool for making tiny images stretch and repeat to create interface elements of any size. It can be particularly effective in fluid layouts and on designs for mobile devices where every byte counts.

RIGHT: `border-image` slices up an image into nine parts using slice guides similar to those in our graphics tools. Slice guides can be set any distance from the top, right, bottom and left sides of an image.

```
a.action {
border-image : url(gloss.png) 10 10 10 10;
border-width : 10px 10px 10px 10px;
}
```

These slices make four corners that are each ten pixels square, and sides that are also ten pixels wide. Because each slice guide is the same distance from all four sides of the image, we can simplify this declaration using shorthand:

```
a.action {
border-image : url(gloss.png) 10;
border-width : 10px;
}
```

When we use only one value, that value will be used for all four borders. If we omit a `border-bottom` value, a browser will use the same value as `border-top`. Likewise, when we omit a `border-left` value, a browser will use the same value as `border-right`.

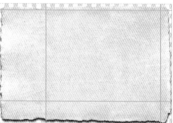

Slice guides don't have to be set at equal distances from the four sides of an image. To make borders asymmetrical, we specify separate values for each of the slice dimensions.

For example, in this next declaration the slice guides will be set running clockwise at: ten pixels (top); twenty pixels (right); forty pixels (bottom); and eighty pixels (left):

```
.asymmetrical {
border-image : url(note.png) 10 20 40 80;
border-width : 10px 20px 40px 80px;
}
```

There are several more CSS `border-image` keywords that help us to fine-tune how images will repeat or even 'stretch' when they fill a border.

```
div {
border-image : url(note.png) 10 stretch;
border-width : 10px;
}
```

Border image stretched to fill a border (bottom)

```
div {
border-image : url(note.png) 10 repeat;
border-width : 10px;
}
```

Tiling a sliced image

```
div {
border-image : url(note.png) 10 round;
border-width : 10px;
}
```

Resizing a slice so that only whole pieces fit inside the border when repeating

```
div {
border-image : url(note.png) 10 space;
border-width : 10px;
}
```

Repeating whole slices and adding space between tiles so that an area is evenly filled

When we need to specify separate `stretch`, `repeat`, `round` or `space` values for each side, we can write multiple keywords on the same line.

```
div {
border-image : url(gloss.png) 10 stretch round;
border-width : 10px;
}
```

Although the CSS `border-image` property is already widely supported by contemporary browsers, most implementations still require us to use vendor-specific prefixes, so we'll add prefixes for Firefox and WebKit browsers, followed by the W3C's official syntax:

```
div {
-moz-border-image : url(gloss.png) 10 stretch round;
-webkit-border-image : url(gloss.png) 10 stretch round;
border-image : url(gloss.png) 10 stretch round;
border-width : 10px;
}
```

Tear up the joint

Let's head back to the 'It's Hardboiled' office. It's been a while and there's a note, ripped from a notebook and pinned to the door. We'll use CSS `border-image` to create its torn edges. The HTML is again pretty damn hardboiled — one HTML5 `article` and paragraphs:

```
<article>
    <p>Hey Malarkey!</p>
    <p>It's been three weeks since I called and you still haven't
    gotten back to me. Have you lost my number? Do you need a
    detective to help you find it?</p>
    <p>Colly</p>
    <p>PS: You still have that umbrella you borrowed from me.</p>
</article>
```

Start styling by giving the `article` dimensions, padding and a background image I made from a scan of a scrap of paper:

```css
article  {
height : 240px;
width : 240px;
padding : 20px;
background-color : rgb(233,227,211);
background-image : url(paper.jpg);
}
```

This note will be seen by everyone. Next, we'll use the CSS `border-image` property to tear it into pieces to make corners, outer edges and a repeating pattern for the centre.

Designing to browser capabilities with Modernizr

Using Modernizr, we can
design the best experience
from the best browsers down,
while still catering for people
who use browsers that aren't
capable of rendering border
images.

Modernizr tests for a browser's ability to render the CSS `border-image` property, appending a class attribute value of `borderimage` to the head element when `border-image` is supported. We can then use a more specific, descendent selector to serve border images to those browsers that have the ability to render them.

Hey Malarkey!

Have you lost my number? Do you need a detective to help you find it?

Colly

PS: You still have that Playboy umbrella you borrowed from me.

To measure how wide the `border-image` slices need to be, we'll drag Photoshop or Fireworks guides in from each side of the image. The numbers we'll find are: twenty pixels from the top; forty pixels from the right; thirty pixels from the bottom; and forty pixels from the left. Set those as `border-image` slices and adjust the widths of each border to match.

```
.borderimage article {
border-image : url(note.png) 20 40 30 40 stretch;
border-width : 20px 40px 30px 40px;
}
```

Finally, remove the background colour and image we served to less capable browsers to allow the page background to show through the alpha-transparent parts of our PNG border image.

```
.borderimage article {
background-color : transparent;
background-image : none;
border-image : url(note.png) 20 40 30 40 stretch;
border-width : 20px 40px 30px 40px;
}
```

Styling a hardboiled business card

We know that not all browsers are capable of rendering border images, but why limit our creative possibilities to these lowest common denominators when we could take the hardboiled approach and make designs that are appropriate to all categories of browsers?

This isn't just any dog-eared scrap of cardboard. It has a decorative border that's been made from Apple keyboard symbols.

We'll round off this chapter by using CSS `border-image` to implement a hardboiled business card. We don't need any fancy HTML to make this card because, as it contains contact information, we should use the hCard microformat which looks like this:

```
<div class="vcard">
    <h3 class="fn org">S.A.Fari</h3>
    <p class="role">Web Inspector</p>
    <h4>Checking all elements</h4>
    <p class="tel">Dial<span class="value">4.0.4 5531.21.10</span></p>
    <p>Member of the WebKit team since 2006</p>
</div>
```

Start by applying styles that will be seen by all browsers, regardless of their abilities. We'll add padding and a solid background colour:

```
.vcard {
padding : 40px 20px 10px;
background-color : rgb(243,243,243);
}
```

Now add styles for CSS border-image capable browsers. We'll first set slicing guides — twenty pixels from each side of the image:

By using the round keyword, we instruct browsers to resize the parts of the decorative image so that only whole pieces of it will fit inside the border.

```
.borderimage .vcard {
border-image : url(safari.png) 20 round;
border-width : 20px;
}
```

To lift our card off the page background, add two RGBa shadows. Although Modernizr tests a browser's support for both box-shadow and RGBa, it's almost guaranteed those capable of rendering border-image also support box-shadow and RGBa.

```
.borderimage .vcard {
box-shadow : 0 2px 5px rgba(0,0,0,.5), 0 20px 30px rgba(0,0,0,.2);
}
```

Changing a border image's width

In every `border-image` example until now, we've made the width of a
border precisely match the size of an image slice, but what happens when
they're different?

When we change a border's width we can control how large the images
they contain will appear. To see this effect in action, reduce the border's width
down to only ten pixels and watch as a browser scales the image to match the
new border width.

```
.borderimage .vcard {
width : 380px;
border-image : url(safari.png) 20 round;
border-width : 10px;
}
```

Making a border's width larger than the size of a slice has the opposite effect.
Scale up a border's width in several increments to see the increase in size of
the border's image. (See overleaf.)

We mustn't forget browsers that aren't capable of rendering `border-image`,
so for them we'll set simpler border styles using Modernizr's `no-borderimage`
class attribute value:

```
.no-borderimage .vcard {
width : 418px;
border : 1px solid rgb(220,220,220);
border-bottom : 4px solid rgb(220,220,220);
}
```

Of course, not every browser supports `border-image`, but that doesn't mean
we should delay using them. By using Modernizr, we can make a design using
`border-image` for the best browsers first, then provide a stylish alternative for
those browsers that are less capable.

border-width : 30px;

border-width : 40px;

border-width : 50px;

border-width : 60px;

Breaking it up

Whether we make our corners rounded, elliptical or fill them with images, with `border-radius` and `border-image`, CSS borders just got interesting. These new properties save us time, solve common implementation problems and open up new creative possibilities for us. Best of all, they're ready for action today in our websites and applications.

Keen to dig up more dirt on CSS3 borders?

You could start by reading the official W3C 'Backgrounds and Borders specification', although I'd recommend that you don't mix it with alcohol.

http://www.w3.org/TR/css3-background/

Otherwise, **Opera's Developer Community** has an excellent introduction to `border-image` (and other CSS3 properties) — 'CSS3 borders, backgrounds and box-shadows' plus an animated demonstration by Vadim Makeev.

http://dev.opera.com/articles/view/css3-border-background-boxshadow/#border-image

http://people.opera.com/pepelsbey/experiments/bdi

Staying at Opera, **Jan Henrik Helmers** has written a fantastic primer, 'Beautiful UI styling with CSS3 text-shadow, box-shadow, and border-radius'.

http://dev.opera.com/articles/view/beautiful-ui-styling-with-css3-text-shadow-box-shadow-and-border-radius

Liam McCabe of CreativityDen's 'The hidden power of border-radius' includes amazing examples of how to create semicircles, quarter-circles and other shapes using `border-radius`.

http://blog.creativityden.com/the-hidden-power-of-border-radius-2

If you want a machine to make your border images for you, use Kevin Decker's `border-image` generator. Feed it the path to your image, use sliders to set your slice guides and border width, then paste the generated CSS into your style sheets.

http://www.incaseofstairs.com/border-image-generator

CSS3 background images

IN THE PAST, setting more than one background image on an element led to presentational junk in our markup. We could have used JavaScript to silently inject them into the DOM but, either way, the end result was the same — we treated HTML like a goon just to satisfy our selfish need for a visual design. Now we can quit abusing our markup because contemporary browsers, including Internet Explorer 9, allow us to use more than one background image.

Multiple background images

Traditionally, if we wanted to use multiple background images on the liquid design of the 'It's Hardboiled' home page, we would have needed two nested elements and applied a different background image to each.

```
<div class="left">
    <div class="right">
        [...]
    </div>
</div>
```

Now our HTML can stay hardboiled and we need use only a single HTML5 `section` element because CSS now allows us to apply two background images to the same element.

```
<section>
    [...]
</section>
```

We'll need two background images for this design: one to position to the left; the other to the right. We can specify both images within a single CSS `background-image` property, separating each image with a comma:

```
section {
background-image : url(section-left.png), ↵
url(section-right.png);
}
```

To save a few bytes, we can write that declaration in shorthand by specifying the source, repeat and position values for both images:

```
section {
background :
url(section-left.png) no-repeat 0 0, ↵
url(section-right.png) no-repeat 100% 0;
}
```

Overlapping background images

When background images overlap, what's the order to specify which of them come to the front and which sit behind? You might think that multiple background images follow the CSS positioning stacking order — where an element furthest down the document source order appears highest, or closer to the viewer (unless `z-index` determines otherwise) — something like this:

```
section {
background :
url(background.png) no-repeat 0 0, ↵
url(middle-ground.png) no-repeat 0 0, ↵
url(foreground.png) no-repeat 0 0;
}
```

You'd be wrong. The *first* image in a list will appear closest to the viewer.

```
section {
background :
url(foreground.png) no-repeat 0 0,
url(middle-ground.png) no-repeat 0 0,
url(background.png) no-repeat 0 0;
}
```

The ability to layer more than one background image, particularly semi-transparent images, opens up a world of creative possibilities and can give our design a real feeling of depth.

Designing to browser capabilities with Modernizr

Now that multiple background images are widely supported in browsers including Safari and Google Chrome, and the latest versions of Firefox, Opera and Internet Explorer 9, there's no reason not to be using them today. But what about less capable browsers? Should we hold off using multiple backgrounds until these browsers 'expire'?

Browsers that aren't capable of rendering multiple background images will ignore any CSS declarations that contain them. But why hand over control of our designs to a browser when Modernizr can help us be hardboiled by serving appropriate designs that are based on a browser's capabilities?

First, let's make an image we can serve to browsers that aren't capable of understanding multiple background images. This image is wide enough for browser widths up to 1,940 pixels and includes a space in the middle to place a heading. We'll apply this image to a section background and centre it horizontally:

```
section { background : url(section.png) no-repeat 50% 0; }
```

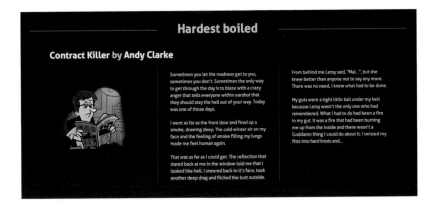

This single image will be seen by people who use browsers not capable of rendering more than one background image.

Modernizr tests a browser's capability to render multiple background images and adds a `class` attribute value of `multiplebgs` to the `head` in capable browsers. With this class we can use a specific selector to declare several background images:

```
.multiplebgs section {
background :
url(section-left.png) no-repeat 0 0,
url(section-right.png) no-repeat 100% 0;
}
```

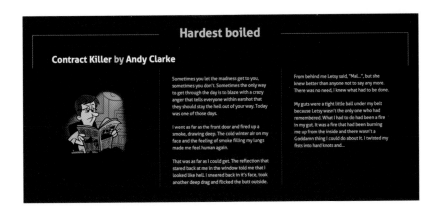

Although the details of this design are different in browsers that have the ability to render multiple background images, people who use less capable browsers will not know that they're missing something.

Everything that's old is new again

In addition to `content-box` and `border-box`, Mozilla has proposed (and also implemented) a third box model type known as a '`padding-box`'. When using `padding-box`, an element's width and height will include padding but not a border. `padding-box` box sizing is not currently part of the CSS3 User Interface Module.

I bet that the box model was one of the first things you learned about CSS. It may also have been one of the first things to trip you up because, in the traditional box model, padding and borders are added to, and not subtracted from, the size of an element.

Add ten pixels padding and a five-pixel border to a one hundred pixels square box and the resulting width and height will be 130 pixels (100px + 20px + 10px = 130px.) This is the default box model in all modern browsers and CSS3 now calls this a '`content-box`'.

In fixed-width designs, this traditional box model rarely causes any problems. But when we're developing flexible designs, this box model causes headaches because CSS has never made it easy for us to mix percentages with fixed units like pixels and ems.

To illustrate this, imagine a box that fills one hundred per cent of the browser window. If that box needs ten pixels padding, what width should we give it? If the same box then needs a five-pixel border, how wide will the box be now? Historically, to work around these difficulties we resorted to nesting one element that used pixels inside another that used percentages.

To help solve the problem of mixing pixel and percentage units on the same element, CSS3 introduced a second box model type — a `border-box` — where padding and borders are subtracted from, not added to, a box's dimensions. This makes it easy to use a one hundred per cent width plus padding and borders set in pixels for this `section`.

```
section {
width : 100%
padding : 10px;
border :
5px solid rgb(229,228,216);
box-sizing : border-box;
}
```

In this example, padding and borders are added to the dimensions of a content-box.

Whereas in a border-box, padding and borders are subtracted.

For now at least, we'll need vendor-specific prefixes for box-sizing in Firefox, Safari and Google Chrome, although Opera and Internet Explorer 9 support it with no vendor-specific prefix.

```
section {
width : 100%
padding : 10px;
border : 5px solid rgb(229,228,216);
-moz-box-sizing : border-box;
-webkit-box-sizing : border-box;
box-sizing : border-box;
}
```

Does the way that border-box draws an element sound familiar? It should, because that is the way that Microsoft calculated box sizes up until Internet Explorer 6. (Did you know that it still does when you trigger that browser's quirks mode?)

Clipping backgrounds

When we combine a background image or colour with a border, by default the background extends underneath the border and out to the edges of a box. CSS3 calls this default behaviour a `border-box` and the CSS `background-clip` property now gives us control over this behaviour:

```
div {
background-color : rgb(246,245,235);
border : 10px dashed rgb(229,228,216);
background-clip : border-box;
}
```

If we specify a box to be a `padding-box`, any background colour or image will be clipped to the outer edges of the box's padding and won't extend behind its border:

```
div {
background-color : rgb(246,245,235);
border : 10px dashed rgb(229,228,216);
background-clip : padding-box;
}
```

Once again we'll need to use vendor-specific prefixes for `background-clip` to work in Firefox, Safari and Google Chrome.

```
div {
background-color : rgb(246,245,235);
border : 10px dashed rgba(229,228,216,.5);
-moz-background-clip : padding-box;
-webkit-background-clip : padding-box;
background-clip : padding-box;
}
```

Defining a background image's origin

You'll no doubt already know about CSS 2.1's `background-position` property. Modern browsers position a background image relative to the outer edges of an element's padding, inside its border. CSS3 calls this default origin a 'padding-box'. CSS3 extends our creative possibilities by providing new properties with several new `background-origin` values:

One of these new `background-origin` properties positions a background image so that it's relative to an element's outer edges, beneath its border. It's called, unsurprisingly, a `border-box`:

```
div {
background-origin : border-box;
}
```

With a `content-box`, a background image's origin will be relative to the outer edge of the content, inside its padding:

```
div {
background-origin : content-box;
}
```

If you need a refresher on CSS 2.1 `background-position` values: `0 0` is the same as left top; `50% 0` is fifty per cent horizontally but still at the top; and `100% 100%` is the same as `right bottom`. You can specify a background image's position using keywords (`left`, `top`, `right`, `bottom`), percentages, pixels and any other CSS units.

Gecko-based browsers including Firefox use the non-standard 'border' instead of `border-box` and 'padding' instead of `padding-box`. For now at least, we need to use both `-moz-` and `-webkit-` vendor prefixes when using CSS3 background-origin.

Sizing background images

Working with large background images can often be a headache and I can't count the number of times that I've resized images in Photoshop while I work on a design. CSS3 has an advanced `background-size` property that gives us far greater control over background image sizes. This can save us time and open up a new world of creative possibilities.

The new `background-size` property takes horizontal and vertical pixel or percentage values, plus optional keyword values of `cover` and `contain`:

```
div { background-size: 100% 50% contain; }
```

Pixel units	Size a background image using pixels (width and height)
Percentages	Specify a background image size as a percentage of the size of the element it is attached to (width and height)
`cover`	A background image's aspect ratio 'covers' an element's background
`contain`	A background image's aspect ratio is 'contained' inside a element

Let's start with a box — it's dimensions are 200 pixels by 310 pixels: Now apply a background image that's the same size as that box:

```
div {
width : 200px;
height : 310px;
background-image : url(store.jpg);
}
```

When both sets of dimensions are identical, there's no problem — but do you hear that? It's the sound of a client changing their mind about a design. Don't worry though, CSS `background-size` will take care of it for us and save us a trip back into Photoshop.

Sizing background images using pixels

The CSS `background-size` property allows us to specify the exact size of a background image using pixels, like this:

```
div { background-size : 200px 310px; }
```

The first value defines the width, the second is height. When we don't specify a height, a browser will automatically choose `auto` and maintain the intrinsic aspect ratio of the background image. In the example, these three values all produce identical results:

```
div { background-size : 200px 310px; }
div { background-size : 200px auto; }
div { background-size : 200px; }
```

If an element changes size, perhaps to 240 pixels by 350 pixels, we can apply those new sizes to a background image and it will scale or stretch to fit. We could even specify a background size that is very different from an element. Here are three examples:

`background-size : 240px 350px;`   `background-size : 120px 175px;`   `background-size : 60px 87px;`

Sizing background images in percentages

CSS now allows us to scale a background image using percentages. In the following series of examples, the first value defines an image's width, the second its height. When we don't specify a height, a browser will automatically choose `auto` and maintain an image's aspect ratio.

`background-size : 100% 100%;`

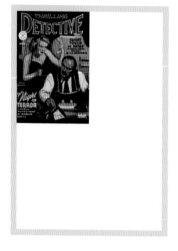

`background-size : 50% auto;`

`background-size : 25%;`

`background-size : auto 100%;`

`background-size : auto 50%;`

`background-size : auto 25%;`

Cover and contain

Let's make something a little more adventurous. It's a promotional panel for the 'It's Hardboiled' store that's designed to promote a very special book. Start with hardboiled HTML — one section that contains a heading and a paragraph.

```
<section>
    <h1>The Phantom Detective</h1>
    <p>The Phantom Detective was the second pulp hero published after
    The Shadow. The first issue was released in February 1933. The
    title continued until 1953, with a total of 170 issues. This is
    the third highest number of issues for a character pulp.</p>
</section>
```

This section will span one hundred per cent of the width of its container, but we'll also need to set padding in pixels, a combination that's been difficult to pull off without nested elements, until now. Don't worry, by declaring border-box we'll make it easy to mix those percentages with pixels:

```
section {
width : 100%;
padding : 40px 80px 40px 280px;
background-color : rgb(29,16,23);
box-sizing : border-box;
}
```

If you're wondering why the large amount of left padding is needed, hold that thought — we'll get to that in just a minute. Now apply a large background image. It's the key to this design and we'll centre it horizontally and fix it to the bottom of the section:

```
section {
width : 100%;
padding : 40px 80px 40px 280px;
background-color : rgb(29,16,23);
background-image : url(cityscape.jpg);
background-position : 50% 100%;
background-repeat : no-repeat;
box-sizing : border-box;
}
```

The result's looking good, but it's not perfect because when a user narrows their browser window, they'll cut off both sides of the background image.

On the right, the background image is cut off when a user reduces the size of the browser window.

CSS now provides two more `background-size` keywords. They both scale an image while maintaining its aspect ratio, which is perfect for just this situation. Somewhat confusingly though, these keywords are called `cover` and `contain`. First, the `contain` keyword which, scales an image so that both its width and height are 'contained' inside the element and not clipped.

This background image is 'contained' inside its element.

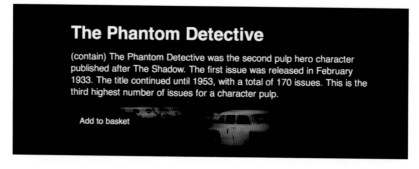

With the `cover` keyword, both the background image's width and height scale to 'cover' the background.

This background image will always cover the element, even when that element changes size — perfect for flexible designs.

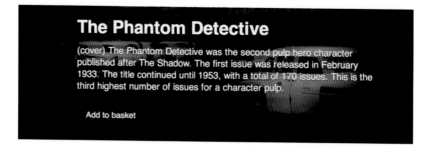

To finish our promotional panel design, we'll add a second background image of a book cover. Any ideas where we'll position it? You guessed it: into the space left by the large amount of left padding, forty pixels from the top and forty pixels from the left.

Separate the position, repeat and size values of each image using commas and remember, the image we specify first will be the one that appears closest to the viewer.

```
section {
background-image : url(cover.jpg), url(cityscape.jpg);
background-position : 40px 40px, 50% 100%;
background-repeat : no-repeat, no-repeat;
background-size : 200px 300px, cover;
}
```

You've probably guessed by now that to enable background sizing in Firefox and WebKit-based browsers we'll need vendor-specific prefixes.

```
section {
-moz-background-size : 200px 300px, cover;
-webkit-background-size : 200px 300px, cover;
background-size : 200px 300px, cover;
-moz-box-sizing : border;
-webkit-box-sizing : border-box;
box-sizing : border-box;
}
```

Our final result — a liquid design accomplished using two background images, the second scales to fit any size container while at the same time maintaining its aspect ratio, the first appears at its native size. Now that's hardboiled.

The Phantom Detective

(cover) The Phantom Detective was the second pulp hero character published after The Shadow. The first issue was released in February 1933. The title continued until 1953, with a total of 170 issues. This is the third highest number of issues for a character pulp.

Add to basket

Authentic Jobs know a thing
or two about how to enrich
their design using multiple
background images.

Authentic Jobs put multiple background images to good use on its subscribe to
search results modal form, a hardboiled unordered list. First, they applied an `id`
of 'methods' onto which to bind their styles:

```
<ul id="methods">
    <li class="email active"><a href="#">Email</a></li>
    <li class="twitter"><a href="#">Twitter</a></li>
    <li class="rss last"><a href="#">RSS</a></li>
</ul>
```

Authentic Jobs then applied two background images: the first a one pixel wide
repeating alpha-transparent PNG; then a one pixel tall GIF format image.

```
ul#methods {
background : transparent url('tabs-gradient.gif') scroll repeat-y 0 0;
background : url('tabs-fade.png') 0 100% repeat-x,
url('tabs-gradient.gif') repeat-y;
}
```

Did you notice that Authentic Jobs first added a single background image for
browsers that don't support multiple background images, followed by the
declaration that contains two images?

Dribbbits

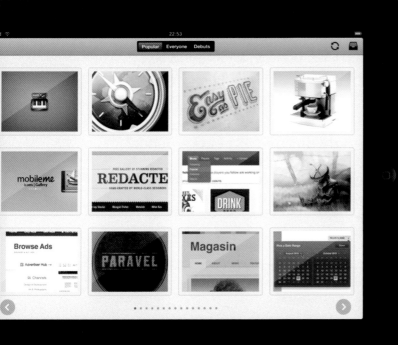

Buy it on the App Store

An elegant way to browse your Dribbble feed.

Introducing Dribbbits for iPad!

With Dribbbits for iPad you can browse Dribbble in a beautiful and exciting way.

Dribbbits is now available in the App Store!

Keep in touch.

Email address...   Update me

Share via Twitter.

You should Tweet this

Remember Dan Cederholm's Dribbble, a site for sharing preview screenshots of designs you're working on? Well Dribbbits' is a native app that lets you enjoy Dribbble on your iPad. Developers Jeremy Swinnen and Cedric Vandendriessche used multiple backgrounds on the app site's header, but there's a twist. The pair combined a repeating bitmap image with a CSS generated gradient:

Don't worry if you're unfamiliar with CSS gradients. You'll learn all about them in the next chapter.

```
#header {
background : url(pattern.png) repeat-x,
-webkit-gradient(linear, 0% 0%, 0% 100%, from(rgb(23, 19, 42)), to(rgb(42, 35, 75)));
background : url(pattern.png) repeat-x,
-moz-linear-gradient(top,  rgb(23, 19, 42),  rgb(42, 35, 75));
}
```

¹ http://dribbbits.webmolecule.com/

Breaking it up

Today, when we need to apply more than one background image to an element, we can keep our HTML hardboiled and free from presentational hacks and JavaScript workarounds by using CSS backgrounds. These properties give us precise control over the size of our background images and how they're rendered behind our elements. These background properties are one of the most interesting and important aspects of CSS3 and already have widespread browser support. Are you using them yet? What are you waiting for? Christmas?

Keen to dig up more dirt on CSS3 backgrounds?

From 2008, **Mozilla Developer Center** explains why 'Background images no longer restricted to original size'.

https://developer.mozilla.org/web-tech/2009/08/04/background-images-no-longer-restricted-to-original-size-explore-the-space-with-background-size

Jonathan Snook has written a thorough, if dry, overview of 'Multiple Backgrounds and CSS Gradients'.

http://snook.ca/archives/html_and_css/multiple-bg-css-gradients

The **W3C** has already started work on a longer-term future version of its 'Backgrounds and Borders Module Level 4'.

http://dev.w3.org/csswg/css4-background

CSS3 gradients

As we know, gradients can bring a two-dimensional interface to life, so they've become a common feature of web designs. Making them in Photoshop or Fireworks isn't difficult and we've all been doing it for years, so why all the excitement about gradients in CSS?

The designs we make today are seen by people using browsers and devices that we couldn't have imagined five years ago. Flexibility in design matters, but bitmap images are inflexible and lack any real ability to scale. File size matters too, and on mobile devices every byte we save can make a big difference to a user's experience.

Gradients without images have been possible in Scalable Vector Graphics (SVG) for some time, but a lack of support from Microsoft (which implemented SVG only in Internet Explorer 9) meant that web designers and developers largely ignored SVG. Now, finally, we have the ability to create gradients using just CSS.

Linear gradients

Why do gradients use the CSS background-image property when they're not images? This may seem illogical, but in practice it makes perfect sense, because CSS backgrounds allow us to apply multiple gradients to an element and mix them with bitmap background images.

In CSS, a linear gradient consists of a gradient line and two or more colours. The line can be horizontal, vertical or at any angle across an element's background. The concept and syntax of CSS gradients shouldn't be difficult to grasp, particularly if you're experienced using Photoshop or Fireworks.

We'll start building a gradient declaration by describing its type — in this case, it's a linear gradient.

```
div { background-image : linear-gradient(); }
```

We can define a gradient's colour values using keywords, hexadecimal values, RGB and HSL, or RGBa and HSLa.

Next, we'll specify a gradient's origin. If we don't, browsers will assume that a gradient will run vertically from top to bottom. The simplest way to define the origin is by using keywords, and we can specify that a gradient runs from: top to bottom; bottom to top; left to right; or right to left. In parentheses, we add the origin, then the start and end colours.

```
background-image : linear-gradient(top, #c8482c, #fff);
```

```
background-image : linear-gradient(right, #c8482c, #fff); }
```

```
background-image : linear-gradient(bottom, #c8482c, #fff); }
```

```
background-image : linear-gradient(left, #c8482c, #fff); }
```

We can create angled gradients by defining an origin using either keywords or an angle in degrees, so: `top left` starts the gradient at the top-left and runs it 45 degrees diagonally towards the bottom right; `bottom left` starts it at the bottom-left and runs it 45 degrees diagonally towards the top-right; and so on.

```
background-image : linear-gradient(top left, #c8482c, #fff);
```

```
background-image : linear-gradient(bottom left, #c8482c, #fff);
```

```
background-image : linear-gradient(-30deg, #c8482c, #fff);
```

```
background-image : linear-gradient(-60deg, #c8482c, #fff);
```

Adding colour stops

Simple gradients come from two main
colours, but designs will often require
more complex gradients that include one
or more colour stops. To help us visualise
what a colour stop is, let's head back into
familiar territory, a graphic editor, in this
case Fireworks. Here, we can add colours
to a gradient using the add colour tool.

Adding a colour stop into a CSS gradient
works in exactly the same way. When
we specify one or more colour stops, a
browser will smoothly blend between them.
　　We might also want to adjust the position of each colour stop along
a gradient's path. We can do this anywhere between zero and one hundred
per cent.

```
background-image : linear-gradient(left, #000, #c8482c 50%, #fff);
```

```
background-image : linear-gradient(left, #000, #c8482c 33%, #ffd822 66%, #fff);
```

```
background-image : linear-gradient(left, #000, #c8482c 25%, #ffd822 50%, ↵
#22aeff 75%, #fff);
```

Writing linear gradients for WebKit

It was the WebKit[1] team who first announced CSS gradients back in 2008 and it based its proposals on work that had already been done on the canvas element. Mozilla followed suit with a proposal for a simpler syntax and this was the syntax that was subsequently adopted by the W3C. There are several differences between these two implementations and, for the time being at least, we need to write CSS gradients using both WebKit's and the Firefox/ W3C's official syntax.

The W3C's gradient syntax[2] (seen in the section above) describes the gradient type as part of the property, but WebKit's older syntax makes that type its first value:

```
div { background-image : -webkit-gradient(linear); }
```

We then define a gradient's direction and WebKit supports numbers, percentages and keywords. I prefer to use keywords because they're simpler to remember and more closely resemble the W3C's official syntax:

```
div { background-image : -webkit-gradient(linear, top, bottom); }
```

The following two values are for the start (from) and end (to) colours in a gradient:

```
div {
background-image : ↵
-webkit-gradient(linear, left top, from(#000), to(#fff));
}
```

And finally, we add one or more (optional) colour stops:

```
div {
background-image : -webkit-gradient(linear, left top,
color-stop(0, #000),
color-stop(0.5 #555),
color-stop(#fff));
}
```

[1] http://webkit.org/blog/175/introducing-css-gradients
[2] http://dev.w3.org/csswg/css3-images

Westciv's CSS gradient generator is a handy tool that creates both linear and radial gradients. Change the start and end colours, adjust the slider controls and watch as the gradients change before your eyes. When we've made a gradient, we can copy the generated styles and paste them into our style sheets.[1]

It's likely that future versions of WebKit will implement the W3C's official gradient syntax. I'll bet my badge on it. I'll also wager that, to ensure backwards compatibility with the countless websites and applications already using its gradients, WebKit will continue to support the older syntax.

Does writing gradient declarations twice take extra time? Yes — welcome to an imperfect world. Should that stop us from using CSS gradients? It should not. This is precisely the kind of situation that demonstrates the importance of vendor-specific prefixes and how they enable browser makers to perfect their implementations while we make creative use of the new properties.

Linear gradients see some action

It's time for gradients to see some hardboiled action and we'll make this happen by adding gradients to the sticky notes on the 'It's Hardboiled' office door that we made back in Chapter 13.

Our markup remains the same hardboiled HTML5 `article` but this time we'll add a related `aside`:

```
<article>
    <ul>
        <li>Hardboiled is attitude</li>
        <li>It's also a lot more</li>
        <li>Don't sugar-coat the truth, don't play it cute</li>
        <li>Find out the truth, no matter how rotten it might be</li>
    </ul>
</article>

<aside class="vcard">
    <p>A fictitious demonstration, designed by Andy Clarke.</p>
    <p>Have something on your mind or just want to say hello, drop me
    a dime</p>
</aside>
```

[1] http://westciv.com/tools/gradients/index.html

We'll start by giving both elements equal dimensions, padding and a solid background colour that's part of our backup plan for less capable browsers:

```
article, aside  {
width : 260px;
height : 260px;
padding : 40px;
background-color : rgb(255,250,150);
}
```

Adding a diagonal gradient

It's time to make our sticky notes more realistic by adding a diagonal gradient consisting of two colours running from top-right to bottom-left in each note. Define the gradient type as linear, then add its direction, followed by start and end colours. We'll write gradient values from the W3C's draft specification first.

```
article, aside {
background-image : linear-gradient(right top, rgb(255,210,105), ↵
rgb(255,250,150));
}
```

Now we'll add Mozilla's implementation — which matches the W3C specification but uses their vendor-specific prefix — followed by WebKit's non-standard syntax with its prefix. We need to make sure the W3C's official declaration comes last so that when WebKit and Mozilla add support for gradients without their vendor-specific prefixes, the official W3C declaration will override anything particular to a vendor:

A fictitious demonstrat
by Andy Clarke.

Have something on your
want to say hello, drop

Hardboiled is attitude

It's also a lot more

Don't sugar-coat the facts, don't play
it cute

Find out truth, no matter how
rotten it might be

Got a story?

It's debatable whether serving less capable browsers a gradient image is worth the time and effort involved in creating one. Whether we serve a gradient image alternative will depend on how much the site design depends on the appearance of a gradient.

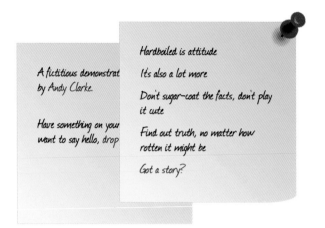

```
article, aside {
background-image : -moz-linear-gradient(right top, rgb(255,210,105), ↵
rgb(255,250,150));

background-image : -webkit-gradient(linear, right top, left bottom, ↵
from(rgb(255,210,105)), to(rgb(255,250,150)));

background-image : linear-gradient(right top, rgb(255,210,105), ↵
rgb(255,250,150));
}
```

Browsers that have implemented CSS gradients, with or without a vendor-specific prefix will render them. Those that aren't capable will render the solid background colour we specified earlier. But why hand control over to a browser when we can play hardboiled and serve an alternative gradient image to less capable browsers using Modernizr?

Designing to browser capabilities with Modernizr

Modernizr will test if a browser is capable of rendering CSS gradients. When they can't, Modernizr will add its no-cssgradients class. We can then use specific descendent selectors to serve a gradient image to those browsers:

```
.no-cssgradients article, .no-cssgradients aside  {
background-image : url(notes.jpg);
background-repeat : no-repeat;
background-position : 100% 0;
}
```

Browsers that are capable of rendering CSS gradients will receive them via a specific selector using Modernizr's cssgradients class:

Adding more depth with a CSS shadow

To give a greater feeling of depth, we'll add a one-pixel border to the right and a two-pixel border at the bottom of each note.

```
article, aside  {
border-right : 1px solid rgb(0,0,0);
border-bottom : 2px solid rgb(0,0,0);
}
```

Modern browsers — including Internet Explorer 9 — have implemented RGBa, which is perfect for creating subtle shadows. Modernizr will test for RGBa support and add its rgba class.

```
.rgba article, .rgba aside  {
border-width : 0;
-moz-box-shadow : 0 2px 5px rgba(0,0,0,.5);
-webkit-box-shadow : 0 2px 5px rgba(0,0,0,.5);
box-shadow : 0 2px 5px rgba(0,0,0,.5);
}
```

When I redesigned CannyBill I made extensive use of CSS3 properties across its interface. Dig into the CannyBill style sheets and you'll find Modernizr helping me to layer colour using RGBa, create `border-radius` rounded corners and CSS gradients used for navigation, buttons and panels.

    For CannyBill's pricing page[1]. I used CSS gradients to add polish to their price options. The HTML is hardboiled, nothing more than an ordered list of options, each one with its own class attribute value applied (`basic`, `small`, `professional` and `enterprise`):

CSS gradients also bring CannyBill's sign-up links to life. First, I added simple styles:

```
a.action {
display : block;
margin-bottom : 1.5em;
padding : 10px 20px 12px;
color : rgb(255,255,255);
text-align : center;
}
```

Then I applied solid background colours to each link. These are visible even in less capable browsers:

```
.basic .action { background-color : rgb(229,195,85); }
.small .action { background-color : rgb(218,109,14); }
.professional .action { background-color : rgb(188,72,72); }
.enterprise .action { background-color : rgb(122,104,166); }
```

Finally, Modernizr tests a browser's ability to render CSS gradients so that I could apply them using a more specific selector:

[1] http://www.cannybill.com/pricing.php

```css
.cssgradients .basic .action {
background-image : -webkit-gradient(linear, left top, left bottom, ↵
from(rgb(229,195,85)), to(rgb(187,160,71)));
background-image : -moz-linear-gradient(left top (rgb(229,195,85)), ↵
(rgb(187,160,71)));
}


.cssgradients .small .action {
background-image : -webkit-gradient(linear, left top, left bottom, ↵
from(rgb(255,153,0)), to(rgb(190,75,26)));
background-image : -moz-linear-gradient(left top (rgb(255,153,0)), ↵
(rgb(190,75,26)));
}


.cssgradients .professional .action {
background-image : -webkit-gradient(linear, left top, left bottom, ↵
from(rgb(188,72,72)), to(rgb(126,49,49)));
background-image : -moz-linear-gradient(left top (rgb(188,72,72)), ↵
(rgb(126,49,49)));
}


.cssgradients .enterprise .action {
background-image : -webkit-gradient(linear, left top, left bottom, ↵
from(rgb(122,104,166)), to(rgb(91,78,127)));
background-image : -moz-linear-gradient(left top ↵
(rgb(122,104,166)), (rgb(91,78,127)));
}
```

Here's how CannyBill's price options are displayed in four
contemporary browsers.

Sign up	Sign up	Sign up	Sign up
30 day free trial	30 day free trial	30 day free trial	30 day free trial
Safari 5	Firefox 3.6	Opera 10.6	Internet Explorer 8

Radial gradients

It's been remarked by some that the CSS Working Group is "a battlefield where vendors fight for competitive advantage." If you need further proof, look no further than CSS3 radial gradients. These gradients were originally proposed and implemented by WebKit. Its proposal was then countered by Mozilla which implemented a very different (and simpler) syntax. The W3C then adopted Mozilla's syntax as the basis for its emerging standard.

To watch every punch and counter-punch as these standards develop, follow the CSS Working Group on Twitter[1] or keep up with the minutes of their meetings on their blog[2]. Pretty, it ain't.

Does all this mean that we should wait until a bloodied victor emerges before we start working with radial gradients? Don't be a mug. Will we need to make changes to our style sheets as the standard develops? Without a doubt. Welcome to the brave new world of CSS3.

Because this standard is, for now at least, a moving target, I'll keep this section intentionally brief and we'll focus on today's practical realities of working with radial gradients.

Defining a gradient type

We'll start describing the type of gradient — this time it's radial:

```
div { background-image : radial-gradient(); }
```

Setting an angle

We first define the gradient line's starting point followed by its angle. If we omit either, a browser will assume that our gradient will radiate outwards from the centre of an element:

---

[1] http://twitter.com/csswg
[2] http://www.w3.org/blog/CSS

background-image : radial-gradient(#c8482c, #ffd822); }

background-image : radial-gradient(top, #c8482c, #ffd822); }

background-image : radial-gradient(right, #c8482c, #ffd822); }

background-image : radial-gradient(bottom, #c8482c, #ffd822); }

background-image : radial-gradient(left, #c8482c, #ffd822); }

background-image : radial-gradient(top left, #c8482c, #ffd822); }

background-image : radial-gradient(top right, #c8482c, #ffd822); }

background-image : radial-gradient(bottom right, #c8482c, #ffd822); }

background-image : radial-gradient(bottom left, #c8482c, #ffd822); }

Next, choose between the two radial shapes, either a circle or an elliptical gradient. The W3C's draft specification makes an ellipse the default shape for a radial gradient if we omit this value.

Now define the size of the gradient by choosing from one of several keywords.

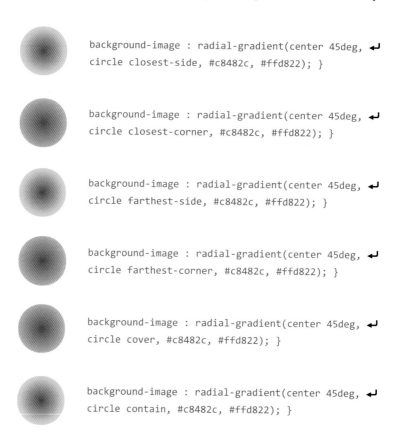

```
background-image : radial-gradient(center 45deg, ↵
circle closest-side, #c8482c, #ffd822); }
```

```
background-image : radial-gradient(center 45deg, ↵
circle closest-corner, #c8482c, #ffd822); }
```

```
background-image : radial-gradient(center 45deg, ↵
circle farthest-side, #c8482c, #ffd822); }
```

```
background-image : radial-gradient(center 45deg, ↵
circle farthest-corner, #c8482c, #ffd822); }
```

```
background-image : radial-gradient(center 45deg, ↵
circle cover, #c8482c, #ffd822); }
```

```
background-image : radial-gradient(center 45deg, ↵
circle contain, #c8482c, #ffd822); }
```

Adding colour stops

Simple radial gradients are made from only two main colours, but if our designs require a more complex gradient we can add one or more colour stops.

```
background-image : radial-gradient(#000, #c8482c 50%, #fff); }
```

```
background-image : radial-gradient(#000, #c8482c 33%, ↵
#ffd822 66%, #fff); }
```

```
background-image : radial-gradient(#000, #c8482c 25%, ↵
#ffd822 50%, #22aeff 75%, #fff); }
```

Writing radial gradients for WebKit

The W3C's official radial gradient syntax[1] differs significantly from the older syntax proposed and implemented by WebKit. As with linear gradients, it's likely that future versions of WebKit will use the W3C's official syntax and that it'll continue to support its older syntax to maintain backwards compatibility — at least for a few versions. Until then, we're stuck with writing multiple declarations.

Radial gradients in the limelight

It's time to put radial gradients in the limelight by combining them with RGBa to shine a spotlight on the door of the 'It's Hardboiled' office. We'll first apply a dark background colour and a wood panel background image:

```
body {
background-color : rgb(23,11,2);
background-image : url(door.jpg);
background-repeat : no-repeat;
background-position : 50% 0;
}
```

This smart wooden panelling will give a good impression to all visitors to the 'It's Hardboiled' office. We'll welcome even those who forget to wipe their feet by using a less capable browser.

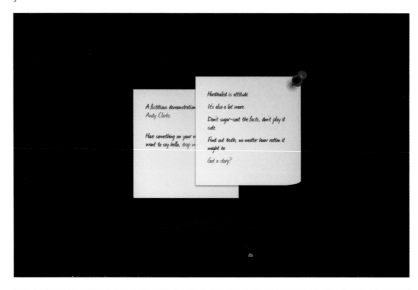

Because CSS gradients use the `background-image` property, we can use them in multiple backgrounds, including bitmap background images or other CSS gradients.

Modernizr tests a browser's capability to render CSS gradients and adds its `cssgradients` class for browsers that can. Using a specific descendent selector, we serve gradients to capable browsers, first using vendor-specific prefixes followed by the W3C's official syntax:

```
.cssgradients body {
background-image : -moz-radial-gradient(center 45deg, circle ↵
farthest-side, ↵
rgba(0,0,0,0) 0%, rgba(0,0,0,.8) 150%), url(door.jpg);

background-image : -webkit-gradient(radial, 50% 50%, 0, 50% 50%, 800,
from(rgba(0,0,0,0)), to(rgba(0,0,0,.8))), url(door.jpg);

background-image : radial-gradient(center 45deg, circle farthest- ↵
side, rgba(0,0,0,0) 0%, rgba(0,0,0,.8) 150%), url(door.jpg);
}
```

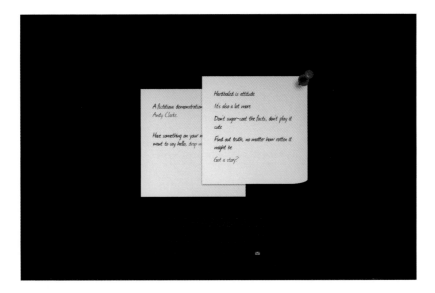

Browsers capable of rendering CSS gradients will overlay this semi-transparent spotlight over the top of the door image.

Breaking it up

CSS gradients may be new, but whether you like your gradients linear, radial or, with multiple background images, a combination of both, they're a flexible tool for creating layered designs with dramatically fewer images. Sure, there are wrinkles to iron out and until they are we'll need to edit our style sheets to accommodate the changes to an emerging specification. But, hey! Who said life was going to be fair?

Keen to dig up more dirt on CSS3 gradients?

'Speed Up with CSS3 Gradients' from **Chris Coyier's CSS Tricks** contains bad advice about using Microsoft's ancient proprietary gradients, but it's otherwise an excellent introduction complete with examples.

http://css-tricks.com/css3-gradients

'CSS gradient syntax: comparison of Mozilla and WebKit' by **Peter Gasston** The first part of an excellent two-part article.

http://www.broken-links.com/2009/11/26/css-gradient-syntax-comparison-of-mozilla-and-webkit

Part two of 'CSS gradient syntax: comparison of Mozilla and WebKit' by **Peter Gasston**·

http://www.broken-links.com/2009/11/30/css-gradient-syntax-comparison-of-mozilla-and-webkit-part-2

Mozilla's explanation of 'CSS gradients in Firefox 3.6' is a comprehensive primer on what is developing into the W3C's draft specification for CSS gradients.

http://hacks.mozilla.org/2009/11/css-gradients-firefox-36

'Using gradients' from the **Mozilla Developer Center** is another thorough introduction from Mozilla.

https://developer.mozilla.org/en/Using_gradients

Hardly a thrilling read but very comprehensive, the 'CSS3 Image Values Module' itself — an emerging standard being worked on by **W3C** CSS Working Group members.

http://dev.w3.org/csswg/css3-images

That was a breeze

In **Hardboiled CSS3**, you learned about web fonts and how we can use them for better type and typography on the web. You learned how to create designs that are layered and full of depth by taking advantage of RGBa colour and CSS `opacity`.

You saw how we no longer need to carve out images to make rounded corner buttons and boxes, and that rounded corners can also be used to create more elaborate shapes to make our designs stand out. If images are your thing, you learned how to add them inside an element's border to create flexible shapes.

Multiple background images, once just a pipe dream, are now a reality and we can use them to add real depth to our designs. Finally, you wound up knowing how to replace many images with CSS3 gradients to make designs that are lighter, faster and more flexible.

MORE HARDBOILED CSS3

You now know that hardboiled CSS helps us to leave behind some of the ways of working we've become accustomed to, making our websites lighter, faster and more responsive as a result. Now it's time to turn up the heat again. In **More hardboiled CSS3**, you'll learn about how to translate, scale, rotate and skew elements using CSS transforms in two and three dimensions. You'll find out how to make state changes smoother with a host of CSS transitions, and finish off by discovering animations in CSS: an emerging standard that has already caught the eye of many of today's top web designers.

CSS3 transforms

DESPITE OUR VERY BEST EFFORTS, CSS layouts can sometimes be a little strait-laced. CSS even calls its basis for layout a 'box model'. While some CSS layout proposals such as Grid Positioning and Template Layout are slowly rotting inside the W3C, there are new tools to help our designs break out of the box. CSS3 calls them two-dimensional and three-dimensional transforms.

Two-dimensional transforms

We'll concentrate mainly on two-dimensional transforms, which have better support in many contemporary browsers, so using them today is a real no-brainer. The basic syntax for transforms is simple:

```
transform : (transform type);
```

There are a number of ways that we can `transform` an element:

- `translate:` moves an element horizontally and vertically
- `skew:` distorts an element horizontally and vertically
- `rotate:` rotates an element
- `scale:` increases or decreases the size of an element

We'll look at each of them, learning how they're implemented and investigating how designers are already putting transforms to good use.

Cross-browser CSS transforms

There's no getting away from the fact that CSS transforms are an emerging standard. But there's already widespread support for them in contemporary browsers; Firefox, Google Chrome, Opera and Safari have all implemented them using vendor-specific prefixes. For the horizontal translation we'll be covering in just a minute, we'll need vendor-specific prefixes for Mozilla, Opera and WebKit, followed by the W3C's official transforms syntax:

```
.vcard {
-moz-transform : translateX(100px);
-o-transform : translateX(100px);
-webkit-transform : translateX(100px);
transform : translateX(100px);
}
```

For all of the examples we're going to cover from now on, I'll use only the W3C's official transforms syntax. I'll leave it up to you to add the corresponding vendor-specific prefixes for Mozilla, Opera and WebKit.

Quite a fistful I know, but necessary, because these vendor-specific prefixes allow each browser maker to perfect their implementations as the standard develops. What about Internet Explorer 9?

For their latest release, Microsoft have made amazing progress in bringing their browser more in line with competitors, but not everything has been possible in this release. Expect CSS transforms to appear in a near-future version (Internet Explorer 10?).

Transform 'translate'

We'll start by moving elements with `translate`. In many respects, this behaves in a similar way to relative positioning, where an element is offset visually but keeps its position in the document's normal flow.

Like CSS positioning, transformed elements also create a new instance of normal flow and become positioning contexts for any absolutely positioned child elements.

`translate` moves elements on the x- and y-axes. We can specify how far they move by using pixels, ems or percentages that are relative to the size of the element. For example, a 100 pixel box translated by 150% moves 150 pixels. Percentages can be particularly useful in flexible designs and on dynamic sites where the size of elements changes.

We'll `translate` an 'It's Hardboiled' business `vcard` one hundred pixels (`100px`) to the right using `translateX` and a distance inside parentheses.

```
.vcard { transform : translateX(100px); }
```

Now translate that card down by 50% with translateY:

```
.vcard {
transform : translateX(100px);
transform : translateY(50%);
}
```

Finally, combine translateX and translateY into a single translate value.

```
.vcard { transform : translate(100px, 50%); }
```

Anthony Calzadilla uses translate and rotate to create his 'Pure CSS3 Animated AT-AT Walker from Star Wars'[1]. Be honest, admit it — Star Wars was the real reason you wanted to learn CSS. Anthony wrote a detailed walk-through of his demonstration[2].

[1] http://www.anthonycalzadilla.com/css3-ATAT/index.html
[2] http://blog.optimum7.com/anthony/website-design/pure-css3-animated-at-at-walker-from-star-wars-2.html

If another element already occupies the space, any translated element will overlap it (it will appear in front of the element if it comes later in the source order, otherwise it will appear behind). As with relative positioning, when we use `translate` the document's normal flow stays unaltered and nothing can flow in to occupy any vacated space.

The best way to learn transforms is to see them in action, so we'll `translate` another business card in several different directions using pixels and percentages. In each example, the dotted box shows the card's original position.

`.vcard { transform : translateX(50px); }`

`.vcard { transform : translateY(50px); }`

`.vcard { transform : translateX(50%); }`

`.vcard { transform : translateY(50%); }`

Transform 'scale'

When we use the scale value, we make elements appear larger or smaller. By how much and on what axes is determined by a scaling factor, which can range between 0.99 and 0.01 to make an element smaller, or 1.01 and above to make it larger. A scaling factor of 1 maintains the intrinsic size of an element. Other elements remain blissfully unaware of the new size and so don't reflow around it.

You can scale elements along the horizontal or vertical axis, or a combination of the two. Next, we'll scale a vcard horizontally by 150% using scaleX. The scaling factor is in parentheses:

```
.vcard { transform : scaleX(1.5); }
```

Now use scaleY to increase its height by 50%:

```
.vcard {
transform : scaleX(1.5);
transform : scaleY(.5);
}
```

Or combine scaleX and scaleY into a single scale value:

```
.vcard { transform : scale(1.5, .5); }
```

To see scale in action, we'll change the size of another business card in several ways. The dotted box is there to remind us of their original sizes:

Look sharp! There's something there that could trip us up if we don't keep our wits about us. Inside those parentheses, the two values must be separated by a comma.

.vcard { transform : scaleX(.5); }

.vcard { transform : scaleY(.5); }

.vcard { transform : scale(.25, .5); }

.vcard { transform : scale(.5, .25); }

dribbble

Do you Dribbble'? I know I occasionally do. Hard man Dan Cederholm added subtle interaction to this design by scaling the colour tags in Dribbble's sidebar².

Dribbbling. We all do it sometimes.

Dan's marked up these colour chips using a list.

As a heavy microformats user, Dan also added rel-tag to each anchor. I've simplified Dan's HTML for this demonstration, so be sure to view his live code on Dribbble to get the full picture.

```
<ul class="color-chips group">
  <li><a href="/tags/red" class="red">Red</a></li>
  <li><a href="/tags/pink" class="pink">Pink</a></li>
  <li><a href="/tags/purple" class="purple">Purple</a></li>
  <li><a href="/tags/blue" class="blue">Blue</a></li>
  <li><a href="/tags/green" class="green">Green</a></li>
  <li><a href="/tags/yellow" class="yellow">Yellow</a></li>
  <li><a href="/tags/orange" class="orange">Orange</a></li>
  <li><a href="/tags/brown" class="brown">Brown</a></li>
  <li><a href="/tags/grey" class="grey">Grey</a></li>
  <li><a href="/tags/black" class="black">Black</a></li>
  <li><a href="/tags/white" class="white">White</a></li>
</ul>
```

Dan floated each list item, then, because he was desperate to move his text off-screen, he indented it by a massive –9,999 pixels, before adding rounded corners using border-radius:

```
.color-chips li a {
float : left;
width : 20px;
height : 10px;
text-indent : -9999px;
}
```

¹ http://dribbble.com
² http://dribbble.com/players/malarkey

```
.color-chips li:first-child a {
border-top-left-radius : 3px;
border-bottom-left-radius : 3px;
}

.color-chips li:last-child a {
border-top-right-radius : 3px;
border-bottom-right-radius : 3px;
}
```

To give each chip its own background colour, Dan targeted the class (red, pink, purple, blue, etc.) that he'd applied to each anchor:

```
a.red { background-color : #c33; }
a.pink { background-color : #ea4c88; }
```

We can remove Dan's classes and use CSS attribute selectors to target each anchor's href. This will make his HTML and CSS more hardboiled.

```
a[href*="red"] { background-color : #c33; }
a[href*="pink"] { background-color : #ea4c88; }
```

Dan increased the size of his chips by 140% (1.4) on mouse-over and added a touch of RGBa box-shadow to enrich the effect.

```
.color-chips li a:hover {
transform: scale(1.4);
box-shadow : 1px 1px 2px rgba(0,0,0,.3);
}
```

Dan Cederholm is a master of design details and Dribbble is a perfect example of how using transform, rounded corners, shadows and RGBa in combination can turn a great design into a classic.

Transform 'rotate'

We can rotate an element between 0 and 360 degrees (clockwise) and even
use negative values to rotate an element anticlockwise. The syntax is quick to
learn. First, declare the rotate value, then the angle — in this case forty-five
degrees (45deg) — inside parentheses:

```
.vcard { transform : rotate(45deg); }
```

```
.vcard { transform : rotate(-30deg); }
```

```
.vcard { transform : rotate(30deg); }
```

When an element is rotated, other elements on a page remain unaware of any change in angle and don't reflow around it. To see `rotate` in action, we'll change the angle of another `vcard` by different degrees. The dotted box is there to remind us of the original position:

`.vcard { transform : rotate(60deg); }`

`.vcard { transform : rotate(90deg); }`

Butterlabel's' designers, Luke Dorny and Scott Boms, love to spread their style on thick. On their home page, the two rotated a contact form to surprise visitors when they mouse-over it.

The Butterlabel home page HTML simply consists of a division, heading and the form element itself, of course.

```
<div id="subscribe">
    <h2>Why not find out when we release things?</h2>
    <form action="http://butterlabel.com" method="post">
        <div>
            <label for="name">Name:</label>
            <input type="text" name="name" id="name" />
        </div>
        <div>
            <label for="email">Email:</label>
            <input type="text" name="email" id="email" />
        </div>
        <div>
            <label for="site">Site:</label>
            <input type="text" name="site" id="site" />
        </div>
        <input type="submit" value="Subscribe" id="submit" />
    </form>
</div>
```

We could make the Butterlabel form hardboiled by adding HTML5 email and url input types.

```
<div>
    <label for="name">Name:</label>
    <input type="text" name="name" id="name" />
</div>

<div>
    <label for="email">Email:</label>
    <input type="email" name="email" id="email" />
</div>
```

' http://butterlabel.com

```
<div>
    <label for="site">Site:</label>
    <input type="url" name="site" id="site" />
</div>
```

Luke and Scott rotated the subscribe division anticlockwise by two degrees (-2deg) and added a soft RGBa shadow that's horizontally and vertically offset by twenty pixels.

```
#subscribe {
transform : rotate(-2deg);
box-shadow : 20px 20px 8px
rgba(0,0,0,.2);
}
```

When a user mouses-over the Butterlabel boys' form — to send them a message, or just for the hell of it — the division straightens up, rotating two degrees (2deg) clockwise:

```
#subscribe:hover {
transform : rotate(0deg);
box-shadow : 1px 1px 1px rgba(0,0,0,0.8);
}
```

Watch the video[1] of the Butterlabel form in action or visit the website and you'll notice that the smooth transition between the two angles takes .3 seconds. You'll learn about how to use CSS transitions like this in Chapter 17.

Why not find out when we release things?

Name:
Your callsign

Email:
name@email.tld

Do you skate?:
◯ Yes.
◯ No.
◯ Are you kidding me?

Do you design?:
◯ Nope.
◯ Sometimes.
◯ All day long!

Site:
http://site.tld

Subscribe

Occasional email newsletters. Your privacy is sacred. You'll never be spammed by us, except to promote ourselves, naturally.

Why not find out when we release things?

Name:
Your callsign

Email:
name@email.tld

Do you skate?:
◯ Yes.
◯ No.
◯ Are you kidding me?

Do you design?:
◯ Nope.
◯ Sometimes.
◯ All day long!

Site:
http://site.tld

Subscribe

Occasional email newsletters. Your privacy is sacred. You'll never be spammed by us, except to promote ourselves, naturally.

Remember the 2010 SXSW Beercamp party'? Me neither. The site's designers, nclud, used a `rotate` transform on the rounded corner date panel we investigated back in Chapter 13. Here's a reminder of the HTML:

```
<div id="date">
    <time class="day_of_week">Monday</time>
    <time class="day">March 15</time>
    <time class="year">Twenty Ten</time>
    <time class="time">Festivities begin at 7:30 PM</time>
</div>
```

To make the date panel swing like the party, nclud rotated the date division anticlockwise by minus fourteen degrees (`-14deg`).

```
#date { transform : rotate(-14deg); }
```

`rotate` changes the angle of all child elements within the date division, so to keep its content readable, nclud straightened the `time` elements by rotating them clockwise by fourteen degrees (`14deg`):

```
#date time { transform : rotate(14deg); }
```

Beercamp was staggering
(or was it just me?)

Don't worry if you're still thirsty. We'll be heading back to the Beercamp party later.

Transform 'skew' — the twisted thing

Skew — another `transform` value — distorts an element on the horizontal axis, vertical axis or both. The syntax is simple, so to demonstrate, we'll skew a `vcard` horizontally by first declaring `skewX`, then the amount, thirty degrees (`30deg`), inside parentheses:

```
.vcard { transform : skewX(30deg); }
```

Now let's combine two axes by also skewing the `vcard` vertically by fifteen degrees (`15deg`) using `skewY`. Longhand values look like this:

```
.vcard {
transform : skewX(30deg);
transform : skewY(15deg);
}
```

We can also use the shorthand `skew` property:

```
.vcard { transform : skew(30deg, 15deg); }
```

The best way to learn skews is to see them in action, so we'll put the skews on another business card by skewing it horizontally and vertically, positively and negatively to demonstrate the effects. In each example, the dotted box shows the card's original shape.

Watch out! If we don't separate those two values with a comma, we could easily end up looking like punks.

```
.vcard { transform : skewY(30deg); }
```

```
.vcard { skew(-15deg, -15deg); }
```

Setting the origin of a transform

Translating (moving), scaling, rotating and skewing are powerful tools for controlling the finer details in a design, but for even greater control we can define the origin of a `transform` on any given element.

Define a `transform-origin` by using either keywords like `top`, `right`, `bottom`, `left` and `center`, or by using pixels, ems or even percentages. Origins normally consist of two values: the first is a point on the horizontal axis; the second is on the vertical. In the next example, we'll `transform` a `vcard` around its right, uppermost corner:

```
.vcard { transform-origin : right top; }
```

The declaration below will give us the same results using percentages:

```
.vcard { transform-origin : 100% 0; }
```

When we use just one value, a browser will automatically assume that the second is `center`.

One of the best ways to understand transform origins is to see their effects in action, so in the next set of examples, the card is rotated by thirty degrees (`-30deg`) anticlockwise around different origin points. You sussed it: the dotted boxes show us the card's original position:

```
.vcard {
transform : rotate(-30deg);
transform-origin : 0 0;
}
```

```
.vcard {
transform : rotate(-30deg);
transform-origin : 50% 0;
}
```

```
.vcard {
transform : rotate(-30deg);
transform-origin : 0 100%;
}
```

```
.vcard {
transform : rotate(-30deg);
transform-origin : 100% 0;
}
```

Combining two or more transforms

Occasionally a design will require us to set two or more transforms on one element. To set multiple `transform` values, string them together and separate each with a space. In this next example, the `vcard` is both rotated by two degrees (2deg) and scaled five per cent (1.05) above its original size.

```
.vcard { transform : rotate(2deg) scale(1.05); }
```

A browser applies these transforms in order — reading from the left. In that last example, it will first `rotate` the `vcard` by two degrees clockwise (2deg), before increasing its size by five per cent (1.05). Watch as we apply a series of transforms, each one building on the last.

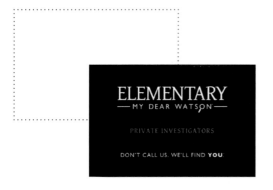

```
.vcard {
transform : translate(100px, 50%);
}
```

```
.vcard {
transform : translate(100px, 50%);
transform : rotate(30deg);
}
```

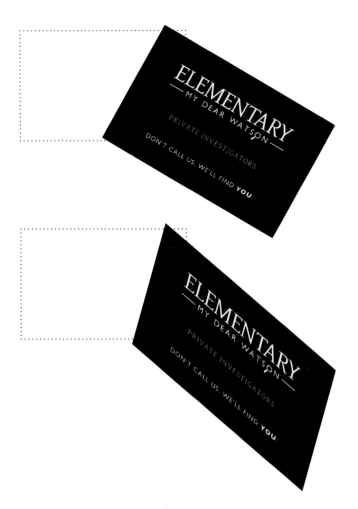

```
.vcard {
transform : translate(100px, 50%);
transform : rotate(30deg);
transform : scale(1.05);
}
```

```
.vcard {
transform : translate(100px, 50%);
transform : rotate(30deg);
transform : scale(1.05);
transform : skew(-15deg, -15deg);
}
```

Transforms see some action

It's time to put transforms to work by scattering those 'It's Hardboiled'
business cards across the detective's desk. To achieve the off-kilter design,
use rotate transforms and fine-tune their origins using the
transform-origin property.

The HTML we'll use is strictly hardboiled and you won't find a single
presentational element or attribute no matter how hard you look. There are
nine microformat vCards, each with its own set of values to describe every
detective's contact information. You won't even find a unique id on any
of the cards. Now that's hardboiled.

```
<div class="vcard">
    <h3 class="org">The No. 1 Lady Boys' Detective Agency</h3>
</div>

<div class="vcard">
    <h3 class="fn org">Shades &amp; Staches Detective Agency</h3>
</div>

<div class="vcard">
    <h3 class="fn org">Command F Detective Services</h3>
</div>

<div class="vcard">
    <h3 class="fn">The Fat Man</h3>
</div>

<div class="vcard">
    <h3 class="fn org">Hartless Dick</h3>
</div>

<div class="vcard">
    <h3 class="fn org">Nick Jefferies</h3>
</div>

<div class="vcard">
    <h3 class="fn org">Elementary My Dear Watson</h3>
</div>

<div class="vcard">
    <h3 class="fn org">Shoes Clues</h3>
</div>

<div class="vcard">
    <h3 class="fn org">Smoke</h3>
</div>
```

Let's start by writing styles that will be common to every vcard. We'll use absolute positioning to arrange them into a grid, then give each one its own coordinates in just a moment. Give all cards the same dimensions and apply the background-size property — you learned about that in Chapter 14 — to ensure that background images will always scale to fit, no matter how large we make the cards.

```
.vcard {
position : absolute;
width : 300px;
height : 195px;
background-size : 100% 100%;
}
```

To crack this design wide open, we'll apply different absolute positioning values to each card that will scatter them across the desk in a rough grid. Of course, each one will need a different background image too, but how? Remember, there wasn't a single presentational id or class attribute value anywhere in our HTML. It's time to get hardboiled again and select each vcard with the rarely used :nth-of-type pseudo-element selector.

Uncovering :nth-of-type

You've likely used an :nth- pseudo-element selector before. Maybe the last time
was :last-child to remove a border from the final item in list. Perhaps it was
adding a border to a paragraph that comes at the start of an article using :first-
child, like this:

```
p:first-child {
padding-bottom : 1.5em;
border-bottom : 1px solid rgb(229,228,216);
font-size : 1em;
}
```

So far, so good. Then some deadbeat goes and drops in another element before the
paragraph, maybe a list or a quotation. Those styles? Poof!

:nth-child selectors are fine in predictable situations (list items in an
unordered list, or rows in a table), but there's a more flexible option when we
need to style elements whose position we can't predict. Wouldn't it be better to
target an element based on its type and position in the document? That's exactly
what an :nth-of-type pseudo-element selector does, making it one of CSS's best-
kept secrets.

Want to target a first paragraph, no matter where it appears in the document
order? Not a problem. How about the thirteenth item in the fourth instance of
an unordered list? :nth-of-type will help you out there too. Target any element,
wherever it appears, without needing id or class attributes. Pretty damn powerful
and very hardboiled, don't you think?

:nth-of-type arguments

:nth-of-type will accept one of several arguments — keywords like odd and even,
a number or an expression. Sound complicated? Not really. I'll walk you through a
few examples.

Imagine you want to add a border under each odd numbered item in a list
(first, third, fifth, seventh, etc.) — :nth-of-type makes that easy. You won't need
to add classes in your HTML or use a JavaScript hack, just the odd keyword:

```
li:nth-of-type(odd) { border-bottom : 1px solid rgb(255,255,255); }
```

In the next example, an `:nth-of-type` selector makes the first paragraph in an article bold, no matter what comes before or after it in the document flow:

```
article p:nth-of-type(1) { font-weight : bold; }
```

Expressions are more complicated and we all scratch our heads the first time we encounter them. My tip is read expressions in reverse, from right to left, so in the example below, 3n+1 will match the first instance of a table row (1) followed by every third row (3n) after that:

```
tr:nth-of-type(3n+1) { background-color : rgb(255,255,255); }
```

6n+3 will match the third element, then every sixth one after that.

```
tr:nth-of-type(6n+3) { opacity : .8; }
```

Sitepoint published a thorough explanation of expressions[1]. Read it with a whisky and maybe some painkillers*.

---

[1] http://reference.sitepoint.com/css/understandingnthchildexpressions
* Legal disclaimer: I advise readers not to mix alcohol and drugs with CSS.

Remember that we applied absolute positioning to every vcard? Let's put that to use by giving each card its own top and left values to form them into a loose grid. Now would be a good time to add background images too.

```
.vcard:nth-of-type(1) {
top : 100px;
left : 0;
background : url(c01.jpg) no-repeat 50% 50%;
}

.vcard:nth-of-type(2) {
top : 80px;
left : 320px;
background : url(c02.jpg) no-repeat 50% 50%;
}

.vcard:nth-of-type(3) {
top : 100px;
left : 640px;
background : url(c03.jpg) no-repeat 50% 50%;
}

.vcard:nth-of-type(4) {
top : 320px;
left : 40px;
background : url(c04.jpg) no-repeat 50% 50%;
}

.vcard:nth-of-type(5) {
top : 270px;
left : 570px;
background : url(c05.jpg) no-repeat 50% 50%;
}
```

```
.vcard:nth-of-type(6) {
top : 320px;
left : 600px;
background : url(c06.jpg) no-repeat 50% 50%;
}

.vcard:nth-of-type(7) {
top : 540px;
left : 0;
background : url(c07.jpg) no-repeat 50% 50%;
}

.vcard:nth-of-type(8) {
top : 560px;
left : 320px;
background : url(c08.jpg) no-repeat 50% 50%;
}

.vcard:nth-of-type(9) {
top : 540px;
left : 640px;
background : url(c09.jpg) no-repeat 50% 50%;
}
```

As we only want the background images to show and not the HTML text, indent every element inside those cards to move them off-screen.

```
.vcard * { text-indent : -9999px; }
```

The design's starting to pull its weight, but that grid looks too stiff.

Let's loosen it up by rotating odd-numbered cards anticlockwise by two degrees (-2deg) by targeting them with an :nth-child selector:

```
.vcard:nth-child(odd) {
transform : rotate(-2deg);
transform-origin : 0 100%;
}
```

Now let's shake things up again, giving every third, fourth and sixth card different rotate values and every sixth card translate values that will nudge them off the grid:

By applying rotate and translate values to a few of the vcards, we make the design appear more natural in browsers that support those properties.

```
.vcard:nth-child(3n) { transform : rotate(2deg) translateY(-30px); }

.vcard:nth-child(4n) { transform : rotate(2deg); }

.vcard:nth-child(6n) {
transform : rotate(-5deg);
transform-origin : 0 0;
}
```

If you're still confused by :nth-child, try the *CSS Tricks* :nth-child Tester[1] to input expressions and watch as they're applied instantly.

[1] http://css-tricks.com/examples/nth-child-tester

I bet you've spotted my deliberate mistake. The fifth card has a portrait orientation whereas all others are landscape. Fix this by rotating that errant card ninety degrees clockwise (90deg). The transform origin rotates the card around its top left corner:

```
.vcard:nth-child(5n) {
transform : rotate(90deg);
transform-origin : 0 0;
}
```

The lonesome portrait format card looks best when we rotate it by ninety degrees clockwise (90deg) so it overlaps other cards.

Now it's time for a few finishing touches. Add not one, but two RGBa shadows using Modernizr's rgba class and two solid black borders using no-rgba:

```
.rgba .vcard {
box-shadow : 0 2px 1px rgba(0,0,0,.8), 0 2px 10px rgba(0,0,0,.5);
}


.no-rgba .vcard {
border-right : 1px solid rgb(0,0,0);
border-bottom : 2px solid rgb(0,0,0);
}
```

Zooming in on the design, soft RGBa shadow adds depth. You could choose to add two simple, solid borders to hint at three dimensions for browsers that don't support RGBa.

Enabling CSS3 selectors in older versions of Internet Explorer

Instead of adding `id` and `class` attributes that act purely as styling hooks, we can now use CSS3 selectors to bind styles to an element — `:nth-child`, `:only-child`, `:nth-of-type`, `:first-of-type`, `:last-of-type`, `:only-of-type` and `:empty` — to name just a few. These selectors have strong support in contemporary browsers, including Internet Explorer 9. What should we do about browsers that don't support CSS3 selectors? Go back to filling documents with presentational markup, making it fatter, slower and less agile? Thankfully, Keith Clark has developed Selectivizr[1], a JavaScript helper that plugs the holes in selector support in older versions of Internet Explorer.

If we're already using a JavaScript library like jQuery, MooTools or Prototype, simply link to Selectivizr on your server and let it do the rest.

```
<script src="jquery.min.js"></script>
<script src="selectivizr.js"></script>
```

Selectivizr works in tandem with most popular JavaScript libraries.

- DOMAssistant 2.7.4 / 2.8.0 http://www.domassistant.com
- Dojo 1.4.1 http://dojotoolkit.org
- jQuery 1.3 / 1.4 http://jquery.com
- MooTools 1.2.4 http://mootools.net
- NWMatcher 1.2.0 / 1.2.1 http://javascript.nwbox.com/NWMatcher
- Prototype 1.6.1 http://prototypejs.org
- YUI 2.8.0 http://developer.yahoo.com/yui

Wrap Selectivizr inside conditional comments and serve it only to the versions of Internet Explorer we need to patch.

```
<script src="jquery.min.js"></script>
<!--[if lte IE 8]>
<script src="selectivizr.js"></script>
<![endif]-->
```

---

[1] http://selectivizr.com

The selectors Selectivizr enables depend on the JavaScript library we use. If our preferred JavaScript library, for example jQuery, includes support for the selectors we need, simply add Selectivizr.

jQuery doesn't currently include support for several useful pseudo-class selectors, so if we need to use :nth-last-child, :only-child or :only-of-type, we'll also need to add DOMAssistant inside our conditional comments.

```
<script src="jquery.min.js"></script>
<!--[if lte IE 8]>
<script src="DOMAssistant-2.0.min.js"></script>
<script src="selectivizr.js"></script>
<![endif]-->
```

Selectivizr is small, fast and essential in helping us to use the CSS3 selectors we need to finally remove those presentational attributes from our HTML. It's already become an integral part of my hardboiled web design toolkit and should now be part of yours too.

Selectivizr currently supports only linked style sheets although we can use @import in our style sheets. Selectivizr will not modify embedded styles.

Back to our 'It's Hardboiled' design. Internet Explorer didn't support the :nth-of-type selector before version 9, but Selectivizr adds support for it in older versions. We'll also need to add remedial styles into an IE-specific stylesheet — we need only four positioning fixes to slap Internet Explorer into behaving:

```
.vcard:nth-of-type(4) {
top : 320px;
left : -20px;
}

.vcard:nth-of-type(5) {
z-index : 2;
top : 300px;
left : 320px;
}
```

The 'It's Hardboiled' author's page rendered by Internet Explorer 8. This design will intentionally look slightly different because that browser has no support for CSS transforms.

```
.vcard:nth-of-type(6) {
top : 320px;
left : 640px;
}


.vcard:nth-of-type(8) { top : 520px; }
```

Designing alternatives

Let's head back to outside the 'It's Hardboiled' office. Nobody's been by, so those notes are still stuck on the door. Remember the HTML? An `article` element and its related `aside`.

Modernizr tests a browser's ability to render CSS transforms. When it can, Modernizr adds its class of `csstransforms` to the `html` element. We'll use a descendent selector to apply a `skew` transform to the `article`, plus new positioning and margin values:

Skewing an element adds visual interest to a design and, before CSS transforms, was only possible by creating images in Photoshop.

```
.csstransforms article {
position : absolute;
z-index : 2;
top : 220px;
left : 50%;
margin-left : -60px;
transform : skew(10deg, -15deg);
}
```

When Modernizr finds support for transforms is lacking, it adds its no-
csstransforms class so that we can adjust those positioning and margin
values, and send incapable browsers an alternative, but still appropriate,
layout:

```
.no-csstransforms article  {
position : absolute;
z-index : 2;
top : 300px;
left : 50%;
margin-left : -60px;
}
```

Just because a browser has
no support for CSS transforms
does not mean we should
avoid using them. This design,
for browsers without support
for the skew transform,
remains totally appropriate.

Three-dimensional transforms

In 2009, Apple announced three-dimensional transforms in Safari running on Mac OS X Snow Leopard. These properties position elements in a three-dimensional space to add even more depth to our designs.

Apple's proposals have been adopted by the W3C and, as I'm writing (October 2010), three-dimensional transforms are currently supported by Safari running on Mac OS X Snow Leopard plus its iOS cousins. With this in mind, our hardboiled examples will only include WebKit's vendor prefix, plus the W3C's emerging standard syntax. You should keep up-to-date with news about Google Chrome, Firefox and Opera as they're sure to include 3-D transforms in future versions.

3-D Safari Sites[1] maintains a list of sites that use 3-D transforms. It's a list mainly of examples and personal sites. Why don't you go one better and develop a show-stopper of a site for a commercial client project?

Putting it all into perspective

Perspective is key in making elements appear three-dimensional. It takes transform properties and places them within a three-dimensional space. To enable perspective, we must apply it to a parent element and not to transformed elements themselves. To demonstrate perspective we won't need special HTML, just a division for each item and a parent hlisting division:

```
<div class="hlisting offer sale group">
    <div class="item">
        <a href="store.html"><img src="f-01.jpg" alt=""></a>
    </div>
    <div class="item">
        <a href="store.html"><img src="f-02.jpg" alt=""></a>
    </div>
    <div class="item">
        <a href="store.html"><img src="f-03.jpg" alt=""></a>
    </div>
    <div class="item">
        <a href="store.html"><img src="f-04.jpg" alt=""></a>
    </div>
</div>
```

[1] http://3dsafarisites.com

To begin styling this three-dimensional interface, set up styles that will be applied by all browsers. Float each item to the left, add margins and a wide, white border to those images:

```
.item {
float : left;
margin-right : 10px;
}


.item:last-child { margin-right : 0; }


.item img { border : 10px solid rgb(220,220,220); }
```

This interface looks neat and tidy, but it won't set your head spinning.

Now rotate the items horizontally by forty-five degrees (45deg):

```
.item {
-webkit-transform : rotateY(45deg);
transform : rotateY(45deg);
}
```

When we rotate these items in two dimensions they appear compressed.

Apply `perspective` to the parent `hlisting` division to transform its child
divisions in three-dimensional space.

```
.hlisting {
-webkit-perspective : 500;
perspective : 500;
}
```

Raising and lowering the `perspective` has this effect on each item:

```
.hlisting {
-webkit-perspective : 300;
perspective : 300;
}
```

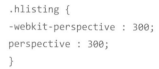

```
.hlisting {
-webkit-perspective : 1200;
perspective : 1200;
}
```

Changing our viewpoint

When we look at an element that's transformed in three dimensions, our default perspective is in the centre, both horizontally and vertically. We can change this `perspective-origin` using either keywords, pixel or em values, or percentages. In percentage terms, `0 50%` places the perspective viewpoint on the left, halfway down, while `50% 0` places it halfway horizontally and at the very top.

```
.hlisting {
-webkit-perspective-origin : 50% 0;
perspective-origin : 50% 0;
}
```

Watch how a different origin changes our perspective on these items:

```
.hlisting {
-webkit-perspective-origin : 0 0;
perspective-origin : 0 0;
}
```

```
.hlisting {
-webkit-perspective-origin : 0 100%;
perspective-origin : 0 100%;
}
```

```
.hlisting {
-webkit-perspective-origin : 50% 100%;
perspective-origin : 50% 100%;
}
```

```
.hlisting {
-webkit-perspective-origin : 100% 100%;
perspective-origin : 100% 100%;
}
```

Hardboiled in 3-D

First, CSS2 gave us the ability to position elements and a stacking order so we can arrange them using z-index. Then CSS3 introduced translate, which moves elements along x- and y-axes. Now, three-dimensional transforms give us translateZ, moving an element closer to or away from the viewer.

To demonstrate translateZ we'll carry on building that three-dimensional 'It's Hardboiled' store interface, but this time we'll flesh out our content by adding a description for each item. This description includes a heading and an 'add to basket' link:

```
<div class="hlisting offer sale group">
    <div class="item">
        <a href="store.html"><img src="fiction-01.jpg"
        alt="The Scarlet Menace"></a>
        <div class="description">
            <h3 class="fn">The Scarlet Menace</h3>
            <a href="store.html" class="action">Add to basket</a>
        </div>
    </div>
    […]
</div>
```

Now apply perspective to the outermost hlisting division, setting this value at 500.

```
.hlisting {
-webkit-perspective : 500;
perspective : 500;
}
```

Now, add width and padding to the descriptions, and position them relatively to move them up by 150 pixels. We'll also add a background colour and border:

Scaling in three dimensions

CSS3 includes other three-dimensional transform properties: `rotateZ` and `scaleZ`. `scaleZ` allows us to scale the element in exactly the same way as `scaleX` and `scaleY`, but along the z-axis. Or we can use the combined `scale3d` property to specify scaling along all three axes at once:

```
.item {
-webkit-transform : scale3d(scaleX, scaleY, scaleZ);
transform : scale3d(scaleX, scaleY, scaleZ);
}
```

```
.item .description {
position : relative;
top : -150px;
padding : 20px;
width : 120px;
background-color : rgb(57,53,70);
border : 10px solid rgb(220,220,220);
}
```

These simple styles will be applied by browsers of all capabilities

With our foundations steady, we'll work through the final components that make the interface appear three-dimensional.

Preserving 3-D

By default, when we apply `perspective` to an element, its children lie flat against a two-dimensional plane. The `transform-style` property gives us the option to either maintain this flattened behaviour, or raise elements off that plane using a value of `preserve-3d`.

All elements lie flattened against a two-dimensional plane by default. Applying `transform-style : flat;` sets this value explicitly.

For this design, we'll apply `preserve-3d` to every `item`, then lift their descriptions into three-dimensional space using `translateZ`. This will make the descriptions appear to be closer to the viewer by eighty pixels:

```
.item {
-webkit-transform-style : preserve-3d;
transform-style : preserve-3d;
}

.item div {
-webkit-transform : translateZ(80px);
transform : translateZ(80px);
}
```

Enhancing depth with box-shadow

To enhance the feeling of depth in this design, add RGBa shadows to the descriptions and images. To make sure that only browsers that are capable of 3-D transforms see these shadow declarations, prefix them with Modernizr's `csstransforms3d` class:

```
.csstransforms3d .item img {
-webkit-box-shadow : -5px 5px 15px rgba(0,0,0,.25);
box-shadow : -5px 5px 15px rgba(0,0,0,.25);
}

.csstransforms3d .item div {
-webkit-box-shadow : -20px 20px 30px rgba(0,0,0,.25);
box-shadow : -20px 20px 30px rgba(0,0,0,.25);
}
```

We can enhance the appearance of depth using `box-shadow` for browsers that are capable of rendering three-dimensional transforms.

Adding interactivity

Our interface is almost complete, but the eagle-eyed among you will have spotted that the items become difficult to read the more that `perspective` increases. To fix this, swing the items back to face the user when they mouse-over them. Do this by resetting the y-axis rotation to zero on `:hover`:

```
.item:hover {
-webkit-transform : rotateY(0);
transform : rotateY(0);
}
```

For good measure, we'll also reduce the amount of `translateZ` from eighty pixels to just five pixels and move the descriptions to the right by twenty pixels:

```
.item:hover div {
-webkit-transform : translateZ(5px) translateX(20px);
transform : translateZ(5px) translateX(20px);
}
```

When these descriptions move to their new positions, the shadows they cast fall in the wrong places. Help these shadows to appear more natural by altering their blur radii and transparency values.

```
.item:hover img {
-webkit-box-shadow : 0 5px 15px rgba(0,0,0,.25);
box-shadow : 0 5px 15px rgba(0,0,0,.25);
}

.item:hover div {
-webkit-box-shadow : 0 10px 15px rgba(0,0,0,.5);
box-shadow : 0 10px 15px rgba(0,0,0,.5);
}
```

Now open this 'It's Hardboiled' store interface in a capable browser and watch as the items change their rotations in three-dimensional space as your mouse passes over them.

Designing to browser capabilities with Modernizr

Three-dimensional transforms in non-WebKit browsers might be some way off, but should we let that cripple our creativity? I hope you're braver than that. Instead, we should provide an alternative, two-dimensional design to browsers that can't yet render elements in three dimensions. We can do this with Modernizr and just two additional declarations.

Adjust the shadow offsets and blur radii for Firefox, Google Chrome, Internet Explorer, Opera and Safari (not running on OS X Snow Leopard), then nudge the descriptions to the right by twenty pixels:

```
.no-csstransforms3d .item img {
-webkit-box-shadow : 0 5px 15px rgba(0,0,0,.25);
-moz-box-shadow : 0 5px 15px rgba(0,0,0,.25);
box-shadow : 0 5px 15px rgba(0,0,0,.25);
}


.no-csstransforms3d .item div {
left : 20px;
-webkit-box-shadow : 0 10px 15px rgba(0,0,0,.5);
-moz-box-shadow : 0 10px 15px rgba(0,0,0,.5);
box-shadow : 0 10px 15px rgba(0,0,0,.5);
}
```

To make sure that only browsers that are incapable of 3-D transforms see these shadow declarations, prefix them with Modernizr's `no-csstransforms3d` class:

Taking a hike

Finally, smooth the transitions between all of the state changes.

```
.item {
transition-property : transform;
transition-duration : .5s;
timing-function : ease-in-out;
}

.item div {
transition-property : transform, box-shadow;
transition-duration : .5s;
timing-function : ease-in-out;
}
```

Wait... what's that?

That's what we call a cliffhanger.

Keen to dig up more dirt on CSS3 transforms?

Edited by representatives from Apple, the **W3C's** 'CSS3 2D Transforms Module'
Working Draft is a dry read made more interesting by the questions they ask
(in red) about how to implement some CSS3 transforms in the future.

http://www.w3.org/TR/css3-2d-transforms

Apple's 'Safari CSS Visual Effects Guide' is filled with information on
transforms, transitions and animations and has more code examples than you
can hang a dirty raincoat on.

http://developer.apple.com/safari/library/documentation/InternetWeb/Conceptual/

SafariVisualEffectsProgGuide/Transforms/Transforms.html

'-moz-transform', from the horse's mouth at **Mozilla Developer Center**, covers
all the bases for making CSS3 transforms work in Gecko-based browsers.

https://developer.mozilla.org/en/CSS/-moz-transform

David Storey and Molly E. Holschlag's 'CSS3 transitions and 2D transforms' is
an excellent overview of CSS3 transforms (and the transitions that we'll cover
in the next chapter), published on **Opera's Developer Community**.

http://dev.opera.com/articles/view/css3-transitions-and-2d-transforms

Although his advice on using Microsoft Internet Explorer proprietary filters
should be ignored, **Jonathan Snook's** 'Text Rotation With CSS' is an otherwise
excellent and practical use of CSS3 transforms.

http://snook.ca/archives/html_and_css/css-text-rotation

John Allsopp's 'CSS3 Transforms Generator' is fantastic visual way of leaning
both two- and three-dimensional transforms with code to cut and paste for
Firefox, Opera and WebKit browsers.

http://www.westciv.com/tools/transforms/index.html

CSS3 transitions

IN WEB PAGES AND APPLICATIONS, changes in state can
have a huge impact on how an interface feels to use.
Make a change too fast and an interaction can feel
unnatural. Make it too slow, even by a few milliseconds,
and an interface will feel sluggish.

Remember when we transformed those links into faux buttons in Chapter
13? We could also have changed their appearance on mouse-over simply by
changing their background and text colours:

```
a.action {
background-color : rgb(143,58,58);
color : rgba(255,255,255,.5);
}

a.action:hover {
background-color : rgb(119,48,48);
color : rgb(255,255,255,);
}
```

By default, these style changes happen instantly, but using CSS transitions,
we can make them change over a specified period of time and control
acceleration and delay. CSS transitions have already been implemented
across a wide range of contemporary browsers and are now part of their
own developing CSS3 module'.

---

[1] http://www.w3.org/TR/css3-transitions
[2] http://www.w3.org/TR/css2/aural.html

A basic transition

CSS transforms currently need vendor-prefixes for WebKit, Mozilla and Opera, in addition to the W3C's standard syntax.

```
a.action {
background-color : rgb(143,58,58);
-webkit-transition-property : background-color;
-moz-transition-property : background-color;
-o-transition-property : background-color;
transition-property : background-color;
}
```

To keep these code examples simpler, I'll include only the W3C's standard declaration. The rest is up to you.

We can trigger transitions using dynamic pseudo-class selectors like :hover, :focus, :active and :target. Our first step is to specify which property or properties we want to transition. On our faux buttons, we need transition only the background colour, so use transition-property to specify this:

```
a.action {
background-color : rgb(143,58,58);
transition-property : background-color;
transition-duration : .25s;
}
```

Transition duration

Transitions change one or more styles over any number of seconds (s) or milliseconds (ms). These time units have, until now, only been used in aural style sheets[2]. To smooth the transition over a quarter of one second, add a duration of .25s.

```
a.action { transition-duration : .25s; }
```

If we set duration at zero (0) or omit the property altogether, there will be no transition and any state changes will happen immediately.

Notice how we include transition declarations on the element to be transitioned and not on a state change such as :hover. Now change the background colour for the link's :hover state:

```
a.action:hover { background-color : rgb(119,48,48); }
```

With this declaration in place, the faux button's background colour will now transition smoothly over a quarter of a second between those two shades of red.

We can apply transitions to any block-level or text-level element, as well as to :before and :after pseudo-elements. Here are some ideas of what you can do with them:

Background	Transition a background-color, CSS gradient or the background-position of a background-image on mouse-over.
Border	Emphasise a warning message by transitioning border-color, border-width or border-radius. We can also use outline for similar effects.
Colour	Smoothly transition text color when an element is moused over, :active or in :focus.
Dimensions	Transition width, height, min-width, max-width, min-height and max-height to make dynamic interfaces.
Font	Ease the transition between font-family, font-size or font-weight. For more control over typography, transition between letter-spacing, word-spacing and line-height values.
Margin and padding	Draw attention to an element by transitioning to new margin and padding values on :target.
Opacity	Add smooth fades and reveals by changing either the opacity or visibility of an element.
Position	Move smoothly between top, right, bottom and left and transition between z-index values to make simple animations from positioned elements.
Transform	Add transitions to transform property types like translate, scale, rotate and skew to bring interfaces to life.

Combining transitions

When we need two or more properties to transition — for example both a background colour and a text colour — separate each property with a comma.

```
a.action {
background-color : rgb(143,58,58);
color : rgba(255,255,255,.5);
transition-property : background-color, color;
}
```

We could otherwise group multiple properties into a single declaration using the all keyword.

```
a.action {
transition-property : all;
}
```

Delaying a transition

In the physical world, many objects we interact with don't turn on immediately upon pressing a button or flipping a switch. By default, CSS transitions start from the moment they're activated — we'll call that the zero point. We can add a sense of physical reality by adding a delay between the zero point and the start of a transition. Specify the amount of delay in either milliseconds (ms) or seconds (s).

```
a.action {
transition-delay : .1s;
}
```

Here, we added a delay of only a tenth of one second (.1s), from the zero point to the start of the background colour change. The same delay will also be applied when a property returns to its original state.

Accelerating a transition

Acceleration depends on the `transition-timing-function` we choose. For example, a `linear` transition will maintain a constant speed across its entire duration, whereas `ease` will gradually slow it down across the style change. Three more keywords are available to vary acceleration still further. They are:

`ease-in`	Starts slowly and gradually increases speed
`ease-out`	Starts quickly and reduces speed over time
`ease-in-out`	Smoothly transition text `color` when an element is moused over, `:active` or in `:focus`.

On our faux button links we'll specify a `linear` timing function:

The W3C's CSS3 Transitions Module [1] also includes the ability to plot a `transition-timing-function` along a custom bezier curve. This mathematical approach to timing is fascinating, but beyond the scope of this book.

```
a.action {
transition-property : background-color;
transition-duration : .25s;
transition-delay : .1s;
transition-timing-function : linear;
}
```

Applying multiple transitions

When we need two or more properties to transition, we can group them into a comma-separated list, then specify duration, delay and timing function values for each. First, we'll write these multiple transitions in longhand.

```
a.action {
transition-property : background-color, color;
transition-duration : .25s, .25s;
transition-delay : .1s, .1s;
transition-timing-function : linear, linear;
}
```

[1] http://www.w3.org/TR/css3-transitions/#transition-timing-functions

When the duration, delay or timing function values are the same, we only need write their value once.

```
a.action {
transition-property : background-color, color;
transition-duration : .25s;
transition-delay : .1s;
transition-timing-function : linear;
}
```

We can also combine all values into one comma-separated string.

```
a.action {
transition : background-color .25s .1s linear, color .25s .1s linear;
}
```

Practical transitions using vendor prefixes

Firefox, Google Chrome, Opera, Safari and a host of browsers on mobile devices have already implemented transitions. Microsoft hasn't yet indicated when transitions will be implemented in Internet Explorer. Should this stop us using transitions today? I hope not, because transitions degrade well and, when we use them appropriately, their absence will have no negative impact on less capable browsers.

For now, as the emerging standard matures, we need vendor prefixes to enable transitions in Mozilla, Opera and WebKit, followed by the official W3C syntax:

```
a.action {
-moz-transition-property : background-color, color;
-moz-transition-duration : .25s;
-moz-transition-delay : .1s;
-moz-transition-timing-function : linear;

-o-transition-property : background-color, color;
-o-transition-duration : .25s;
-o-transition-delay : .1s;
-o-transition-timing-function : linear;

-webkit-transition-property : background-color, color;
-webkit-transition-duration : .25s;
-webkit-transition-delay : .1s;
-webkit-transition-timing-function : linear;

transition-property : background-color, color;
transition-duration : .25s;
transition-delay : .1s;
transition-timing-function : linear;
}
```

That's quite a handful. Thankfully, we can squash that down to just four shorthand declarations:

```
a.action {
-moz-transition : background-color .25s .1s linear, color .25s .1s ↵
linear;
-o-transition : background-color .25s .1s linear, color .25s .1s ↵
linear;
-webkit-transition : background-color .25s .1s linear, color .25s ↵
.1s linear;
transition : background-color .25s .1s linear, color .25s .1s linear;
}
```

Transitions see some action

In the previous chapter we built a 3-D interface for the 'It's Hardboiled' store and I left you with a cliffhanger. Glance back over your shoulder if you need a recap, because now it's time to add transitions and rotate items forty-five degrees (45deg) in three-dimensional space. Then, to ensure that users can read our text, we'll turn the items back to face the viewer on :hover:

```
.item {
transform : rotateY(45deg);
transform-style : preserve-3d;
}
```

```
.item:hover { transform : rotateY(0); }
```

Set up this way, the transition will happen instantly. To make our interface feel more fluid, add transitions, first by defining transform as the property to transition:.

```
.item { transition-property : transform; }
```

Next, specify that the transition will take three quarters of one second (.75s) with an ease-in-out timing function:

```
.item {
transition-duration : .75s;
timing-function : ease-in-out;
}
```

When we need to shave a few bytes off our style sheets, we can combine these properties into a single shorthand declaration:

```
.item { transition : transform .75s ease-in-out; }
```

To give this 3-D interface added realism, use translateZ to make the descriptions appear to be closer to the viewer by eighty pixels. Then move it back and to the left, adjusting the strength of its shadow on :hover:

```
.item div {
transform : translateZ(80px);
box-shadow : -20px 20px 30px rgba(0,0,0,.25);
}
```

```
.item:hover div {
transform : translateZ(5px) translateX(20px);
box-shadow : 0 10px 15px rgba(0,0,0,.5);
}
```

We'll transition all of our state changes over a half of one second (.5s) and delay them by a fifth of one second (.2s).

```
.item div {
transition-property : transform, box-shadow;
transition-duration : 5s, 5s;
transition-delay : .2s, .2s;
timing-function : ease-in-out, ease-in-out;
}
```

Both transitions share the same duration, delay and timing function values, so we could simplify this declaration by combining two values into one:

```
.item div {
transition-property : transform, box-shadow;
transition-duration : .5s;
timing-function : ease-in-out;
}
```

Our design now feels more fluid and a user's interaction with it is more akin to what they might experience in the physical world.

Pulp fiction

Dave Shea's CSS Zen Garden[1] proved beyond any doubt that visual designs need not be tied to specific markup. With a hardboiled attitude and today's selectors and properties, we have more creative opportunities available than Dave could have imagined when he planted the Garden.

If you or your clients aren't ready for three-dimensional interfaces yet, we can use transitions to create an entirely different 'It's Hardboiled' store page.

This new interface won't require any changes to our HTML.
Here's a reminder:

```
<div class="hlisting offer sale group">
    <div class="item">
        <a href="store.html"><img src="fiction-01.jpg"
        alt="The Scarlet Menace"></a>

        <div class="description">
            <h3 class="fn">The Scarlet Menace</h3>
            <ul>
                <li>Volume 1 Number 3</li>
                <li>Issue #3</li>
                <li>May 1933</li>
            </ul>
            <a href="store.html" class="action">Add to basket</a>
        </div>
    </div>
[…]
</div>
```

To start laying the foundations for this design, float the items to the left
and give them dimensions and margins. We'll also establish each one as a
positioning context for its positioned child elements:

```
.item {
position : relative;
float : left;
height : 320px;
width : 220px;
margin : 0 10px 10px 0;
}
```

Forget everything you've read about absolute positioning being inflexible or unsuitable for dynamic content. With careful planning, absolute positioning can give us precise control, even in the most demanding situations. First, absolutely position the images inside their parent division and give them a solid white border:

```
.item img {
position : absolute;
border : 10px solid rgb(220,220,220);
}
```

Now make the descriptions wider than their containers and use negative absolute position values to move them to the left. Finish styling those descriptions by giving them a border and an RGBa background colour:

```
.item .description {
position : absolute;
width : 200px;
top : 0;
left : -10px;
padding : 10px;
background-color : rgba(57,53,70,.9);
border : 10px solid rgb(220,220,220);
}
```

Layering descriptions over images.

To create the bubbles, reposition the descriptions above the top of the images. To ensure that active bubbles always appear closest to the viewer, give them a higher z-index:

```
.item:hover .description {
top : -80px;
z-index : 3;
}
```

Next, add depth with two RGBa shadows, separating the values of each with a comma:

```
.item:hover .description {
box-shadow : 0 2px 5px rgba(0,0,0,.5), 0 8px 10px rgba(0,0,0,.25);
}
```

Adding depth with box shadows.

With our description bubbles inflated, hide them from view simply by making them fully transparent. We can reveal them again on :hover:

```
.item .description { opacity : 0; }
```

```
.item:hover .description { opacity : 1; }
```

By default, the changes in position and opacity will happen instantly, but we can use transitions to make it feel more fluid. First define top and opacity as the two properties to transition, followed by a half-second (.5s) duration and a timing function that slows the transitions as they progress:

```
.item .description {
transition-property : top, opacity;
transition-duration : .5s;
transition-timing-function : ease-out;
}
```

Now our bubbles slide and fade into view when a user mouses-over an item.

These bubbles now render correctly in a wide array of contemporary browsers. But what about less capable ones — those that haven't implemented either transitions or opacity? How do they handle this interface?

Browsers that don't support transitions will safely ignore them and we should remember that, as Dan Cederholm reminded us, websites don't need to be experienced exactly the same in every browser'.

Designing to browser capabilities with Modernizr

Modernizr tests for opacity support and adds either its opacity or no-opacity
class depending on the results. We'll use the latter to move the descriptions
under the images for opacity-impaired browsers:

```
.no-opacity .item { height : auto; }

.no-opacity .item img {
position : static;
float : left;
margin-bottom : .5em;
}

.no-opacity .item .description {
position : static;
width : auto;
top : auto;
left : auto;
padding : 0;
background-color : transparent;
border-width : 0;
text-align : left;
}

.no-opacity .item:hover .description { top : auto; }
```

Using Modernizr to provide
an alternative design for
browsers without support for
opacity.

Volume 1 Number 3
Issue #3
May 1933

Add to basket

Volume 1 Number 3
Issue #5
July 1933

Add to basket

Volume 4 Number 1
Issue #10
December 1933

Add to basket

Volume 4 Number 3
Issue #12
February 1934

Add to basket

Panel game

This next interface has an entirely different look and feel. Clicking on a book reveals a panel that contains its description. We'll build the panels using CSS positioning, `opacity` and transitions. We can reuse our HTML from the last example, but this time we'll need a unique `id` for each `item` so that we can address their fragments directly:

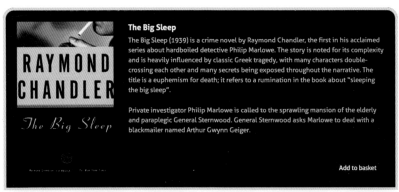

Here's an early look at the 'It's Hardboiled' store interface we're building. [1]

```
<div class="hlisting offer sale group">
    <div id="s01" class="item">
        <a href="store.html"><img src="fiction-01.jpg"
        alt="The Scarlet Menace"></a>
        <div class="description">
            <h3 class="fn">The Scarlet Menace</h3>
            <a href="store.html" class="action">Add to basket</a>
        </div>
    </div>
    [...]
</div>
```

[1] http://hardboiledwebdesign.com/v/c17-05

We'll also need an anchor that points back to its parent item:

```
<div id="s01" class="item">
    <a href="#s01"><img src="store-01.jpg" alt="The Big Sleep"></a>
</div>
```

Start adding dimensions to the hlisting division, then establish it as a
positioning context for any positioned child elements by applying relative
positioning without any offsets.

```
.hlisting {
position : relative;
height : 500px;
width : 710px;
}
```

It's time to get hardboiled by adding rounded corners and a linear gradient:

```
.hlisting {
border-top-left-radius : 10px;
border-top-right-radius : 10px;
background-image : linear-gradient(left top, rgb(240,240,240),
rgba(255,255,255,.1));
}
```

Next, size those inline images and position them so that they fit neatly at the
bottom of the panel. Later we'll use those same images as backgrounds, so they
need to be larger than they appear initially.

```
.item img {
position : absolute;
top : 330px;
width : 100px;
height : 150px;
}
```

```
#s01 img { left : 0; }
#s02 img { left : 120px; }
#s03 img { left : 240px; }
#s04 img { left : 360px; }
#s05 img { left : 480px; }
#s06 img { left : 600px; }
#s07 img { left : 720px; }
#s08 img { left : 840px; }
```

With planning, absolute positioning gives us fine control, even in the most demanding situations.

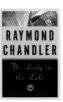

We don't want our descriptions to show until a user clicks on a book cover, so make every description small enough to position behind its respective cover. Setting overflow to hidden will make sure that long content won't escape and ruin our design:

```
.item .description {
position : absolute;
top : 335px;
width : 100px;
height : 150px;
overflow : hidden;
}
```

```
#s01 .description { left : 0; }
#s02 .description { left : 120px; }
#s03 .description { left : 240px; }
#s04 .description { left : 360px; }
#s05 .description { left : 480px; }
#s06 .description { left : 600px; }
```

Now tuck the descriptions behind the images by giving them a lower z-index and, to make sure they're not seen until we want them, set opacity to zero (0) so they'll be fully transparent:

```
.item img { z-index : 2; }

.item .description {
z-index : 1;
opacity : 0;
}
```

Earlier, we twisted the knife by pointing an anchor to its parent item. It's this anchor and the :target pseudo-class selector that make it possible to trigger the transformation of each description. Reset the descriptions' opacity and position, then resize them to fill the top of the listing panel. Add padding including a wide space on the left that will soon be filled with a background image.

```
.item:target .description {
opacity : 1;
top : 0;
left : 0;
width : 460px;
height : 290px;
padding : 20px 20px 0 220px;
}
```

Now to set background and border properties, common to every description:

```
.item:target .description {
background-color : rgb(241,239,232);
background-repeat : no-repeat;
background-position : 20px 20px;
background-size : auto 270px;
background-origin : padding-box;
border : 5px solid rgb(220,220,200);
border-top-left-radius : 10px;
border-top-right-radius : 10px;
}
```

Next, add a unique book cover background image to each description:

```
#s01:target .description { background-image : url(store-01.jpg); }
#s02:target .description { background-image : url(store-02.jpg); }
#s03:target .description { background-image : url(store-03.jpg); }
#s04:target .description { background-image : url(store-04.jpg); }
#s05:target .description { background-image : url(store-05.jpg); }
#s06:target .description { background-image : url(store-06.jpg); }
```

The panels are almost complete. When a user clicks on a book cover, a panel that contains its description will appear above. [1]

---

[1] http://hardboiledwebdesign.com/v/c17-09

Now we'll use transitions to make the interaction seem smoother and bring our interface to life. For each description, we'll transition four properties — top, width, height, and opacity — separating them using a comma:

```
.item .description {
transition-property : top, width, height, opacity;
}
```

Finally set a duration for each property:

```
.item .description { transition-duration : .5s, .5s, .75s, .5s; }
```

The changes to top, width and height will last half of one second (.5s) — the opacity change will last three quarters of one second (.75s)

Designing for landscape and portrait formats

When our HTML is hardboiled, we can more easily adapt our designs to satisfy the demands of different browsing environments including devices such as the iPad that can switch between portrait and landscape formats. While the layout we just made works fine in portrait, it doesn't fit so well into the iPad's landscape format.

You'll learn more about implementing orientation-specific layouts using CSS Media Queries later in Chapter 19. For now, let's set up a static layout optimised for a landscape format. You should be pleased to learn that this doesn't involve changing our HTML, just our CSS.

We'll start this alternative layout by changing the height of the `hlisting` division, from the previous example:

```css
.hlisting {
position : relative;
height : 330px;
width : 710px;
}
```

Next, resize those inline images and position them to form a new grid on the panel's left side:

```css
.item img {
position : absolute;
width : 100px;
height : 150px;
}
```

```css
#s01 img { top : 0; left : 0; }
#s02 img { top : 0; left : 120px; }
#s03 img { top : 0; left : 240px; }
#s04 img { top : 170px; left : 0; }
#s05 img { top : 170px; left : 120px; }
#s06 img { top : 170px; left : 240px; }
```

Laying out images into a grid.

Now we need to make the descriptions small enough to position behind their respective images:

```
.item .description {
position : absolute;
width : 100px;
height : 10px;
overflow : hidden;
}
```

```
#s01 .description { top : 0; left : 0; }
#s02 .description { top : 0; left : 120px; }
#s03 .description { top : 0; left : 240px; }
#s04 .description { top : 170px; left : 0; }
#s05 .description { top : 170px; left : 120px; }
#s06 .description { top : 170px; left : 240px; }
```

Set up the basis for transitions by giving each description a lower z-index than the corresponding images and set their opacity to zero (0):

```
.item img { z-index : 2; }

.item .description {
z-index : 1;
opacity : 0;
}
```

Use the :target pseudo-class selector to reset the opacity to one (1) and reposition and resize the descriptions to fill the right side of the panel. Also, add twenty pixels padding, a solid background colour and a border to complete the look:

```
.item:target .description {
top : 0;
left : 360px;
width : 390px;
height : 280px;
padding : 20px;
opacity : 1;
background-color : rgb(57,53,70);
border : 5px solid rgb(220,220,220);
}
```

For this interface, we'll use just two transition properties — height and opacity:

```
.item .description { transition-property : height, opacity; }
```

Set a duration for each transition property; half a second (.5s) for the change in height and three quarters of one second (.75s) for opacity:

Providing an alternative layout
for a landscape orientation.[1]

```
.item .description { transition-duration : .5s, .75s; }
```

To learn more about the creative possibilities that CSS transitions bring,
we'll round off this chapter by studying how two designers have already been
using them.

[1] http://hardboiledwebdesign.com/v/c17-12

Luke Dorny isn't afraid of making use of the most up-to-the-minute techniques, so on his personal site, Luke used CSS transitions to enhance his Twitter feed section':

Designers like Luke Dorny are proving every day that a subtle use of CSS transitions can have a huge effect on making an interface feel special.

```
<section id="twitter_div">
    <ul id="twitter_update_list">
        <li>@Malarkey I hear Smashing Magazine is a favourite</li>
        <li>@Malarkey But you live in a freakin' spaceship</li>
    </ul>
</section>
```

Using CSS transitions, Luke specified the background colour to change over two and a half seconds (2.5s), gradually picking up speed before finally tailing off. He then applied those same values to his shadow:

```
#twitter_div {
background-color : rgba(225,225,202,0);
box-shadow : 0 0 15px rgba(35,0,0,0.5);
transition : background-color 2.5s ease-in-out 2s, box-shadow 2.5s
ease-in-out 2s;
}
```

Luke included two time-based values — first a duration, then a two-second (2s) delay. Luke could also have written this, because the second time value — the delay — can be written anywhere in this shorthand string, as follows:

```
transition : background-color 2.5s 2s ease-in-out,
box-shadow : 2.5s 2s ease-in-out;
```

Staying with Luke and his work for a moment, we'll head back to the Butterlabel site we saw in the last chapter. Here, Luke and Scott Boms rotate their contact form, then return it to a fully upright position on :hover to help their users input information more easily:

```
#subscribe {
transform : rotate(-2deg);
box-shadow : 20px 20px 8px rgba(0,0,0,.2);
}

#subscribe:hover {
transform : rotate(0deg);
box-shadow : 1px 1px 1px rgba(0,0,0,0.8);
}
```

If the changes in rotation and the density of the shadow were to occur instantly, the effect would be jarring, so the Butterlabel partners spread their transition over a third of one second (.3s), gradually slowing it down across its duration:

This simple effect makes their interface feel more natural and also adds the element of surprise.

Why not find out when we release things?

Name:
Your callsign

Email:
name@email.tld

Do you skate?:
○ Yes.
○ No.
○ Are you kidding me?

Do you design?:
○ Nope.
○ Sometimes.
○ All day long!

Site:
http://site.tld

(Subscribe)

Occasional email newsletters. Your privacy is sacred. You'll never be spammed by us, except to promote ourselves, naturally.

```
#subscribe {
transition : transform .3s
  ease, box-shadow .3s ease;
}
```

Before we leave their site for the last time, let's see how Luke and Scott keep their visitors amused with a fake progress bar on Butterlabel's 404 page. The HTML is simple — a container division and two paragraphs, one with an id attribute applied:

expect. Instead of growing, it shrinks when a user moves over the parent division. To achieve this, Luke and Scott gave the bar an initial width of 150 pixels:

```
div.action p#progress-bar {
position: absolute;
left : 35px;
bottom : 36px;
height : 10px;
width : 150px;
background : transparent url(progress-bar.gif) repeat 100% 0;
text-indent : -1000em;
}
```

Then they transformed it to only ten pixels over a period of three seconds (3s):

```
div.action p#progress-bar { transition : width 3s ease; }
div.action:hover p#progress-bar { width : 10px; }
```

404 pages are so often overlooked, but Butterlabel's design keeps us inspired down to the very last detail.

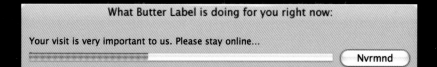

To confuse their visitors some more, this transition slows down as it progresses.

Breaking it up

How a web page or application 'feels' can have a huge impact on how often people use it. You learned from two talented designers how to add subtle transitions that can both delight a user and add the element of surprise to make using an interface more enjoyable.

On three different interfaces for the 'It's Hardboiled' store, the same HTML underpinned three very different interfaces using transitions tailored to make them appropriate for the lower capabilities of some browsers, without compromising the experience of people who use the best, most up-to-date browsers. Now that's hardboiled.

Keen to dig up more dirt on CSS3 transitions?

What better place to start than at the **W3C's** 'CSS3 Transitions Module'? It's a blast!

http://w3.org/TR/2009/WD-css3-transitions-20091201

David Storey and Molly E. Holschlag's 'CSS3 transitions and 2D transforms' is an excellent overview of CSS3 transitions, published on **Opera's Developer Community**.

http://dev.opera.com/articles/view/css3-transitions-and-2d-transforms

More from **Opera** — 'CSS3 Transitions support in Opera Presto 2.3' is a technical guide to transitions that includes a comprehensive list of animatable properties.

http://opera.com/docs/specs/presto23/css/transitions

Jason Cranford Teague knows a thing or two about CSS, having served on the CSS Working Group. His 'CSS Transitions 101' published on Web designer Depot is an excellent primer.

http://webdesignerdepot.com/2010/01/css-transitions-101

Trent Walton is a class act. In his authoritative 'CSS Three In Transition', Trent considers when transitions and animations are used best.

http://trentwalton.com/2010/03/22/css3-in-transition

CSS3 keyframe animations

CALL ME OLD-FASHIONED if you like, call me a shady character; hell, you can even call me a dumb mug. But no matter how sophisticated computer animation gets, for me it can never top the charm of the golden age cartoons I watched every day when I got home from school. Frankly, you can keep your *Shrek* — give me *The Perils Of Penelope Pitstop*[1] any afternoon.

Hanna–Barbera made animated shorts like these for over thirty years and it's their cartoons from the late '60s and early '70s that fascinate me most. The studio made five-minute episodes for a tenth of the budgets of other studios, and to keep costs to a minimum and their releases flowing, Hanna–Barbera stripped animation back to its bare essentials and animated only what was absolutely necessary to spin a story. I was fascinated to find out that shorts at that time might have averaged 26,000 individual drawings; Hanna–Barbera's, on the other hand, averaged only 1,200[2]. Their animations may have been low-fidelity but you have to admit their cartoons are still high-fidelity entertainment.

Animation on the web has traditionally been low-fidelity and shares a common ground with the early work of Hanna–Barbera. Compare the animation techniques of *The Perils Of Penelope Pitstop* with *The Goddamn George Liquor Program*[3], which was one of the first Flash cartoons made for the web. You'll track down both on YouTube.

Such web-delivered keyframe-based animations have always been the domain of Flash because equivalents couldn't easily be created using open standards. That's until now, with support for the CSS3 Animations Module in WebKit-based browsers[4]. This is certainly a breakthrough and other browsers are likely to follow suit soon.

---

[1] http://en.wikipedia.org/wiki/The_Perils_of_Penelope_Pitstop
[2] http://en.wikipedia.org/wiki/Hanna-Barbera_Productions
[3] http://en.wikipedia.org/wiki/The_Goddamn_George_Liquor_Program
[4] http://www.w3.org/TR/css3-animations

Keyframe animation

'Keyframes' are defining moments inside the timeline of an animation. They're moments when an object changes from one state to another; for example, its position, direction, size, shape, rotation or colour. Now, imagine we want a shadow to move across the 'It's Hardboiled' office door.

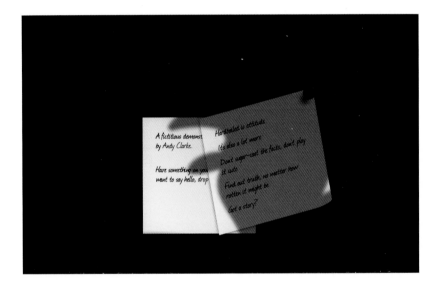

With CSS animations we can specify one or more positions for that shadow and the animation will transition smoothly between these positions.

CSS animations have three component parts: an at-rule containing the name of an animation; definitions of the different keyframe states; and then various animation properties. The at-rule looks like this:

To keep these code examples simpler, I'll include only the W3C's standard declaration. Adding vendor-specific prefixes is up to you.

```
@keyframes shadow {
0% { left : 0; }
25% { left : 475px; }
50% { left : 950px; }
75% { left : 1425px; }
100% { left : 1900px }
}
```

We've called this animation `shadow` and we'll use the name to reference it later. Each percentage refers to an animation keyframe plus the values of each property at each point (in this case, moving an element by varying its `left` position value). With the animation defined, we can define its other properties, like:

`animation-name`	The name of the animation, as defined in the at-rule.
`animation-duration`	The length of time an animation takes to complete one iteration. We can specify a duration in seconds (`s`) or milliseconds (`ms`).
`animation-timing-function`	Similar to a CSS transition's timing function, animation timing functions control acceleration. A `linear` animation will maintain a constant speed throughout its entire duration, whereas `ease` will gradually slow down as the animation progresses
`animation-iteration-count`	The number of times an animation will be played from beginning to end. We can specify whole numbers (1, 2, 5, 10, etc.) or use the keyword `infinite` when we need animations to play continuously. The default value is 1, so we won't need to include this property when an animation will play only once.
`animation-delay`	The length of time between an animation being triggered and when it starts to play. We can specify this optional delay in seconds (`s`) or milliseconds (`ms`).
`animation-direction`	The direction an animation plays. The default `normal` keyword plays each iteration forwards, from start to finish. `alternate` first plays an animation forwards, then in reverse from the end back to the beginning.

These may seem complicated, but when you get used them, you'll be animating like a pro in no time. To help get a better understanding, lets walk through the creation of our animated shadow.

Defining an animation

We'll start by stating the name of the animation inside the at-rule:

```
@keyframes shadow { }
```

Next, add the properties to be animated as well as the keyframes when changes will occur. We can use percentages 0% and 100%:

```
@keyframes shadow {
0% { right : -100%; }
100% { right : 100%; }
}
```

or the keywords from and to

```
@keyframes shadow {
from { right : -100%; }
to { right : 100%; }
}
```

Hold on one Goddamn minute! Why did we add a per cent symbol to a zero value? Surely zero is zero, regardless of the unit? That is true of most values in CSS (pixels, ems, line-height, etc.), but it's important to add % when we're animating or our animations won't play. When we need more precision, specify any number of keyframes between 0% and 100%.

```
@keyframes shadow {
0% { right : -100%; }
25% { right : -50%; }
50% { right : 0%; }
75% { right : 50%; }
100% { right : 100%; }
}
```

In that example, we're moving an element by changing its `right` position value in five increments, but there are plenty more properties we could animate:

background-color	background-image (gradients)	background-position
background-position	border-bottom-width	border-color
border-left-color	border-left-width	border-right-color
border-right-width	border-spacing	border-top-color
border-top-width	border-width	bottom
color	crop	font-size
font-weight	height	left
letter-spacing	line-height	margin-bottom
margin-left	margin-right	margin-top
max-height	max-width	min-height
min-width	opacity	outline-color
outline-offset	outline-width	padding-bottom
padding-left	padding-right	padding-top
right	text-indent	text-shadow
top	vertical-align	visibility
width	word-spacing	z-index

We might animate the background colour or border on a form element to make it blink when a user fails to complete all required fields. We could also animate the opacity of a warning message so that it fades away after a few seconds, as 37signals do so well in their applications. We can even animate z-index to shuffle the stacking order of photographs on a portfolio site.

With an animation defined, apply it to one or more elements. For the hardboiled detective's shadow, our HTML will consist of just one empty division we have given an id of shadow.

We'll position this absolutely, add a semi-transparent background image, and then apply the shadow animation:

```
.shadow {
z-index : 3;
position : absolute;
top : 0;
right : -100%;
width : 880px;
height : 1000px;
background-image : url(shadow.png);
background-repeat : no-repeat;
background-position : 0 0;
}
```

Controlling the animation

How long will it take for that shadow to walk across the screen? Whoever's casting it is moving slowly, so set the animation's duration to twenty seconds (20s):

```
.shadow { animation-duration : 20s; }
```

This shady character is in no hurry and the speed he moves at is linear — it doesn't speed up, doesn't slow down:

```
.shadow { animation-timing-function : linear; }
```

Whoever he is, whatever his plans, this shadowy figure is certainly persistent — he walks by that door ten times:

```
.shadow { animation-iteration-count : 10; }
```

Finally, to keep anyone who might be watching on their toes, we'll delay his walk for five seconds (5s) before the animation starts playing.

```
.shadow { animation-delay : 5s; }
```

Walking across the 'It's Hardboiled' door.

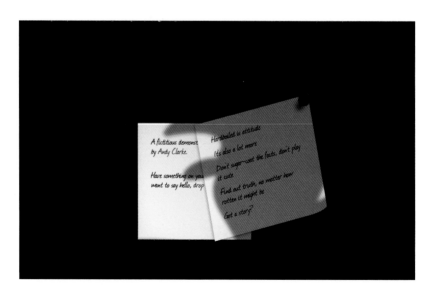

Designing to browser capabilities with Modernizr

Modernizr tests for a browser's ability to render CSS animations. When a browser can, we isolate animations by using a descendent selector from Modernizr's cssanimations class.

When animations aren't supported, provide an alternative design descending from Modernizr's no-cssanimations class.

```
.no-cssanimations .shadow {
left : 50%;
margin-left : -440px;
}
```

Some designers and developers have already embraced CSS animations, so let's study how they have been using them to learn more about their creative possibilities.

massiveBLUe

On his Massive Blue' portfolio, Sam Brown uses RGBa to blend the colour of elements with his backgrounds. On his home page, Sam uses CSS keyframe animations to cycle through seven background colours. Sam started by defining the background colour of his pages in an external style sheet.

This background colour will be displayed by all browsers regardless of their animation abilities.

```
body {
background-color : #39f;
}
```

He then defined an animation named colours in an embedded style rule. This cycles through the default and six additional background colours.

```
@keyframes colours {
0% { background-color: #39f; }
15% { background-color: #8bc5d1; }
30% { background-color: #f8cb4a; }
45% { background-color: #95b850; }
60% { background-color: #944893; }
75% { background-color: #c71f00; }
90% { background-color: #bdb280; }
100% { background-color: #39f; }
}
```

Sam wanted his animation to change the background colour once every minute (60s) in an infinite loop, so he set the animation's iteration count to infinite.

CSS animations needn't be over the top; they can be subtle. The technique that Sam Brown used can be applied to any element.

```
body {
animation-name : colours;
animation-duration : 60s;
animation-iteration-count : infinite;
}
```

' http://massiveblue.com
² http://hardboiledwebdesign.com/v/c18-05

Designer Tim Van Damme is never afraid to make use of new technologies and for his Made By Elephant portfolio site[1] he used CSS animations to make his current status message pop. Tim started with just a single wrapper division, containing a heading and a paragraph.

Tim Van Damme was one of the first designers to experiment with CSS animations. He wrote an article including several clever examples in a 2009 article on 24ways.[2]

```
<div id="wrapper">
    <h1>Made by Elephant</h1>
    <p>Made by Elephant is currently not accepting any new projects.
    If you want to get in touch you can always shoot me an email.
    Follow Tim on Twitter or read his overrated blog.</p>
</div>
```

This animated status message pops using a scale transform. Tim defined an at-rule animation name he called pop; then, to achieve a natural looking result, Tim changed the scaling factor in three, irregularly spaced keyframes — at 0% (from), 85% and at 100% (to).

```
@keyframes pop {
from { transform : scale(.1); opacity : 0; }
85% { transform : scale(1.05); opacity : 1; }
to { transform : scale(1); }
}
```

You might have noticed that Tim animated two properties to make his status message pop: a scale transform; and opacity. There's no limit to the number of properties we can combine to build an animation. Simply list each one in order, inside a single keyframe.[3]

Tim applied his pop animation to the wrapper division, setting it to play once with an iteration count of one. The animation lasts for a second (1s) and accelerates towards its end.

```
#wrapper {
animation-name : pop;
animation-duration : .5s;
animation-iteration-count : 1;
animation-timing-function : ease-in;
}
```

[1] http://madebyelephant.com
[2] http://24ways.org/2009/css-animations
[3] http://hardboiledwebdesign.com/v/c18-06

If you've no idea what Jon's
handbag-raising antics are
all about, read his blog entry
about the origins of
oo00.eu[3] and watch the video
clip from the classic BBC
Shooting Stars game show.

Jon Hicks' has an eye not only for great design but also for the absurd. Jon's oo00.eu[2] (that's two Os, two zeros and a European Union) used CSS animations, HTML5 audio and web fonts to raise his handbag at any "comment of a bumptious, snide or haughty nature". To "dislodge a pilgrim from the edge of time", Jon used two elements — one image and an empty division to create his shadow:

```
<div id="bag">
  <img src="handbag.png" alt="handbag" id="ooooh">
  <div id="shad"></div>
</div>
```

Jon's animation consists of not one, but two transform properties — scale and rotate — and his handbag shakes between three degrees clockwise (3deg) and anticlockwise (-3deg). Jon also defined individual position values in each of his nine keyframes:

```
@keyframes ooh {
0% { top : 0px; transform : scale(1.0) rotate(0deg); }
5% { top : -100px; transform : scale(1.0) rotate(1deg); }
10% { top : -100px; transform : scale(1.0) rotate(-3deg); }
15% { top : -100px; transform : scale(1.0) rotate(3deg); }
20% { top : -110px; transform : scale(1.3) rotate(-6deg); }
25% { top : -100px; transform : scale(1.0) rotate(3deg); }
30% { top : -100px; transform : scale(1.00) rotate(-2deg); }
35% { top : 0; transform : scale(1.0)rotate(0deg); }
100% { top : 0; transform : scale(1.0)rotate(0deg); }
}
```

Jon positioned the handbag image absolutely and applied his ooh animation — setting it to play for three iterations over six seconds (6s):

[1] http://hicksdesign.co.uk
[2] http://oo00.eu
[3] http://hicksdesign.co.uk/journal/the-handbag-has-been-raised

```
#ooooh {
position : absolute;
top : 0;
-webkit-animation-name : ooh;
animation-name : ooh;
-webkit-animation-iteration-count : 3;
animation-iteration-count : 3;
-webkit-animation-duration : 6s;
animation-duration : 6s;
}
```

Two bags against one is strong! To make the waving bag more realistic, Jon
added an animated shadow using an empty division and an alpha-transparent
PNG background image. Jon animated the shadow division's opacity from
fully opaque to semi-transparent and back again over five keyframes:

```
@keyframes shadow {
0% { opacity : 1 }
5% { opacity : .4 }
30% { opacity : .4 }
35% { opacity : 1 }
100% { opacity : 1}
}
```

Finally, he applied this shadow animation and made
sure that its opacity changes in time with the
movement of the bag by using the same iteration
count and duration:

```
shad {
-webkit-animation-name : shadow;
animation-name : shadow;
-webkit-animation-duration : 6s;
animation-duration : 6s;
-webkit-animation-iteration-count : 3;
animation-iteration-count : 3;
-webkit-animation-timing-function : ease-in-out;
animation-timing-function : ease-in-out;
}
```

CSS animations see some action

In the last few chapters, we used transforms and transitions to make interfaces for the 'It's Hardboiled' store. Now we'll build on everything you've learned so far to make one final interface that combines transforms, transitions and CSS animations.

We won't need to write new markup for this new interface. Instead we can reuse the markup pattern we've been using throughout. It's hardboiled — just a series of divisions wrapped a single container.

For this interface we'll need one extra wrapper division inside each item to which we'll apply our three-dimensional transforms. I wish this presentational element wasn't needed, but we shouldn't beat ourselves up if our HTML is already stripped bare and there's simply no other way to achieve a result we need.

Inside each item we include a book cover, plus a description containing extra information:

```
<div id="s01" class="item">
    <div class="inner">
        <a href="#s01"><img src="store-01.jpg" alt=""></a>
        <div class="description">
            <h3 class="fn">The Big Sleep by Raymond Chandler</h3>
            <p>[…]</p>
            <a href="store.html" title="Add The Big Sleep" ↵
            class="action">Add to basket</a>
        </div>
    </div>
</div>
```

We'll start styling this interface by floating every item to the left and giving them dimensions and margins. We'll also establish them as positioning contexts for their absolutely positioned images and descriptions:

```
.cssanimations .item {
float : left;
position : relative;
height : 330px;
width : 220px;
margin : 0 20px 40px 0;
}
```

Position the images absolutely and give them a solid border:

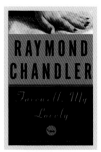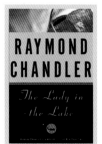

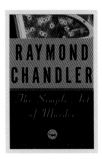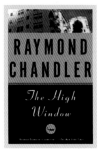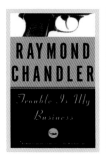

By default, the descriptions will appear in front of, and obscure, the cover images.

```
.cssanimations .item img {
position : absolute;
border : 10px solid rgb(255,255,255);
}
```

Then position those descriptions, giving them dimensions, padding and a solid background colour and border:

```
.cssanimations .item .description {
position : absolute;
width : 160px;
height : 270px;
padding : 20px;
background-color : rgb(57,53,70);
border : 10px solid rgb(220,220,220);
}
```

In this interface, each item will be rotated around 180 degrees (180deg) to reveal its description. As the rotation must appear three-dimensional, we'll add perspective to each item:

```
.cssanimations .item {
perspective : 400;
}
```

Make the transform appear three-dimensional by preserving its description's 3-D appearance:

```
.cssanimations .item .inner {
transform-style : preserve-3d;
}
```

We'll declare transform as the transition property, then the duration of the transition. We'll choose one second (1s):

```
.cssanimations .item .inner {
transition-property : transform;
transition-duration : 1s;
}
```

We won't want the descriptions to appear until after the transitions have been triggered, so rotate them horizontally by 180 degrees (180deg) to make them disappear behind the cover images:

```
.cssanimations .item .description {
transform : rotateY(180deg);
}
```

Now hide the back of the book covers using the backface-visibility property so that when items are rotated, a user will only see the descriptions and not the images in reverse:

```
.cssanimations .item img {
backface-visibility : hidden;
}
```

Finally, trigger the rotating transition using the :target pseudo-class selector. This transition will start immediately that any item becomes the target of a link.

```
.cssanimations .item:target .inner {
transform : rotateY(-180deg);
}
```

Sweating the details

Our interface is shaping up, but there are still details we need to sweat. When items are rotated to show their descriptions, we lose the visual link between the written text and its associated book cover image.

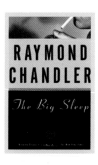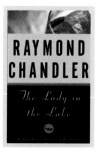

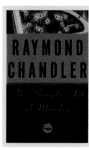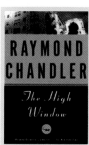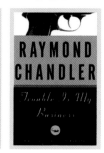

Let's fix that now.

A small image could help restore the balance but we haven't included a thumbnail in our HTML. With lateral thinking, background sizing properties and CSS generated content, we can add faux thumbnail images without changing our markup.

We'll use the `:before` pseudo-element to insert a one pixel square transparent image before the heading. Float the generated image to the left, give it dimensions, then add a solid white border:

```
.cssanimations .item .description h3:before {
content : url(ihatetimvandamme.png);
display : block;
float : left;
width : 60px;
height : 90px;
margin : 0 10px 5px 0;
border : 5px solid rgb(220,220,220);
}
```

This generated placeholder image won't appear in the DOM, but we can style it as if it was.

The placeholder image may be transparent, but we can see already how the descriptions are now shaping up. Next, apply individual background images to each description, making use of the `id` attributes we gave each `item`. Size the background images to match the transparent placeholder and position them over the top to create the illusion that the thumbnails have been styled with the borders we added to the placeholder image:

```
.cssanimations .item .description {
background-repeat : no-repeat;
background-position: 25px 25px;
background-size : 60px 90px;
}
```

These faux thumbnails improve both the look and usability of the flipped descriptions but they make less sense when we can see the larger covers.

We gave items their own `id` attributes so we can reuse their inline image sources as background images:

```
.cssanimations .item#s01 .description {
background-image : url(store-01.jpg); }

.cssanimations .item#s02 .description {
background-image : url(store-02.jpg); }
```

```
.cssanimations .item#s03 .description {
background-image : url(store-03.jpg); }

.cssanimations .item#s04 .description {
background-image : url(store-04.jpg); }

.cssanimations .item#s05 .description {
background-image : url(store-05.jpg); }

.cssanimations .item#s06 .description {
background-image : url(store-06.jpg); }

.cssanimations .item#s07 .description {
background-image : url(store-07.jpg); }

.cssanimations .item#s08 .description {
background-image : url(store-08.jpg); }
```

By using Modernizr's added `cssanimations` class in our declarations, our faux thumbnails will only be visible in browsers that have implemented CSS animations. Less capable browsers will ignore these declarations and won't display the thumbnail background images.

Flipping the bird

It's time to add an animation which plays when the 'It's Hardboiled' store first loads. This will spin every `item` and display their descriptions to show users that extra content is hidden behind every book cover.

Set up an animation called `bookflip`. This will rotate an element horizontally from zero degrees (`0deg`) to 180 degrees (`180deg`) and back again over three keyframes:

```
@keyframes bookflip {
from { transform : rotateY(0deg); }
50% { transform : rotateY(180deg); }
to { transform : rotateY(0deg); }
}
```

Apply the `bookflip` animation to each item's `inner` container. It will only flip once, last for two seconds (2s) and accelerate before tailing off.

```
.cssanimations .item .inner {
animation-name : bookflip;
animation-duration : 2s;;
animation-iteration-count : 1;
animation-timing-function : ease-in-out;
}
```

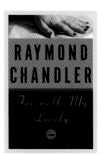
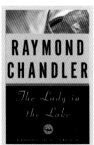

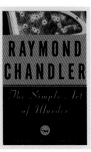
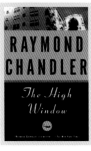
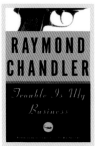

Targeting a rotation

To create a staggered sequence of bookflip animations, set delays that start each animation half a second (.5s) prior to the previous animation completing a rotation:

```css
.cssanimations .item#s01 .inner {
animation-delay : 1s;
}

.cssanimations .item#s02 .inner {
animation-delay : 1.5s;
}

.cssanimations .item#s03 .inner {
animation-delay : 2s;
}
.cssanimations .item#s04 .inner {
animation-delay : 2.5s;
}

.cssanimations .item#s05 .inner {
animation-delay : 3s;
}

.cssanimations .item#s06 .inner {
animation-delay : 3.5s;
}

.cssanimations .item#s07 .inner {
animation-delay : 4s;
}

.cssanimations .item#s08 .inner {
animation-delay : 4.5s;
}
```

Designing for a browser's capabilities

Apple's proposals for CSS animations have been adopted by the W3C, but animations in non-WebKit browsers like Firefox, Opera and Internet Explorer might be some way off. Should the newness of CSS animations prevent us from using them for the millions of people who use WebKit-based browsers on desktops, laptops, tablets and smartphones? Of course not.

Instead we can design alternative, appropriate experiences for people who use browsers that have different or lower capabilities. This hardboiled approach helps us to create engaging experiences for better browsers and not be limited to the capabilities of less capable ones.

Modernizr's `no-cssanimations` class allows us to serve an alternative design to browsers that can't render CSS animations. Three extra declarations are all we need for this alternative design.

Using a selector descended from `no-cssanimations`, we'll float each `item` to the left, but this time give them a width that's capable of fitting both the cover images and descriptions side-by-side:

```
.no-cssanimations .item {
float : left;
height : 330px;
width : 450px;
}
```

Now simply float the images and descriptions so that they fit along side each other:

```
.no-cssanimations .item img,
.no-cssanimations .item .description {
float : left;
}
```

Now apply a background colour and a border and, to prevent odd looking double borders between elements, remove the left border from the descriptions:

It shouldn't come as a surprise to learn that we'll use Modernizr to test a browser's ability to render CSS animations. This will help us isolate animations using a descendant selector from the cssanimations class Modernizr adds.

```
.no-cssanimations .item img,
.no-cssanimations .item .description {
border : 10px solid rgb(220,220,220);
}

.no-cssanimations .item .description {
width : 170px;
height : 270px;
padding : 20px;
background-color : rgb(240,240,240);
border-left-width : 0;
}
```

Of course, this design of our interface won't look exactly the same in browsers that support CSS animations and others like Internet Explorer that don't. This should be perfectly acceptable for two reasons.

First, the design looks great in every browser and is appropriate to any browser's capabilities. This is one of the fundamental principles of the hardboiled approach. Second, users won't know about the differences between browsers. Ignorance is bliss.

Designing an appropriate alternative for less capable browsers.

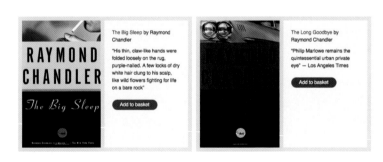

Breaking it up

Why settle for static designs when we can make them pop and delight our users using CSS keyframe animations? These properties may be experimental, but they're part of the W3C's standards development process and many talented designers are already making the most of them.

Using emerging standards such as these means designing from the top down, for the best browsers first. Does that mean that people who use older, less capable browsers get a different experience? Yes it does, but don't regard these differences negatively. Instead, we should embrace them as ways to make our creativity shine.

Keen to dig up more dirt on CSS3 animations?

Why not start with the blog post that first introduced CSS Animations, posted by WebKit's Dean Jackson on the **Surfin' Safari** blog?

http://webkit.org/blog/324/css-animation-2

Keep on top of the **W3C**'s CSS3 Animations Module as the emerging standard develops.

http://www.w3.org/TR/css3-animations

The animation section of **Apple**'s 'Safari CSS Visual Effects Guide' is a great companion to this book as it covers in more detail how to trigger events using JavaScript for both desktop operating systems and touch devices like the iPad, iPhone and other WebKit based smartphone browsers.

http://developer.apple.com/safari/library/documentation/InternetWeb/Conceptual/

SafariVisualEffectsProgGuide/Animations/Animations.html#//apple_ref/doc/uid/TP40008032-CH6-SW1

Tim Van Damme's 'CSS Animations' article for 24ways demonstrates how to accomplish several animated visual effects.

http://24ways.org/2009/css-animations

Zurb's explanation of how to combine CSS animations with RGBa colour to create 'Radioactive Buttons' shows how we can use CSS animations now to enhance a user's interaction with our sites and applications.

http://www.zurb.com/playground/radioactive-buttons

CSS3 Media Queries and multi-column layout

I'M OFTEN ASKED how I explain to my clients why a website can't and shouldn't look (or be experienced) exactly the same in every browser. In the past, that's been something of a tough sell, but over the last few years it's become a whole lot easier.

When I wrote *Transcending CSS*[1] in 2006 the mobile web wasn't the booming phenomenon we know today. There were no iOS or Android devices and very few mobile browsers could render websites anywhere near close to a desktop experience. People thought about websites mostly in terms of desktop browsers.

Today, it's different, as users have amazing browsing experiences on a multitude of devices, including desktop browsers, smartphones, tablets and more. This creates challenges about how we should design for different screen sizes, resolutions and interfaces, including those that we touch, as well as point to with a mouse. More than that, it calls into question what it really means to design for the web today.

I don't intend this chapter to be a complete guide to mobile web design — to attempt that would be dumb — but we'll round off this book by exploring two hardboiled CSS3 modules that will make designing responsive layouts a whole lot easier — Multi-column Layout and Media Queries.

---

[1] http://transcendingcss.com

CSS3 multi-column layout

You've probably guessed from its title that the CSS3 Multi-column Layout Module' provides a standardised way to create multiple-column layouts with CSS, without us needing to use the float and positioning methods we've all come to know.

We'll dive right in with a multi-column layout example from the 'It's Hardboiled' home page. On the latest story, columns reduce the measure and help to make the content more readable. To achieve this, we'd traditionally add a fixed number of divisions, then float them to create columns.

```
<div>
    <img src="hentry-01.jpg" alt="">
    <p>Sometimes you let the madness get to you, sometimes you don't.
    Sometimes the only way to get through the day is to blaze with a
    crazy anger that tells everyone within earshot that they should
    stay the hell out of your way. Today was one of those days.</p>
</div>

<div>
    <p>I went as far as the front door and fired up a smoke, drawing
    deep. The cold winter air on my face and the feeling of smoke
    filling my lungs made me feel human again.</p>
</div>

<div>
    <p>That was as far as I could get. The reflection that stared back
    at me in the window told me that I looked like hell. I sneered
    back in it's face, took another deep drag and flicked the butt
    outside.</p>
</div>
```

¹ http://www.w3.org/TR/css3-multicol/

There's nothing inherently wrong with this familiar technique. It's easy to implement and, for the most part, reliable. That's why we see it used on countless websites. Today, though, the disadvantages of using this technique are beginning to outweigh the advantages: we can no longer rely on a user employing a traditional, landscape format browser.

Columns in the modern age

The iPad is currently one of the most talked about devices and Apple makes a feature of the device's ability to display websites in landscape and portrait formats. When we hold an iPad in portrait mode (or use a low resolution monitor), it makes sense for the latest story on the 'It's Hardboiled' home page to be presented in two columns.

The measure — the line length — works best with two columns in the iPad's portrait orientation.

Turn the iPad into landscape mode (or use a larger monitor) and two columns work less well, because the line length now makes reading less comfortable. In landscape format, three columns and a narrower measure make more sense.

Three columns and a narrower measure make the text more readable in the iPad's landscape format.

When we develop pages using the traditional, floated division method, our options for adapting a layout to work best in different orientations are limited. Sure, we can change divisions' widths or prevent them from floating, but adding or removing columns entirely, without making changes to the structure of our markup, is impossible. That's why we need to look beyond traditional techniques to help our sites adapt more easily.

Wouldn't it be amazing if layouts could automatically change the number of columns to optimise a user's reading experience? Guess what? With CSS columns they can.

Out with the old and in with the old

When I sat down to write about CSS columns for this book, I read back what I'd written in *Transcending CSS* four years ago. I can clearly remember my frustrations that only Firefox (1.5) supported them.

Today, the situation is far better because Safari and Google Chrome have also implemented large parts of the CSS3 Multi-column Layout Module. I'm optimistic that columns will soon be a part of Opera too.

The fact that CSS columns have been implemented in WebKit is a huge deal because it's WebKit that powers the browsers that millions of people use on their desktop and mobile devices: iPhone, iPod Touch and iPad all use iOS's WebKit engine. RIM's Blackberry browser runs WebKit, as does Palm/ HP's webOS. Google's Android uses WebKit and so does its Chrome browser on the desktop. The widespread use of WebKit is now a major reason to use CSS columns to make our page layouts more flexible and adaptable today.

Column widths and counts

Changing the number of CSS columns and column widths so that they adapt to different layouts and orientations is easy. We can implement columns in two ways, either by defining the number of columns or their width. Let's rewrite the HTML of our latest 'Its's Hardboiled' story, removing those presentational divisions to leave only the structured content. We'll include an HTML5 `article`, `header` and `footer` and apply the `entry-content` class from the hAtom microformat:

```
<article>
    <div class="entry-content">
        <header>
            <h3>Contract Killer by Andy Clarke</h3>
        </header>

        <img src="hentry-01.jpg" alt="">
        <p>Sometimes you let the madness get to you, sometimes you
        don't. Sometimes the only way to get through the day is to
        blaze with a crazy anger that tells everyone within earshot
        that they should stay the hell out of your way. Today was one
        of those days.</p>
```

```
<p>I went as far as the front door and fired up a smoke,
drawing deep. The cold winter air on my face and the feeling
of smoke filling my lungs made me feel human again.</p>
<p>That was as far as I could get. The reflection that stared
back at me in the window told me that I looked like hell. I
sneered back in it's face, took another deep drag and flicked
the butt outside.</p>

<footer>
    <time datetime="2010-11-20" class="updated published">
        20th November 2010
        <span class='value-title' title="2010-20-11">
        </span>
    </time>
</footer>
    </div>
</article>
```

With the divisions removed, define the number of columns we need for an optimal line length — let's start with a count of three:

```
.entry-content { column-count : 3; }
```

In a flexible, percentage-based layout, the columns' widths will change dynamically to fit inside their parent element. Or we can specify a precise width for columns, and a browser will then create as many columns as it needs to fit inside a parent:

```
.entry-content { column-width : 220px; }
```

If a parent gets wider, a browser will add new columns. When it narrows, a browser will remove them, one at a time — all the while reflowing text to fit.

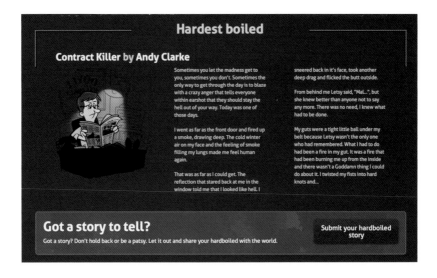

White space is also an important factor in improving readability, so we'll insert gaps (gutters, to many of us) and rules between columns. Our gaps will be eighty pixels wide, filled with one pixel solid white rules:

```
.entry-content {
column-gap : 80px;
column-rule : 1px solid rgb(255,255,255);
}
```

CSS columns are fast and easy to implement, but there's no getting away from the fact that they have patchy support.

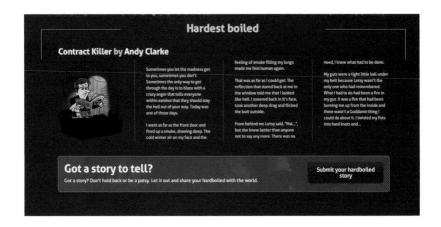

Writing vendor prefixes

Firefox and WebKit have both implemented CSS columns using their own vendor-specific prefixes, so we'll add prefixes for Mozilla and WebKit, followed by the W3C's official syntax:

```
.entry-content {
-moz-column-width : 220px;
-moz-column-gap : 80px;
-moz-column-rule : 1px solid rgb(255,255,255);
-webkit-column-width : 220px;
-webkit-column-gap : 80px;
-webkit-column-rule : 1px solid rgb(255,255,255);
column-width : 220px;
column-gap : 80px;
column-rule : 1px solid rgb(255,255,255);
}
```

That's quite a handful I know, but these vendor-specific prefixes are necessary while browser makers perfect their implementations. What's to complain about, really? We might have to write column declarations a few times but, hey, is that really so bad?

TweetCC', is a site I made that allows Twitter users to add Creative Commons licences to their tweets? On TweetCC's home page, I divided the 'about' section into three columns:

```
#content div {
column-count : 3;
column-gap : 20px;
column-rule : 1px solid ↵
rgba(255,255,255,.1);
}
```

Using CSS columns meant that I didn't need to calculate the widths, margins or padding of presentational divisions.

I also didn't worry about making columns equal in height as CSS columns will always be the height of the tallest column.

Trent Walton divided the tag navigation on his search page into four CSS columns. Trent's tags use only a simple unordered list instead of presentational divisions or other hacked elements:

```
<section class="tag_list">
    <ul>
        <li><a href="/tag/analytics/">Analytics</a></li>
        <li><a href="/tag/animation/">Animation</a></li>
        <li><a href="/tag/apple/">Apple</a></li>
        <li><a href="/tag/chrome/">Chrome</a></li>
    </ul>
</section>
```

Did you spot that Trent used 'tag spaces' in his URLs? He could make his HTML hardboiled by adding the rel tag microformat you learned about in Chapter 9.

Trent divided the nested list into four CSS columns, with twenty pixel gaps:

```
.tag_list {
column-count : 4;
column-gap : 20px;
}
```

| Articles | Notes | Info | Search |

Search [   ] **Go**

Popular search terms: CSS, CSS3, Design, Paravel, Webkit

Tags

Analytics	DesignSwap	Markup	The Many Faces Of
Animation	Dribbble	Mobile	Twitter
Apple	Firefox	Multi·Touch	Typography
Chrome	Food	Opera	UX
CMS	HTML5	Opinion	W3C
Conferences	Illustration	Paravel	Web Fonts
CSS	Internet Explorer	Personal	Webkit
CSS3	iPad	Rdio	
Design	iPhone	Safari	

Flexible media and robot ninjas

Where were we? Oh yeah. On the 'It's Hardboiled' home page. It now has a flexible design that adapts as the browser or device width changes. Columns are added and removed, and text will reflow between them. But what about fixed-width assets like images or videos? Can we make them become flexible too? Yes we can.

Did you notice that the columnised content includes an image in the first column? If this image is too small, the neatness of our grid will be broken. When it's too large, it will spill into neighbouring columns and spoil the design. What can we do to solve this?

We could just open Photoshop and bust images down to fit the column width, but this will take time and when we don't know how wide a flexible column will be, we can't make images to fit. It's time to go back to the drawing board. Or is it? Lucky for us that Ethan Marcotte, the 'Unstoppable Robot Ninja', has devised a solution to the fluid media problem'. Best of all, Ethan's solution doesn't require anything more than some clever CSS.

No matter how big an image's intrinsic width is, make sure it never exceeds the width of a column by setting its maximum width (`max-width`) to one hundred per cent (we'll make our image files 400 pixels wide to allow for almost any column width):

```
img { max-width : 100%; }
```

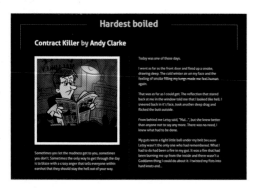

---

[1] http://unstoppablerobotninja.com/entry/fluid-images

This simple rule has an added bonus. When an image's width is changed to fill a container, its height also changes to maintain its original aspect ratio.

Our images look better with a border, this time set in pixels — but mixing pixels and percentages can be tricky. We can make life easier by enclosing images in another element, and HTML5 has the perfect one ready to use: it's the figure element you learned about in Chapter 8:

```
<figure>
    <img src="hentry-01.jpg" alt="">
</figure>
```

Now add a solid white border to the figure:

```
figure { border : 10px solid rgb(255,255,255); }
```

The image will now scale to fit inside a flexible column and we'll never have to worry about it becoming too large and breaking our layout.

What about video? Ethan's technique works for other types of media too, including HTML5 videos and Flash player content. We simply need to add three more elements to our declaration: `video`, `object` and `embed`:

```
img, video, object, embed { max-width : 100%; }
```

If you use any browser on a Mac, they do a fantastic job of resizing images and other media when we use Ethan's technique. It's a shame that the same can't be said for Internet Explorer on Windows, as that browser pixelates images to the point that they become unusable. This is a real problem, especially when images contain fine details or text. Once again, Ethan's robot ninja is unstoppable and he/it (I'm never sure) has devised a JavaScript workaround that restores images to their detailed glory in Internet Explorer:

```
<!--[if IE]>
    <script src="imgsizer.js"></script>
<![endif]-->
```

You can download Ethan's script' and read the background to it and the techniques he uses².

Designing for a browser's capabilities

It would be wrong to ignore browsers that are incapable of rendering CSS columns altogether, especially when we can use Modernizr to test for column support and use its classes to make an alternative design that's appropriate to a browser's abilities. When a browser is able to render columns, Modernizr adds its `csscolumns` class. Otherwise it adds — you guessed it — `no-csscolumns`.

Let's deal with that image. We purposely made it large to allow for flexible column widths, but when there is no CSS column support, this huge image will dominate our design. We can fix this by giving the `figure` element that contains it a width of 300 pixels, then float it left or right:

---

[1] http://unstoppablerobotninja.com/demos/resize/imgSizer.js
[2] http://unstoppablerobotninja.com/entry/fluid-images

I often choose right to preserve a clean left-hand reading edge.

```
.no-csscolumns figure {
float : right;
width : 300px;
}
```

When there are no columns, however, any text will span the full width of the layout and make the measure too wide. To compensate, increase the font size from .82em to 1em and add a wide right margin to create a narrower measure:

```
.no-csscolumns p {
margin-right : 400px;
font-size : 1em;
}
```

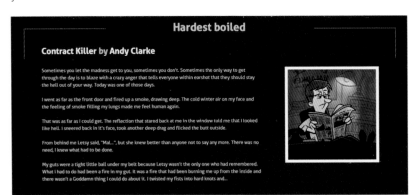

As these rules descend from Modernizr's no-csscolumns class, they will be seen only by browsers that don't have the ability to render CSS columns.

CSS Media Queries

CSS2 introduced media types that already give us the ability to specify different style rules — and even entirely different style sheets — based on a type of device. In the example below, the styles in main.css will only be applied on screen, while a printer will use styles from the print.css style sheet.

Serving alternative style sheets to screens and printers is as simple as adding a media attribute:

```
<link rel="stylesheet" media="screen" href="main.css">
<link rel="stylesheet" media="print" href="print.css">
```

Media Queries in CSS3' now make it possible for us to define precisely which styles get applied under which circumstances. They work by querying a device's features including its:

aspect-ratio	color	orientation	device-aspect-ratio
device-height	device-width	resolution	height
monochrome	max-width	width	max-height

Enabling CSS3 Media Queries to deliver styles based on a device's features involves adding one or more arguments to a style sheet link, an embedded style or inside an external style sheet. Let's start by switching to an entirely new screen style sheet when a browser's width exceeds 800 pixels.

```
<link rel="stylesheet" media="screen and (min-width : 800px)" ↵
href="800.css">
```

We could choose to load this specific style sheet in addition to a primary screen style sheet, so place the media query link to 800.css lower in the source order and use the cascade to override any rules in main.css:

' http://w3.org/TR/css3-mediaqueries

Proportional leading with CSS3 Media Queries

Responsive, percentage-based layouts that use CSS columns cry out for fine control over typography. One of the most effective ways to improve readability is to adjust text size and leading (`line-height`) in relation to the width of the measure (text column width). CSS3 Media Queries allow us to precisely control leading, using a query of the window or device's width and descendant CSS selectors. First, we'll set `line-height` to 1.6 when the minimum overall window width is 1,000 pixels:

```
@media screen and (min-width: 1000px) {
.entry-content p {
line-height : 1.6; }
}
```

We'll reduce the line height in increments, starting with a maximum width of 900 pixels and a `line-height` of 1.5:

```
@media screen and (min-width: 900px) {
.entry-content p {
line-height : 1.5; }
}
```

Finally set `line-height` to 1.4 when the minimum overall window width is 800 pixels:

```
@media screen and (min-width: 800px) {
.entry-content p {
line-height : 1.4; }
}
```

Using a contemporary browser, one that supports CSS3 Media Queries, resize the window and watch the `line-height` change automatically.

Typefaces have been designed with different x-heights and need different amounts of line-height to help them stay readable, but CSS doesn't provide a way to specify variable line-height if a font in the stack is not installed. Read more about this problem in my 'Lead Pipe' article[1] and Phil Oye's jQuery solution, Font Unstack[2]

[1] http://stuffandnonsense.co.uk/blog/about/lead_pipe
[2] http://stuffandnonsense.co.uk/blog/about/font_unstack

```
<link rel="stylesheet" media="screen" href="main.css">
<link rel="stylesheet" media="screen and (min-width : 800px)" ↵
href="800.css">
```

Alternatively, we can keep media-related styles inside the same style sheet. Let's build a query that adjusts a paragraph's `line-height` when a browser's width exceeds 800 pixels. To ensure this style is only applied when reading on `screen`, use the screen media type and the `and` combinator:

```
@media screen and (min-width: 800px) {

.entry-content p {
line-height : 1.5; }

}
```

Targeting small screens

When we left the main story on the 'It's Hardboiled' home page, we'd specified the columns to be 220 pixels wide. A browser will automatically create as many columns as it can to fill a container:

```
.entry-content {
column-width : 220px;
column-gap : 80px;
column-rule : 1px solid rgb(255,255,255);
}
```

To make the story more easily readable on a mobile phone, we only need one column, so we'll create a media query that targets a maximum device width of 480 pixels, as most mobile phone screens are this width or below.

In these circumstances, reset the CSS column width to `auto` and specify just one column:

```
@media only screen and
(max-device-width: 480px) {

.entry-content {
column-width : auto;
column-column-count : 1; }


}
```

This query should be placed at the bottom of a linked or embedded style sheet so that the rules they contain override styles above them. Alternatively, we can place these styles in an external style sheet linked from the `head` of any document, like this:

```
<link rel="stylesheet" media="only screen and ↵
(max-device-width: 480px)" href="480px.css">
```

You might think that this is an iPhone-specific layout, but in fact it will render well in Opera Mini and on Android-powered devices too.

In 2010, Clearleft used CSS3 Media Queries to deconstruct the design for the smaller screens we find on many smartphones. We can learn a lot from how they used two media queries: the first targets all devices that have widths lower than 480 pixels; and the second, browser window widths up to 800 pixels. Each set of queries has been separated using a comma:

```
@media all and (max-device-width: 480px), all and (max-width: 800px)
{

[...]

}
```

Clearleft placed these media queries at the bottom of its style sheet so that the style rules they contain will override core styles. First, they reset all position, float, (min) width and (min) height values:

HOME   SCHEDULE   WORKSHOPS   SPONSORS   LOCATION   OFFERS

dConstruct 2010

**3RD SEPTEMBER 2010
BRIGHTON, ENGLAND**

SOLD OUT!

£125 + VAT

DESIGN & CREATIVITY

Now in its sixth year, **dConstruct 2010** brings together leading industry figures to explore the power of design thinking and show how we can all become just a little bit more creative.

SPEAKERS INCLUDE:
BRENDAN **DAWES**
DAVID **MCCANDLESS**
HANNAH **DONOVAN**
JAMES **BRIDLE**
JOHN **GRUBER**
MARTY **NEUMEIER**
MERLIN **MANN**
SAMANTHA **WARREN**
TOM **COATES**

LATEST NEWS

20 AUGUST
Suspending Disbelief

We're thrilled to announce that as part of dConstruct 2010 we have teamed up with Lighthouse, a leading arts agency in the

13 JULY
Conference Sold Out

A week after going on sale, tickets for the dConstruct conference are now sold out. If you've missed out then you can join the

2 JUNE
dConstruct Tickets

Tickets for dConstruct 2010 will go on sale at 11am UK time on Tuesday 6th July. dConstruct tickets are always hotly

```
@media all and (max-device-width: 480px), all and (max-width: 800px) {

div.overflow-catch * {
overflow : visible;
position : static;
float : none;
clear : both;
width : auto;
height : auto;
min-width: 0;
min-height: 0; }

}
```

Then they added other override styles for specific elements.
For example, in their core styles, the site's clever speaker
carousel uses a mix of absolute positioning, floats and CSS
sprites to create its innovative interface. Roll your mouse over
each of the speaker photos and a full colour version and the
speaker's name fades into view.

On smaller screens, dConstruct 2010's speaker carousel
makes little sense, so Clearleft hid it completely from view by
setting its display property to none:

```
@media all and (max-device-width: 480px), all and ↵
(max-width: 800px) {

.speaker-carousel {
display : none; }

}
```

dConstruct 2010 makes the most of the space available on smartphones and
other small displays. By using the cascade and placing CSS3 media queries at the
end of our stylesheets, we can overwrite any earlier CSS style rules designed for

You spin me right round, baby, right round

Whether or not you believe that the iPad qualifies as revolutionary, we should now think differently about the design of our sites and how they can adapt to the iPad and devices like it. To target the iPad specifically, use CSS3 media queries to target that device's maximum width of 1,024 pixels:

```
<link rel="stylesheet" media="only screen and (max-device-width: ↵
1024px)" href="ipad.css" type="text/css">
```

Users can hold an iPad in landscape or portrait format, so making sure our websites offer users the best possible experience in both formats makes sense.

With CSS3 media queries, in combination with CSS columns, we can change a page's layout based on the orientation of a device. If the browser height is larger than its width, the device is in portrait mode. If the width is larger, it's in landscape mode.

When we left the 'It's Hardboiled' main story, we had specified a fixed column width for desktop browsers, followed by a query that reduced the layout to just one column on smaller screens up to 480 pixels. To optimise the design for landscape and portrait formats, we'll add two more media queries.

The first sets the number of columns to two when a device is in portrait orientation:

```
@media screen and (orientation:portrait) {

.cols { column-column-count : 2; }

}
```

The second adds a third column if a device is in landscape orientation:

```
@media screen and (orientation:landscape) {

.cols { column-column-count : 3; }

}
```

Again, these queries should be placed at the bottom of a linked or embedded stylesheet, or we can place their styles in an external stylesheet, like this:

```
<link rel="stylesheet" media="all and (orientation:portrait)" ↵
href="portrait.css">

<link rel="stylesheet" media="all and (orientation:landscape)" ↵
href="landscape.css">
```

If you have an iPad or similar device, switch from portrait to landscape format and watch as the CSS3 media queries change the number of columns.

Simon Collison's site attracted adoration and critical acclaim when he redesigned it in February 2010. Take a look at Simon's site in a wide browser and his primary navigation, an unordered list of tiles, is arranged in a single row of four. Never one to let sleeping dogs lie, in June of that year, Simon updated his site, this time using CSS3 media queries, to make it more 'responsive.' Now, using a contemporary browser that supports CSS3 media queries, reduce the width of the browser window and watch as Simon's navigation layout switches first to two rows of two, and then to a single column. Simon achieved this by changing the width of his page division in response to several device and window widths, using four queries:

```
@media (min-device-width:1024px) and (max-width:989px),
screen and (max-device-width:480px),
(max-device-width:480px) and (orientation:landscape),
(min-device-width:481px) and (orientation:portrait) {

div#page { width:468px; }

}
```

Let's run through each of Simon's queries line by line.

1. Devices with a minimum width of 1,024 pixels and windows with a maximum width of 989 pixels.
2. Screens that have a maximum device width of 480 pixels.
3. Devices with a maximum width of 480 pixels and are also in landscape orientation.
4. Devices with a minimum width of 481 pixels and are also in portrait orientation.
5. When one of the above criteria are met, resize the page division to 468 pixels.

But Simon doesn't stop there. He adds a further set of queries that result in a narrower width again:

```
@media (min-device-width:1024px) and (max-width:509px),
(max-device-width:480px) and (orientation:portrait) {

div#page { width:306px;

}
```

With these two queries, Simon's page division shrinks to 306 pixels wide when viewed with:

1. devices with a minimum width of 1,024 pixels and windows with a maximum width of 509 pixels.
2. devices with a maximum width of 480 pixels which are also in landscape orientation.

Resize a browser window, or use a device that matches Simon's criteria and watch as his navigation switches to two rows of two.

In 2010, Jon Hicks made his portfolio site and journal responsive by using CSS3 media queries to restructure his entire layout in three, two and one columns. Jon's hardboiled HTML5 includes a nav element, followed by a floated content division that contains two more divisions that he floated to create columns in wide browser windows. They are main and side:

Investigate Hickdesign's style sheets and you'll find that Jon is among many leading designers who are now serving the Universal Internet Explorer 6 CSS stylesheet that you learned about in Chapter 6.

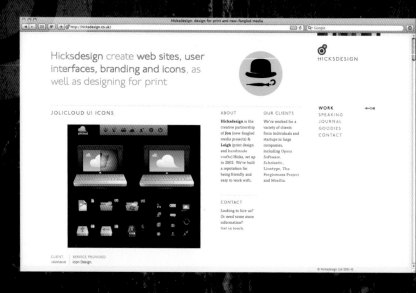

```
<div class="page">
    <nav>
        <ul>
            <li><a href="/">Work</a></li>
            <li><a href="/speaking/">Speaking</a></li>
            <li><a href="/journal/">Journal</a></li>
            <li><a href="/goodies/">Goodies</a></li>
            <li><a href="/contact">Contact</a></li>
        </ul>
    </nav>
```

```
            <p>Hicksdesign is the creative partnership of Jon
            (new-fangled media projects) and Leigh (print design
            and handmade crafts) We've built a reputation for
            being friendly and easy to work with.</p>

        </section>

      </div>

    </div>

</div>
```

Three columns work well in wider browser windows,
but to make sure that his design responds equally well
in narrower windows and on smaller screens, Jon used a
series of six CSS3 media queries.

For screens that are smaller than 600 pixels, including
smartphone screens, Jon removed all floats on his nav, main
and side divisions:

```
@media handheld and (max-width: 480px),
screen and (max-device-width: 480px), screen and
(max-width: 600px) {
nav, #main, #side {
float : none; }
}
```

When browser windows have a minimum width of 920 pixels, Jon's content division shrinks in size from its default 100% to 76%:

```
@media screen and (min-width: ↵
920px) {

#content {
width : 76%; }
```

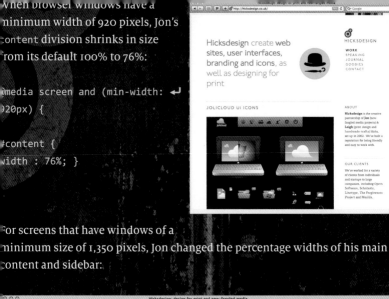

For screens that have windows of a minimum size of 1,350 pixels, Jon changed the percentage widths of his main content and sidebar:

```
@media screen and (min-width: 1350px) {

#main {
width : 60%; }
#side {
width : 32%; }


}
```

And for screens that have windows of a minimum size of 1,500 pixels, Jon
changed the margins on his outer page division:

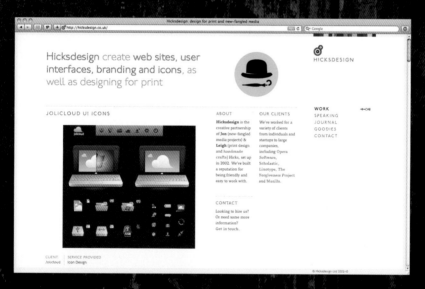

```
@media screen and (min-width: 1500px) {

.page {
margin : 0 8% 0 12%; }


}
```

Ever the perfectionist, Jon's incredible attention to detail led him to adjust only the letter-spacing and capitalisation on second-level headings when his design is rendered by a device, such as the iPhone, where the maximum device width is 480 pixels:

```
@media only screen and (max-device-width: 480px) {

h2 {
letter-spacing : 0;
text-transform : capitalize; }


}
```

For the iPad — where the minimum device width is 768 pixels and the maximum is 1,024 pixels — Jon changed the margins and padding on the body element to allow more space around his content:

```
@media only screen and (min-device-width: 768px) and (max-device-
width: 1024px) {
body {
margin : 0;
padding : 66px 24px 24px 24px; }
}
```

Jon's layered CSS3 media queries are testament to his desire to make his design look fantastic, no matter what device his prospective clients and readers of his journal use. Such a complicated set of queries can present problems however, particularly in how we test on a range of devices, some of which we don't own or have regular access to.

Hicksd
interfac
well as designing for print

JOLICLOUD UI ICONS

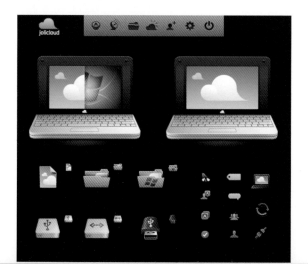

HICKSDESIGN

ABOUT

Hicksdesign is the creative partnership of **Jon** (new-fangled media projects) & **Leigh** (print design and handmade crafts) Hicks, set up in 2002. We've built a reputation for being friendly and easy to work with.

OUR CLIENTS

We've worked for a variety of clients from individuals and startups to large companies, including **Opera Software**, **Scholastic**, **Linotype**, The **Forgiveness Project** and **Mozilla**.

CONTACT

Looking to hire us? Or need

WORK
SPEAKING
JOURNAL
GOODIES
CONTACT

Testing media queries

If you're the proud owner of an iOS, Android or other device where the browser supports CSS3 media queries, upload files to a server to test the results. But what about testing on devices you don't own, as there are many more smartphone varieties than there are desktop browsers?

With the introduction of its iPhone 4, Apple increased the resolution of the phone's Retina display to 326ppi, double that of previous iPhone models. To help you serve double resolution images and other styles to the iPhone 4, use a CSS3 media query.

```
<link rel="stylesheet" media="only screen and
(-webkit-min-device-pixel-ratio: 2)" type="text/css" ↵
href="iphone4.css">
```

Aral Balkan has written 'How to make your web content look stunning on the iPhone 4's new Retina display'.[1]

ProtoFluid[2] is a web application that gives us options to test designs in either a Google Nexus One smartphone, iPhone, iPad and Motorola Droid. Simply add a URL, select from ProtoFluid's preset devices and screen sizes or input your own, press 'launch' and let ProtoFluid handle the rest.

ProtoFluid is also a fantastic tool for demonstrating the possibilities of media queries to clients who may not yet appreciate the benefits of designing tailored experiences.

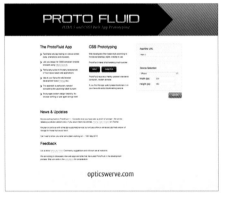

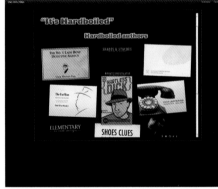

More good news. If you use the Firebug extension for Firefox, WebKit's Web Inspector or Opera's Dragonfly, make changes directly to your HTML or CSS and see the media query results instantly inside ProtoFluid.

[1] http://aralbalkan.com/3331
[2] http://protofluid.com

Breaking it up

With new devices available, the one-size-fits-all approach to web design that we've stuck with for so long is no longer relevant. It's now essential that the designs that we create are responsive to the different ways that users access our content.

CSS3 columns have been implemented in many desktop browsers and on many more mobile devices. CSS3 media queries have been implemented in many contemporary browsers and devices. Opera was one of the first but lacks support for orientation. Google Chrome and Safari both support them and they are also supported in Safari on iOS. Mozilla implemented CSS3 media queries in Firefox 3.5 and now, at last, Microsoft has implemented them in Internet Explorer 9.

Keen to dig up more dirt on CSS3 Media Queries?

Chris Coyier has published an excellent 'Different Stylesheets for Differently Sized Browser Windows' tutorial and screencast on CSS Tricks along with a plethora of examples and files to download and customise.

http://css-tricks.com/resolution-specific-stylesheets

If you're interested in optimising sites for the iPhone, **Sitepoint's** 'iPhone Development: 12 Tips To Get You Started' is (as you might guess from the title) a fantastic place to start.

http://articles.sitepoint.com/article/iphone-development-12-tips

If Sitepoint's article whetted your appetite for iPhone design, move right along to **Apple's** own Safari Web Content Guide and specifically its section on 'Optimising Web Content for iPhone'.

http://developer.apple.com/safari/library/documentation/AppleApplications/Reference/SafariWebContent/OptimizingforSafarioniPhone/OptimizingforSafarioniPhone.html

Ryan Seddon's 'How to use CSS3 Orientation Media Queries' is currently one of the best orientation tutorials and his 'CSS3 Chameleon' demonstration is worth the price of admission alone.

http://1stwebdesigner.com/tutorials/how-to-use-css3-orientation-media-queries

That was a breeze

In **More hardboiled CSS3**, CSS transforms translated, scaled, rotated and skewed elements in not two but three dimensions, creating designs that were previously not possible using CSS alone. CSS transitions made state changes smoother and simple animations possible and, for more complicated effects, CSS keyframe animations brought designs to life in the best browsers. Finally, CSS columns and media queries made designs responsive to new browsing environments and devices.

It's time to get hardboiled

So, we've made it to the end of the book. But really, it's just the beginning. I closed off my last book, *Transcending CSS*, with, "So what's next? The future." This time, it's different. The future's already here.

The web's not the same place it was four years ago, two years ago, even one year ago, and the one-size-fits-all approach to web design we've clung to since the web began isn't relevant anymore. Today's myriad of web-enabled devices and browsers with varying capabilities mean it's now essential that we design websites and web applications that are tailored and responsive to the different ways that people access what we create. Changing the tools and techniques we use and, most importantly, the ways we think about and approach design is now essential: we have to embrace that change, or be left behind.

For web professionals, change means finding new ways to work and leaving behind many familiar methods and workflows. It means learning new technologies — such as HTML5 forms, and CSS3 selectors and properties — and re-evaluating older ones, putting them to new uses. It also means re-examining some of the canons of modern web design, such as progressive enhancement and graceful degradation, questioning their relevance and how we apply their principles in a modern context.

Change is always tough, not only for us but for the people, companies and organisations that we work for. Those people often pay our salaries or invoices so it can be hard sometimes to push for the change that we need. But make no mistake: push for change we must, if we're going to make the best work that we can — work that is effective and long-lasting, work that we can be proud of.

For the hardboiled heroes in the detective stories that I love, rules are there to be remade when that means going to work, catching the killer, seeing that justice is done by any means necessary. As web professionals, jamming a pistol into a guy's temple or ramming a fist into his guts isn't all part of a day's work, but we can learn a lot from those hardboiled heroes. Who makes the rules? We do. Who lives by those rules? We do. Whose responsibility is it to make damn sure that the work that we do on the web is the best that it can be, so that everyone — us, our bosses and customers and their users — will benefit? It's ours. It's what we're paid to do. It should be our passion too.

Some people say that websites must look the same in every browser. To hell with that. This attitude makes many of us think that we can't make use of new and emerging technologies like HTML5 and CSS3 today, and we have to wait for some day in the future when all browsers support the same technologies the same way at the same time! It ain't gonna happen. It's best that we, and the people we work for, learn to live with that reality and move on.

Using HTML5, microformats and WAI-ARIA roles means that our markup can be leaner, fitter, more flexible and more adaptable to anything the web can throw at it. Their semantics mean that more people can access what we publish from anywhere, using anything they choose, from PCs to smartphones and other types of device that we haven't imagined yet.

CSS3 selectors and properties give us the power to use better, less presentational HTML with fewer images, to create designs that are responsive to browsers of all capabilities. With this variety of tailored designs at our disposal come new opportunities to show our creative skills and new opportunities for business.

It's time to seize those opportunities, grab them with both hands.

It's time to get hardboiled